When Students Have Power

When Students Have Power

Negotiating

Authority in a

Critical Pedagogy

Ira Shor

The University of Chicago Press

Chicago and London

IRA SHOR is professor of English at the Graduate
School of the City University of New York. He is the
author of five books, including *Empowering Education,*
also published by the University of Chicago Press.

The University of Chicago Press, Chicago 60637
The University of Chicago Press, Ltd., London
© 1996 by Ira Shor
All rights reserved. Published 1996
Printed in the United States of America

05 04 03 02 01 00 99 98 97 96 1 2 3 4 5

ISBN 0-226-75354-9 (cloth)
     0-226-75355-7 (paper)

Library of Congress Cataloging-in-Publication Data

Shor, Ira, 1945–
    When students have power: Negotiating authority in a critical
pedagogy / Ira Shor.
        p.   cm.
    Includes bibliographical references (p.   ) and index.
    ISBN 0-226-75354-9 (cloth: alk. paper). — ISBN 0-226-75355-7
(paper: alk. paper)
    1. Critical pedagogy—United States. 2. College teaching—United
States. 3. Educational anthropology—United States. 4. Working
class—Education (Higher)—United States. I. Title.
LC196.5.U6S566   1996
370.11′5′09747—dc20   96-15983
                                                            CIP

The paper used in this publication meets the minimum
requirements of the American National Standard for
Information Sciences—Permanence of Paper for Printed
Library Materials, ANSI Z39.48-1984.

In memory of Jim Berlin, 1942–1994.

Scholar, mentor, friend.
Father, husband, athlete.
Brilliant, productive, congenial,
  working-class.
Always missed, always
  remembered.

"Students must learn to locate
the beneficiaries and the victims
of knowledge, exerting their
rights as citizens in a democracy
to criticize freely those in
power."

—James Berlin, "Postmodernism, the College Curriculum,
and Composition," in *Composition in Context*

And in honor of the living—

Bill Bigelow, Linda Christensen,
Debi Duke, Stan Karp, Deborah Menkart,
Bob Peterson, Rita Tenorio—Educators,
leaders, authors, visionaries.

"When we dream alone, it remains only a
dream. When we dream together, it is not just
a dream. It is the beginning of reality."

—Dom Helder Camara, Archbishop of Brazil

"Many of my students have never been asked their opinions about anything in high school."
—African-American woman, graduate student in my doctoral seminar, teacher of freshman writing

"[W]hat I thought the students would want to learn was in fact astonishingly different from what *they* decided they wanted to learn . . . I was astounded by the difference between what I had anticipated the areas of study would be and what the students themselves decided they needed to know."
—JoAnne Reid, teacher, in *Negotiating the Curriculum* (1992, p. 103)

"[T]he fragmented curriculum fits the school's primary goal: the control of students. By cutting up the curriculum into bits and snippets and by testing students continually on those bits, teachers keep control of their classes."
—Linda McNeil, *Contradictions of Control* (1986, p. 205)

"Knowledge is power only to those who have it or can purchase it and who already have power enough to put it to use."
—Richard Ohmann, *English in America* (1976, p. 311)

"Let us imagine what it would be like if the history and culture of working-class people were at the center of educational practices. What would students learn?"
—Janet Zandy, *Women Studies Quarterly* 22, nos. 1 and 2 (Spring/Summer 1995), p. 3

Contents

Preface and
Acknowledgments

This book tells about an experiment in power-sharing that changed me and my practice. It takes place at an unlikely site in a disturbing time—inside my crumbling commuter college in fiscally desperate New York, when the go-go 1980s burst and the no-go 1990s brought a high tide of conservativism that undermined many public schools and campuses. From this location, I will report an unsettling exercise in democratic dreaming that brought me and the students into power-sharing, sometimes called negotiating the curriculum, shared authority, or cogovernance—what Seth Kreisberg (1992) called "power with" instead of "power over."

My story begins in a wretched basement room packed with stressed-out working-class students who have come for a required study of "Utopia," of all things. The students found themselves in the curious position of being compelled to study Utopia while enchambered underground in an airless cinderblock room too small for the overenrolled class. I found myself in the peculiar situation of teaching an allegedly "empowering" and "liberatory" course to people more or less forced to be there and wishing they weren't. I suppose this bizarre arrangement could be considered a sanity test to find out just how much teachers and students will put up with or can take. Then again, I like to think of this strange experience as a tale of two cities—two cities at war, really, a culture war in an age of conservative restoration, I'd call it, with one city old, familiar, neurotic, and controlling, while the other appears new, unpredictable, risky, and transformative. I see myself and this class traveling between the two warring towns, sometimes in both at the same time, sometimes split into groups inhabiting one town or the other, sometimes outside of the walls of both, wandering the heath at night, like Lear in the storm.

The students, waterproof veterans of culture war and the irrational disciplines of schooling, were used to the unreasonable but were not expecting the unexpected. They had become resilient experts in the skill most taught by mass education—spitting out and spitting back the official syllabus force-fed to them year after year. While waiting once again to swallow and expel knowledge like tasteless pumpkin seeds, they were also ready to knit yet another teacher's name (mine) into their long sweaters of remembrance.

For twenty years before this story begins, I had been experimenting with critical teaching. Despite my apparent credentials in alternative pedagogy, I was not prepared when power-sharing led to a surge of student demands. Suddenly, this group was released into desires for power and democracy, a release I had invited without knowing where it could lead. When a struggle for control burst into the open, I got a new on-the-job lesson about the power relations at the heart of every social experience, especially education. Yet, that heart of power can be so deeply mystified, denied, or buried that it becomes a latent volcano barely disturbing the surface with erratic pulsations until finally an eruption overwhelms the unreasonable order of things. There is a message in all of this worth rescuing: namely, that power is a learning problem and learning is a power problem, which is the moral of this tale, a theme that Dewey and Freire on separate continents at separate times warned about years ago.

John Dewey, the patron saint of American education, so honored, invoked, and ignored, impatiently asked eighty years ago, "Why is it, in spite of the fact that teaching by pouring in, learning by a passive absorption, are universally condemned, that they are still entrenched in practice?" (*Democracy and Education*, p. 38). His word "still" echoes loudly to me, speaking of his deep frustration in 1916 (when the book was published and schooling was relatively new in society), a frustration over the teacher-talk, one-way transmission of knowledge, and undemocratic relations dominating education. Dewey insisted that "education is not an affair of 'telling' and being told, but an active and constructive process." Two decades later, in *Experience and Education*, he confirmed his conviction that the central strength of progressive practice was its inclusion of students in the making of their education while the central defect of traditional schooling was its exclusion of students from constructing purposes for their learning. How would Dewey feel today, if he could witness undemocratic authority and teacher-centered practice still entrenched from kindergarten through high school and on to graduate school?

In this story about a Dewey-Freire model of democratic power relations, I will try to make my writing itself an experiment about the experiment. That is, I want this personal report to cross genres. On the one hand, I will draw on creative nonfiction and literary narrative to produce "teacher lore," an emergent genre in composition studies (North 1987; Downing, Harkin, and Sosnoski 1994). On the other hand, I will include extensive materials from the students and the curriculum by using the genres of ethnographic reporting and classroom inquiry. For this, I'll be doing some "thick description" of college, classroom, and community experience, as urged by Clifford Geertz (1973), along with discourse analysis of the classroom "speech community" as recommended by Dell Hymes (1974), combined with teacher-research into methodology and learning as described by Dixie Goswami and Peter Stillman (1987) as well as by C. H. Knoblauch and Lil Brannon (1993). Further, I will situate this "blurred genre" narrative and research (Geertz 1983) in a cultural studies approach to everyday life, drawing out issues of class, race, and gender through sociological, economic, and historical frameworks on one side and subjective experience on the other. The intersection of the social and the subjective in cultural studies helps me to understand the meaning of ordinary events, like parking lots, bad teeth, hamburgers, and classroom chairs, connecting the global with the local, the ideological with the personal (Hall 1980; Johnson 1987). By thus crossing genres, I want to avoid a traditional voice of academic discourse, which Peter Elbow (1991) argued denies its own subjectivity, which James Berlin (1988) claimed denies its own ideology, and which Lillian Bridwell-Bowles (1992) said denies the diversity of positions actually at work in the academy. Others have presented innovative narratives in voices that are cross-generic, cross-cultural, or "heteroglossic" (Bakhtin 1981), such as Gloria Anzaldua (1987), Pat Belanoff (1990), Keith Gilyard (1991), and Victor Villanueva (1993), so this book is not the first effort in that direction. Lastly, in terms of the "speech genre" (Bakhtin 1986) of my text, I will also be in dialogue with myself, hoping to be self-critical, interrogating my own position while also trying to represent fairly and to present extensively the positions of the students (through examples of their own productions and expressions).

In telling this story, cross-generic writing and an openly subjective voice feel authentic to me, but they are also risky and revealing so that I feel more vulnerable. Still, I'd rather not hide the vexations of this strange experiment in critical teaching, a personal story of ups and downs that mixes humor and social critique, creative nonfiction and ethnography, conversational style and pedagogical theory. How well this works is for each reader to decide. In the past, my books have experimented with mixed discourses (like the "talking book" with Paulo Freire, the first of that kind), so this is a long-term interest of mine.

Finally, I want to acknowledge and thank several colleagues who read the manuscript and offered good feedback—Diane Tedick, Bill Bigelow, and Linda Christensen. Thanks also to Caroline Pari for helping me assemble the bibliography and to Leo Parascondola for proofreading. And, I am grateful to John Mayher for his suggestion that I focus on narrative after he read and enjoyed the story introducing my previous book, *Empowering Education* (1992). John wrote in *Uncommon Sense* (1990) about the dramatic changes needed in education to fulfill its democratic mission. He said that "The security and comfort of the preset curriculum in which one knows in the fall what the year will entail is gone forever, since until one has met one's students, it is impossible to determine what they will need or will want to work on . . . [W]e must substantially change our conceptions of the nature and processes of schooling" (pp. 37, 1).

And so, there once was a teacher who mistook a basement for Utopia, until all of a sudden . . .

ONE

The Siberian Syndrome: Students as Exiles in the Culture War of the Classroom

A Utopian Hole at the End of the Universe: Encountering the Unlikely, the Unruly, and the Unpredictable

It was a day of high anxiety. It was a day of high hopes. And it was a day of low architecture. Once more it was the first day of class at my budget-broken, concrete campus for working students on Staten Island, New York City's faraway forgotten land, the outer fifth borough on the edge of a decaying urban universe. After twenty years of teaching there, I was about to offer again a course called "Utopias," which I had been tinkering with for over a decade. I had no clue that this course, this semester, with these students, would teach me disturbing lessons not only about power and knowledge but also about critical pedagogy, in whose experimental arms I had grown up as an educator.

Around me loomed conditions that were slightly less than paradise. My cement and weedy campus bordered a roaring expressway, with tractor-trailers zooming by and huge, white City sanitation trucks rumbling to the world's largest garbage dump just down the road, aptly and ironically named the "Fresh Kills Landfill." (This legendary noxious dump joined the also-famous Great Wall of China as the only human-made structures on Earth visible from the moon.) On the first day of the term, I could hear the straining engines and smell the diesel of the garbage trucks as I made my way to one of the College's windowless rooms, my venue for the next class in Utopian vistas.

Thinking of the cinderblock room I was approaching, I felt only more

1

uncertain about my plans for the Utopia course. New York and the eighteen campuses of the City University were writhing in a nonstop fiscal crisis that began in 1972 and grew desperate in the 1990s, forcing thousands of nonelite students out of classes they needed and pushing hundreds of professors into early retirement. Students, teachers, and their families were under attack, unable to fight back effectively, losing ground and feeling pain. We became a phantom university as full-time students and faculty gave way to less visible part-time students and adjunct instructors, the first paying too much for too little and the second being paid too little for too much.

To make matters only worse, most of the students at my College of Staten Island had grown up in some of New York's most conservative neighborhoods, very white enclaves where the men don't eat quiche and neither do the women. They tend to be achingly traditional and proudly insubordinate at the same time. Furthermore, as conditions declined year by year on campus and in the City, a regressive political climate hung like London fog on a windless night. The degradation of New York encouraged in people a siege mentality of self-centered anxiety, impatience, and intolerance—not a good emotional base from which to inspire spacious Utopian vision. In such hard times and narrow political circumstances, I felt uncomfortably obliged to test civic values and critical pedagogy, because the moment required some challenge to the social forces pushing dehumanized thought and feeling.

But, conflicted and uncertain, I asked myself, "Does 'Utopia' make sense in such a time of malaise? What could this airy theme accomplish in a stridently conservative age?" Banging against cemented walls could weaken my most important resource—hope—which I felt evacuating my heart and fleeing south to my toes. I searched for the optimism which had pulled me through two decades of critical experiments during a time I call "the conservative restoration" (see *Culture Wars*, 1986) following the activist sixties. I worried, that first day, about inviting students to question business as usual, to imagine and implement alternatives, to share authority with me, to codevelop the syllabus, to disrupt our routine roles and expectations, to talk back to the reactionary age. In a time and place whose dreamcoats are embroidered in the colors of the status quo, I would have to say that Utopia is not a sensible theme and that critical questioning is unlikely. But . . .

A common weakness of intellectuals who receive more education than is healthy for human beings is our trouble recognizing the obvious and doing the sensible. So, without a rational reply to the apparent inappropriateness of Utopia in such a time and place, I could only turn to my toes where my residue of hope encamped. An intuition came to me when I did, as I was stepping to that first Utopia class—namely, that I should count on the unpredictable and the unknown, even on the unruly habits of some students, because human possibilities are not fully occupied by the dominant forces or trends of any age. There is always a shadow life evolving marginally or awaiting renaissance, I counseled myself (wishing I had a confirming mirror in which to read my lips). These hoped-for and worked-for possibilities which seek unexpected openings despite the limits of an age have been called "untested feasibility" by Paulo Freire (1994). Freire described "limit-acts" which push against the borders of what's possible, to test what is feasible. His notion of "untested feasibility" was formulated differently by Michel Foucault (1980), who wrote that "there is indeed always something in the social body, in classes, groups and individuals themselves which in some sense escapes relations of power, something which is by no means a more or less docile or reactive primal matter, but rather a centrifugal movement, an inverse energy, a discharge" (p. 138). Put yet another way, Raymond Williams (1977) emphatically argued that *"no mode of production and therefore no dominant social order and therefore no dominant culture ever in reality includes or exhausts all human practice, human energy, and human intention"* (p. 125, italics in original).

Thus, I advised myself to search for the untested and unpredictable openings at the margins and in the cracks of the group I was approaching, where I might find territory less captured by the status quo, where some critical thought, civic ideals, and democratic relations were possible even in conservative times. For teachers like me, this experimental search for transformative openings involves a risk-taking "praxis" (action relating theory to practice, in a specific context that challenges limiting situations). The story in this book is about the surprises I encountered as a result of some action against the limits.

Testing the limits by practicing theory and by theorizing practice in a real context is harder and more risky than theorizing theory without a context. So, on the first day of class, as a long-term resident of academe's low-rent district, I feel especially uncertain. The context of Day One in class recycles the problem of making critical knowledge *with* the students, not handing it *to* them (as if such a thing were even possible). In this project, the dissonances I feel with the institution, the students, and the political climate take shape as a clash between a restrictive present and a reinvented future—call it, if you like, the hopeful challenging the actual in the name of the possible.

As it turned out, I couldn't imagine that my offer to negotiate the curriculum, to relinquish unilateral authority, to share power, would threaten to dissolve the Utopia class itself. Not to get ahead of the story, but I should say that I nearly lost the class. Perhaps life and learning are too full of surprises, but that Utopia class focused a spotlight on how critical pedagogy is a constantly evolving process which calls for continual change and growth, in me and the students. The Utopia class obliged me to become more critical and experimental than I had been before. It called out from me and the students some mutually trans-forming actions I hadn't seen before. Student resistance and acceptance drove me to test new methods I hadn't imagined. This, then, is a per-sonal story about what happened when students shared authority in some disturbingly unexpected ways, when the power of knowledge was connected to the knowledge of power.

The Possible Confronts the Actual: Situating Utopia in a Place and a People

I mentioned that the Utopia class met in a dismal windowless room I knew all too well. It was more like a buried chamber than a classroom, deep in the bowels of a gray and aging three-story structure called B-Building. "B," never honored with a proper name, was the middle link connecting equally unnamed buildings "A" and "C," all set in a con-crete quadrangle. This drab architecture and design—cold, colorless, unadorned, uninviting, nameless, uninspiring—communicated an en-vironmental message of low status and minimal expectations. Such a space had no apparent history to pass on, few glories to savor, and small futures to offer most of the working students who passed through its chain-link fences and stainless steel doors, unlike the empowered aes-thetics radiating from the pampered grounds, distinctive gates, and ar-chitectural adornments of elite campuses. This typical working-class campus on Staten Island, a humble abode of slightly higher education, originally opened in 1967 as a community college built for a mere 2,200 students, but was soon stretched and strained to accommodate a raucous 10,000-plus after the determined student protests of 1969 brought Open Admissions to a reluctant City University, which had no tuition and no budget crisis until large numbers of working students and stu-dents of color enrolled in the 1970s, after which we were upgraded to senior college status and downgraded to poverty status.

Sometimes, in my other encounters with legendary B Building, I had at least lucked out and taught on the top third floor, with light coming through the unwashed windows. But this semester it was back to the dungeon. Down a dimly-lit florescent flight of stairs, I found B-34, a windowless box.

Fortunately, my time in such rooms was drawing to a close. A new campus was inching to completion like the beast in Yeats's poem, in a remote part of Staten Island, even closer to the dump, on the former site of the old Willowbrook Center, a notorious bedlam for the mentally ill until it was exposed, condemned, and closed a while back. With the lives once tormented there gone, the vast grounds and buildings lay in ruins, until my College seized them with imperial plans and a fistful of New York State bonds to renovate the acreage. I tried to imagine teaching Utopia at a place famous for mistreating the unfortunate, after all these years in my present shabby quarters. In another way, I read the move to scandalous Willowbrook as an unintended vote of confidence in the students and faculty, who had stayed borderline sane despite impoverishment across two decades of conservative assaults on the public sector.

Knowing my way, I got to B-34 a little early, expecting a big class and the usual small troubles—lost students, unregistered or late students, perhaps a last-minute room change, perhaps another class showing up at the same time, etc. Going through a brown-painted steel door with a wire-mesh window on it, I found myself inside, watching thirty-five mostly white young college students enter and seat themselves (twenty-four women, eleven men, including three female Hispanics, one male African-American, and one young woman from Greece). They looked like the people I've come to know in this predominantly white working-class campus, unlike the students I meet when I'm invited to speak at more elite colleges around the country.

It's hard to fix the "working-class look" of these students without falling into stereotypes. Their human variety is wonderful and substantial from student to student, not just in their "look" but also in their personalities, levels of maturity, academic desires, ethnic family histories, work conditions, voices, and intellectual development. Still, I know them when I see them and I can see them with my eyes closed by now, after twenty years plus at this job. I would describe these students as:

- predominantly white ethnic (largely Italian and Irish, the hyphenated Americans appealed to rhetorically by traditional politicians);
- first-generation collegians, first in their families to come to college, with few books at home and few academic traditions in their backgrounds, often baffled at the language, requirements, and rituals of

higher education (described like this by one adult woman graduate in her College commencement address: "I had no idea of what classes I needed, or even of what all those abbreviations and numbers meant. No one in my family had ever attended college; there was no one whom I could ask for help in deciphering the words that were stranger than Greek to me: pre- and corequisites, core and distribution requirements, credits and equated credits, GPA's—I almost gave up.");

• traditional, family-oriented (living at home, dating, married, divorced, or marriage-minded, with the older students often raising families of their own; invisible homosexuality, vocal homophobia, especially among the male students);

• younger in day classes and older in the evening and weekend sessions, with significant generational differences between the two constituencies;

• occupying a very narrow political spectrum from dominant/aggressive conservatives to marginal/moderate liberals, but often cynical about "politics" as a waste of time and a feedbag for corrupt officials;

• more numerously female than male, with unorganized/nonideological feminism increasing among the women (since the 1980s, women have been outnumbering men in general at U.S. undergraduate colleges and the number of female Ph.D.'s graduating each year from U.S. universities will soon equal the number of male Ph.D.'s for the first time among Americans);

• moderately ambitious (hoping for midlevel careers in business, government, communications, health care, engineering, education);

• often employed in low-to-middle wage jobs while going to school (fire, police, sanitation and parks departments, nonuniformed municipal offices, sales, clerical, security, delivery, direct mail, health care, small business employees in bars, restaurants, home services, cleaning and clothing stores);

• hardworking (often raising kids and employed twenty to sixty hours a week, moonlighting, while enrolled in several college courses);

• pride on the job in doing their work well; knowledgeable about their jobs (quick learners when it matters to them in real contexts);

• wise about earning a living, resilient in making a life in hard times, don't feel that life has been easy for them but not inclined to complain about it, suspicious of affirmative action as "going too far" (they figure out the angles, try to "beat the system," don't whine or feel sorry for themselves or for so-called oppressed groups);

• smart but not sophisticated or academic; intelligent but not belletristic, scholastic, bohemian, or cosmopolitan as students tend to be on elite campuses (my students are *in* college but not *of* college insofar as the elite discourses of professors and high culture are alien to their ways of knowing and speaking);

• media-drenched but not well-informed about events (watching TV more than reading newspapers, some ignoring public events altogether for lack of time or interest, with virtually no access to alternative media except in a few classes like mine);

• unpredictably literate about special subjective interests (car repair, home-building, World War II battles, adoption, crime, religious cults, intermarriage, specific diseases like *lupus*, the multiple uses of hemp, taxidermy, etc.);

• shrewd and manipulative when they need to be, largely unimpressed by professors and intellectuals, not easily persuaded, not pushovers (my doctorate, rank, authority, politics, and publications don't awe most of them);

• eating a bad diet (hamburgers, hot dogs, french fries, processed food, beer, soda, coffee, sweets, cigarettes) and displaying poor health (frequent flu, coughs, colds, bloodshot eyes, bad complexions, allergies, obesity);

• enjoying good stories, a good laugh, and comradery, which display their generally resilient temperaments.

Even though these general identities fill the classroom, I would say that there is no *stereotypical* working-class student. Their *typical* traits and social conditions are identifiable, but this general reality does not exhaust their individual differences. Their diversity can produce a group personality in one class very different from the personality of another class. In any small sample of students constituting a single class, they can display widely varying age spans, employment profiles, gender mixes, racial and ethnic backgrounds, skin colors, family situations, career choices, academic development, and resistance/openness to critical-democratic pedagogy. In fact, these mostly white working students are striking in their individuality (and belief in individualism). On the one hand, many have internalized the corporate religions of consumerism ("being" is "buying") and self-reliance (making it on your own, pulling yourself up by your own bootstraps, looking after number 1, you have no one to blame but yourself for your failures and troubles, the world doesn't owe you a living, etc.). On the other hand, they have multiple voices and body shapes, many facial expressions, skin colors, and speech mannerisms, diverse hobbies, tastes, job experiences, attitudes about gender and racial prejudice. Still, some things always make a global impression on me as I look out at a large group of students like those in the Utopia class—the makeup, jewelry, and perfume used by some of the women, the look of the men's and women's hair, the cut, color, fabrics, and quality of their clothes, the corporate and celebrity names on their shirts and jerseys, the particular femininity and masculinity in the way men and women carry themselves, the heaviness of their searching gazes as they fix their stares on me (wary, wondering what to expect from this teacher), the great range of the apparent "whiteness" in their ethnic skin colors and the ill-health reflected in their faces (reminding me of my own bad complexion and stringy hair when I was a working-class teenager), the frequency of bad teeth (discolored, uneven, broken, recalling for me the teeth I had lost from my own working-class mouth in a society where good dental care is very expensive). All in all, they look and sound like people who come from working homes, whose fate it is to sell their labor every day to make ends meet, working too many hours and earning too little, able to save peanuts and to invest less, with little or no authority on the job or in the halls of government, little or no power to control the decisions that affect them at work and in their communities. These are some of the "working-class" markers to me, recalling for me the looks, sounds, and laboring conditions of the people I grew up among. With little power, or wealth, or cosmopolitan flair, the students staring back at me in the Utopia basement did not remind me of the Stanford or Berkeley undergraduates I have met.

But, even though I think of them as "working-class," they generally don't think of themselves in those terms, which is a large gap between our understandings. This is a grand cultural canyon separating us— how I have learned to see and name them, myself, and our teaching/ learning relationship versus how they have learned to see themselves, the teacher, and what it means to be a student who works for a living. "Class" is an invisible identity in American life, denied and dismissed (Zandy 1990 and 1995; Dews and Law 1995). School and media don't educate working people about their working-class identities or about acting as critical citizens (Cohen and Solomon 1995; Herman and Chomsky 1988). For example, school history texts generally are silent on the connections between labor history and inequality (Anyon 1979, 1980, 1981; Loewen 1994). Not learning their own working-class history and situation, working students are schooled for a public life as "middle-class" consumers, employees, audiences, spectators, and occasional voters. They do identify themselves ethnically as Italian or Irish or Polish or Puerto Rican, racially as white or black, and genderly as male or female, but economically they hope to stay in or to become part of the "middle class," that is, people who can buy what their kids need, pay their bills, and live with some security and dignity (Ehrenreich 1989; DeMott 1990). The official Utopia of middle-class life is an apparently attainable dream that represents to them social respect, self-esteem, material comfort, and job security.

Yet, for these middle-American Dreamers, the captions "ordinary" or "common" or "average" or "mediocre" strike me as inappropriate. These students are nobody's fools. They are complicated, smart, tough, humorous, enterprising, and capable, expressing a range of voices and personalities. Living from paycheck to paycheck, they are not of the elite, not in their incomes, options, goals, experiences, faces, teeth, thought, dress, food, information resources, or speech. They are urban ethnic working-class students. They have no choice but to work for a living and little choice in deciding to attend my low-budget, distressed commuter college; they could benefit from a big pay raise, shorter hours on the job, a long vacation in a quiet spot with good air and good food, and a readable book on working-class history (Zinn 1980; Brier 1992).

They intrigue me, but how close can a teacher like me get to understanding their typicality and their diversity? That's an ongoing research question for me. By that, I mean it's an open question for my classroom and community inquiry, year after year, from course to course. Having lived among my students, renting upstairs apartments in their neighborhoods, playing basketball with the men in the parks, eating in the diners and bakeries they frequent, shopping in the refrigerated malls and vast supermarkets they trek through, using the local GPs who dispense what serves as their medical care, and observing them in class after class, I get a little closer each year. While I'm Jewish and not Italian or Irish like most of them, I've been observing their non-elite characters for a long time from the perspective of a teacher-researcher with my own working-class roots. My identity reflects that of the "anxious and uprooted" scholarship boys and girls (Hoggart 1957) who left crowded homes and teeming urban neighborhoods to study at picturesque university towns where we lost touch with our roots (for accounts of the gains and losses of such upward mobility, see Ryan and Sackrey 1984; Rose 1990; Tokarczyk and Fay 1993; Zandy 1990, 1995; Brodkey 1994; Dews and Law 1995). While I'm an upward climber from the South Bronx working class who went from the Bronx High School of Science to the handsome elite Universities of Michigan and Wisconsin, my students at Staten Island generally don't claim working-class identities and do not win scholarships to the green grounds of fancy campuses. My school and social experiences are thus very different from theirs, and so are my politics, but I once shared their dreams of middle-class Utopia when I first started on a climbing path. So, if we don't share politics, at least we occupy a significant past as well as a conflicted pedagogical present where a culture war gets underway every opening day of class.

The Opening Day: Utopia Meets the Siberian Syndrome

Anxious and uprooted, I breathed deeply in B-34, hoping to get some oxygen to my brain in this airless hole of a room. The students watched me with expectant gazes and mixed complexions, waiting for the professor to do education to them, like other teachers who had done it to them before, shellacking them with knowledge until their faces shined like maple tabletops.

Inside the basement chamber, the Utopia story really begins with how the students chose seats. It all starts with classroom chairs and the pattern of their seating preferences. In my teaching, I have been interested in the cultural study of institutional furniture (see my exercises with classroom chairs in *Critical Teaching and Everyday Life*, originally published in 1980). When I first took a cultural studies approach to education in the 1970s, examining such things as campus parking lots as interferences to critical thought, I found that the students' relationship to seating is a significant text revealing the power relations embedded in schooling, or the social power "circulating" in the discipline of school, as Foucault (1980) put it. The chairs in B-34 were old friends, the same fiberglass seats I wrote about when I first experimented with critical teaching by asking students to analyze the ideology of classroom furniture twenty years before. This was a revealing and hilarious exercise, to discover that we were sitting on power relations and didn't even know it. These cheap, drab, tubular aluminum/fiberform seats are ubiquitous in the College, unlike the comfortable upholstered furniture chosen by the administration for itself. The fiberglass chairs are uncomfortable because the hard sitting area is too small for many students attending this College, especially when they arrive with textbooks, notebooks, shoulder-bags, purses, attache cases, winter coats, etc., for which there is too little room on the chair, on the small desk area, or around the chair on the floor. The class hour is invariably punctuated by the sound of falling books, papers, purses, pens, soda cans, coffee cups, etc. These cheap chairs do make it possible to save money on furnishings, but they represent a depressant environmental message to students about the institution's respect for them, about the quality of learning intended for them in this place, and about the limited impact this College's degree will have on their future careers in the job market. Holistically viewed, people who count in school and society don't get educated on chairs like this, in a room like this, in a place like this, in a curriculum that barks rules and bellows facts at them. Classroom furniture helps discipline students into a status quo of inequality. The socialization into inequality is an environmental outcome of the look, sound, and feel of the place as well as a pedagogical outcome of an uncritical, anti-dialogic curriculum which silences discussions of class, among other central issues (Anyon 1983; Sizer 1984; hooks 1994).

Significantly, in the basement chamber of B-34, for me the teacher there was a different chair provided, one without arms or a small formica desk attached to it. Mine had some black leatherette upholstery on it to cushion my bottom. This minimal attention to my comfort and authority, this noticeably different and upgraded chair, was placed in a special spot of power, at the front of the room near the blackboard, behind a (low-budget) symbol of authority—a cheap formica-veneered steel desk. The thirty-five students had unupholstered fiberglass and aluminum chairs set in rows facing my desk. The power relations of this setting are normal and routine, dispiriting, but not exceptional. The ideology and discipline they represent fade into the background, allowing the experience to assume a business-as-usual quality, the normative routines we expect.

Under these circumstances, a kind of epistemic illusion is delivered by the traditional syllabus: culture is presented as nature. That is, what has been socially and historically constructed by a specific culture becomes presented to students as undebatable and unchangeable, always there, timeless. Like plants growing toward sunlight, students are expected to sit in rows facing the lecturing teacher at the front, the unilateral authority who tells them what things mean, what to do, and how to become people who fit into society as it is. This classroom design is an architecture of control that helps teachers assert their authority to transmit an official syllabus to the students, but as Luke Menand (1995) has humorously explained, "There is nothing more counterproductive than single-mindedly hammering your own views into the heads of your students. Students' heads have been designed through millions of years of evolutionary development to be impervious to hammering.

When you hammer, as everybody does, in desperation, at some point or other in the course of a semester, students go completely rote on you" (p. 61).

Students are creative, intelligent beings, not plants or blank slates or pegboards for teacherly hammering. So, their complex minds and creative desires conflict with architectures of control in curricula that present knowledge and society as finished and fine the way they are. In these classroom "contact zones" (Pratt 1991) of unequal power, students adapt through various means of accommodation and resistance. For example, in the Utopia class, they did not randomly seat themselves as they entered the basement room. For most of the students, certain areas of the room are choice while others are apparently the last resort. As is their habit, most students typically filled the two far corners of the room first, farthest from where the teacher sits. While a few students sat near the front, the decisive majority of both men and women preferred the two classroom territories I fondly call "Siberia, East and West," as distant from me the teacher (the center of authority and academic discourse) as they could be. Their seats of choice were as close to the two rear corners as possible, as far from the front of the room as the cramped space allowed. B-34 was a smallish classroom, perhaps fifteen by twenty feet, so they didn't have a grand opportunity to sit truly far from me. But, they did the best they could, enacting what I call their "Siberian Syndrome," that is, their learned habit of automatically filling the distant corners first, representing their subordinate and alienated position, which drives them to seek the remote seats of any classroom they inhabit. Most of the students have learned socially to construct themselves as intellectual exiles as far from the front of the room as they can be. Heading to the rear of the Utopia basement that day, they took the process in contradictory directions at the same time— by going North to Siberia they helped constitute my sole authority at the front of the room while undermining my authority by sitting as far away as they could from me. They appear to be rejecting authority and submitting to it at the same time.

This Siberian Syndrome is dominant and characteristic, but not universal or uniform. It appears in class by degrees, along a spectrum of response. While most students avoid the front of the room, a handful do want to sit near me, and I will have more to say on this small group of front-seaters, referring to them as "scholasticons" because they identify with school discipline while expressing their own novel forms of resistance. Of those who avoid the teacher's desk at the front, some are more aggressively in exile than others. The more distant and de-

tached I will be calling "the deep Siberians." Lastly, those who go toward the back but don't fight for the most distant corner seats I will
refer to as "the mid-Siberians." On the whole, this decisive student
preference for the Siberian corners seems to be a widespread syndrome
in education, as I discover when I speak to groups of teachers around
the country. When I have asked teachers to guess how most students
prefer to seat themselves in my classes, they correctly and invariably
describe the Siberian Syndrome. Many report witnessing the same race
for the corner seats in their own classes. One education commentator,
Ron Gross, acknowledged this pervasive syndrome: "Anyone who has
stood at a podium recognizes that all classrooms have the same topogra-
phy: Seated down front are the few students who share their teacher's
enthusiasm, while the back rows are inhabited by the majority, who
virtually dare the instructor to force some culture down their throats"
(quoted in Graff 1992, p. 98). Gerald Graff added his thoughts on this
phenomenon by saying that "The stark division between the enthusias-
tic front-bench minority and the disaffected back-bench majority is indeed a persistent feature of classroom life" (p. 99). Of course, unlike
the Siberian exiles of czarist Russia and of the former USSR, these
students have not been arrested for political activity or social crimes;
they have not been ordered into a distant territorial jail by a totalitarian
regime; in theory, in law, they are free to sit wherever they want in
class. Which only begs the question—Why, then, in fact, do they race
for the corners if they are "free" to sit near the front? Why do most
avoid the front and prefer the rear? Why are the seats near the teacher
the least desirable to students and the last to fill up?

A syndrome is a repetitive pattern of behavior developed through
social experiences and institutional practices. Seating choices patterned
into a Siberian Syndrome cannot be described as "free" even though
we do not live in a totalitarian state like the czarism and Stalinism
that gave Siberian exile its legendary status. Essentially, the Siberian
Syndrome is one form of student agency in the contact zone of mass
education. It is a defensive reaction to the unequal power relations of
schooling, which include unilateral authority for the teacher and a curriculum evading critical thought about the history, language, and cultures of the students. Facing unilateral authority that disempowers
them politically and disables them intellectually, most students in my
classes position themselves in the Siberian corners where they can carry
out a variety of guerilla resistances I will enumerate shortly. Given the
outlaw status of their home dialects and community cultures in school,
they construct themselves as subordinates who can't escape authority

but won't cooperate fully with it either—hence, the contradictory position of Siberian exile, being inside and outside of school discipline simultaneously, receiving and rejecting official supervision at the same time, an unhealthy pattern of agency and dependency worthy of the name "syndrome."

Thus, what I call *the Siberian Syndrome* is the students' reactive desire to crowd themselves in the distant corner seats, a socially constructed response to unequal power and institutional discipline. The Siberian Syndrome is a metaphor representing cultural conflict in undemocratic classrooms. The students' apparent acceptance of subordination by occupying the margins is accompanied by other resistances to authority, including outright confrontation with the teacher-authority. Their Siberian resistance comprises what I would describe as *self-protective negative agency* because they are in a symbolic state of intellectual exile, pushed away from learning and pushing it away in response. In the form of resistance represented by the Siberian Syndrome, the students' race for the corner seats reflects a micropolitical struggle between them and the teacher, and, more generally, a larger conflict between nonelite students and schooling in an unequal society. The Siberian Syndrome expresses the students' subordination to the teacher who has the right to govern alone, to make the syllabus, to discipline and punish students according to non-negotiated standards, to be the predominant "rhetor" or speaker who solely enforces what Michel Foucault (1980) called the "regime of truth"—the appropriate forms of discourse, evaluation, subject matter, questions, and interpretations concerning knowledge or behavior. On all matters, from attendance rules to paper deadlines to acceptable dialect and discourse to textbook choices, authority is unilateral. Empowered institutionally by the system but not constitutionally through negotiation with students, the teacher cannot escape problems of resistance and control. In such a non-negotiable regime, students are intellectual and political exiles who grow more cleverly distant and resistant as they age.

Democracy or Hierarchy? Critical Learning versus Siberian Conflict

The Utopia students I watched heading for Siberia began developing their syndrome long before they reached the cinderblock and windowless walls of B-34. For years, they had been learning that their place in school and society was marginal and subordinate. Schooled to follow orders and to fit into lesser places, they reenact and reconstitute their marginality in each new class by heading immediately for the far corners, from which marginal space they can more easily resist the very process marginalizing them (which, I am arguing, they accommodate to and resist at the same time). Affectively, the issue could be posed in terms of their disgust with this version of social and intellectual life, their despair about their educational experience (my class will be their next bout of official academic processing). Facing another classroom in their long socialization through schooling, most, but not all, prefer to keep their distance by a visible race for the limited number of seats in Siberia. Outside of class, in contrast to their Siberian behaviors in schooling, students push to the front of the line when there is something they like or want that is meaningful (like front-row seats at concerts, ballgames, etc., and front-line spots for job interviews). They move to the corners and to the rear when they feel awkward, disrespected, defensive, mistreated, angry, bored, uninvolved, threatened, hopeless, or powerless. Those few scholasticons (like myself) who identify with teachers and schooling move toward the front row because they feel competent in making the system work for their upward mobility, and it does for some.

As the Utopia students went for the corner seats, I knew that this was not a happy state of affairs. It's a sadly conflicted way to launch a new semester, especially in a course called "Utopia," with its themes of community and empowerment. I wish student-teacher relations were congenial instead of conflicted, but, how could they be mutual given the process of mass education—skill-drilling and vocationalism (Kohl 1984; Rose, 1990); teacher-talk, didactic lecturing, memorizing, short-answer testing, unilateral authority, and dull textbooks (Cuban 1984; Goodlad 1984); grossly unequal funding for wealthy and working-class schools (Kozol 1991); a "sorting machine" (Oakes 1985; Spring 1989; Oakes and Lipton 1990) tracking out some elite winners from the many losers. Still, no matter how routine it has become, I am not casual about the Siberian Syndrome. It still amazes me when I watch students enact it at the start of each term. What is stunning about the student preference for Siberia is how automatic it has become before they even reach high school or college.

Remember that the class constructed itself in the Siberian Syndrome before I had uttered a word on that first day of class. I gave no instructions on where to sit. The students who raced to the rear of the room and avoided the empty seats near me have learned that the back is their place given their subordinate position in the traditional classroom. In an unequal, non-negotiated institution, students enact Siberia on the first day of class in the presence of a new teacher they have never met, without having heard me speak. Insofar as I am "the teacher," I am already part of their experience before they experience me. I already exist in their imaginations as part of their subordination to school authority, inside an education system that has been driving them to the rear. They know me before they meet me. They have met me every year before we arrived in this basement chamber. They met my prototypes and precursors in the classrooms they already attended. Before I even say a word, they expect the teacher to be a unilateral authority. They expect an authoritarian rhetorical setting: teacher-talk, teacher-centered standard English, an official syllabus with remote subject matter, and unilateral rule-making. This non-negotiated rhetoric prescribes the knowledge to be learned and the rules to be followed. Such a long-term prescriptive process has moved them to Siberia without the need for me to issue any commands or directions. They have internalized a political compass that compels them to go North into exile. All in all, their race for the Siberian seats emerges from their being talked at, talked about, talked around, and talked down to, but rarely talked *with* in traditional schooling.

Because such a thing as the Siberian Syndrome occurs before I have said anything in class, I argued in *Empowering Education* (1992b) that critical-democratic teachers start at "less than zero" when we begin a negotiated curriculum—with "less than zero" meaning that the status quo presents opening obstacles to critical thought and democratic process. We do not begin with a clean slate free from history, society, or cultural conflict related to gender, race, and class, when we attempt to reconstruct power relations. Critical pedagogy is a "social-epistemic" rhetoric (Berlin 1988) that acknowledges the existing political obstacles to critical thought; it teaches about and against the power relations opposing the transformation of unequal power.

Less than Zero in Siberia: Deploying Critical-Democratic Pedagogy

I often wonder how to use my teacherly authority when faced by the Siberian Syndrome. As the teacher, I'm supposed to go to the front and assert the authority vested in my position. Students expect this (Boomer et al. 1992). This is what teachers learn to do as their routine professional behavior, their "teacherhood." Students enact their "studenthood" by filling the room from Siberia forward. Yet, although subordinate, studenthood is hardly passive, as I suggested above, because the students are actively constructing their apparent passivity and withdrawal, which is not really passive and not exactly withdrawn. As

Foucault (1980) argued, domination is not simply an "interdict," a pro-hibitive "no" that leads to passivity; rather, dominant power "circu-lates," an idea I mentioned before, so that the targets of authority have roles to perform, things to do and say, in constructing their own subor-dinate position. This agency is what Henry Giroux (1983 and 1988) has discussed from a postmodern perspective on student resistance to schooling. Exercising various kinds of agency in an unequal setting where they lack formal authority, students also resist/engage/manipu-late the teacher, the process, and the institution through their informal power, as Theodore Sizer (1984) and Peter McLaren (1988) have also argued. Students are constructing the subordinate self at the same time that they are resisting and undermining it, while believing that their "real selves," "real lives," are somewhere else, not contaminated or controlled by this dominating process.

In such cultural conflict, there is no simple way critical-democratic pedagogy can transform the anti-intellectual stalemate of an unequal status quo. With students having learned to prefer the rear long before the Utopia class even began, my offer of transformative pedagogy started from a point of dramatic teacher-student alienation, the legacy of inequality which Freire (1970) posed as the first problem of libera-tory learning: "Education must begin with the solution of the teacher-student contradiction, by reconciling the poles of the contradiction so that both are simultaneously teachers *and* students" (p. 59). What is especially instructive is that these power problems are social and histor-ical, not personal peculiarities; that is, they already exist in class before the teacher's introduction of the syllabus, before the presentation of formal academic subject matter, before the teacher utters a single word, because education is a social activity formed within the cultural conflicts in society at large. Reflecting inequality in the larger society, teacher-student alienation becomes an interference to academic study and criti-cal thought. It stands in the way of students embracing intellectual work. Thus, before "teaching the conflicts" (Graff 1992; Lazere 1992b) among scholars in any field, we first need to face the always already-existing conflicts between students and the teacher, between students and the institution, between students and the economic system (class, gender, racial inequities), and between the students themselves (over issues of race, gender, sexual orientation, ethnicity, age, physical abil-ity, appearance, choice of major, career competitiveness against each other for grades, etc.). If I begin a course immediately by introducing canonical subject matter or academic conflicts in a field, I am bypassing and pre-empting the destructive power conflicts which already exist in the room before any formal material is presented. Teaching any disciplinary material, including the academic conflicts among scholars, before negotiating the curriculum with students to share power, only frontloads the process with official authority which confirms students as silenced spectators in an education being done to them for their own good, not being done by them or with them. After a negotiated curriculum is underway and authority is being shared, teaching the academic conflicts in any field could be very useful.

Thus, to bypass the political conflicts represented by the Siberian Syndrome is to miss the power relations interfering with critical learning in the first place. The shape of authority shapes the experience of knowledge-making; by transforming unilateral authority, teacher and students begin creating a mutual learning process as the best condition for the introduction of any formal academic subject matter. The Siberian Syndrome results from a destructive knowledge-making process. As long as a struggle for authority exists in a classroom or an institution, the disciplinary learning hoped for in any curriculum will be damaged.

But, in terms of transforming undemocratic power relations, I cannot instantly shed or deny the authority I bring to class. Many students won't allow that. They expect me to install unilateral authority; in some ways, they prefer it or want it, more than just expect it. Yet, it is risky to hand over authority to the students all at once (see Hyde, "Chapter 5," in Boomer et al. 1992). That could be bewildering and unproductive, even arrogant. It would be naive for me to act as if I can walk away from teacherly authority and simply dump power into the students' laps. I cannot end the Siberian Syndrome by a single (Utopian!) command or an automatic transfer of authority to students because many of them

- don't want to share authority (it's easier for them do it the old-fashioned teacher-centered way; it's more demanding to take responsibility for their education);
- don't like the negotiating process (they don't feel authoritative, or they believe in traditional authority, perhaps respecting teachers and elders, or they feel uneducated and want the teacher-expert to tell them what things mean and what to do, so they can absorb as much knowledge as possible);
- don't know how to use authority or to negotiate the curriculum (few, if any, democratic models have crossed their experience; they have rarely or never practiced codeveloping the syllabus before and have become authority-dependent);

- don't understand the explanatory discourse I use to introduce power-sharing (my political frameworks and academic idiom may not make sense to them);
- don't trust my sincerity or the negotiation process even if it appeals to them (there are risks in taking an unknown road with a more powerful official stranger as a guide);
- are reluctant to take public risks by speaking up in an unfamiliar process, because they are shy, or lack confidence in their voice or appearance, or feel at risk because they are female or minority and prefer not to draw attention to themselves in a masculinist or white environment.

Unlikely as it seems, I am trying to be a critical-democratic teacher in a setting where critical inquiry and power-sharing have virtually no profile in student experience. Faced by this democratic vacuum in everyday life, I have no choice but to use my institutional authority to ease into a process of shared power. Whatever authority I inherit through my status as a tall, veteran, white male professor enables my asserting a process that attempts to transform my initial unilateral position. I invite students to invent with me a negotiated curriculum in a mutual process that repositions us, opening the chance to pass through the membranes separating them and me, Siberia and the front of the room. Needless to say, there are serious limits to such use of unilateral authority to create democratic relations; my invitation of power-sharing to students is an unsolicited attempt to distribute some authority to people who are not expecting it, to negotiate a mutual relationship with a group that has not asked for mutuality. So, my transformative overtures begin as an outside overlay not emerging from inside their own agendas, the implications of which I will examine later on. Because the students bring no transformative agendas to class, it's up to me to inaugurate a critical-democratic project, which means that such a novel program will have uneven, unpredictable results, depending on how students accept or reject my invitation to share authority and depending on how well I introduce these possibilities and navigate the surprises.

In initiating and guiding this difficult change, I try to speak plain English, but I am the product of two elite universities. Also, I came of age during a previous time of social activism when youth and hope were synonyms. I developed as a critical teacher through years of classroom experiments and have become part of the English and education professions. Can my language and development cross paths with theirs? There is no simple answer, of course. The students' openness to my proposals and their very comprehension of my discourse vary from class to class, in terms of their willingness to pay attention to my words, to puzzle out the meanings, and then to talk back to my invitation to negotiate. As I said early on, students do not come to class expecting a negotiated curriculum, power-sharing, or an invitation to critique the status quo. Because their prior school experiences have developed the Siberian Syndrome in most of them, the negotiation process has to proceed by developing their undeveloped democratic arts and desires. They arrive with little practice in democratic rhetoric. They do know how to follow or to frustrate authority (sometimes by doing both at the same time!) but not how to assume authority. In this situation, students and teachers can only learn how to negotiate by negotiating, on-the-job, in-process. We don't come to class with the discourse habits suitable for reconstituting power relations. We have to invent that discourse as we invent the process and, by doing so, reconstruct our social selves.

This in-process invention calls upon me to behave like an authority who is a legitimate teacher, someone who knows something worth learning, who knows how to teach what I know, who knows how to listen to students and how to be fair with grades and assignments, and who can maintain order. These are some minimal markers that reassure students of my competence and of the intellectual seriousness of the course. If I deny these professional signs of authority, I will broadcast incompetence or carelessness. This will tell them that they are in an "anything-goes" class where I lose their respect and confidence, thus inviting frivolous disregard for the work, or even chaos. My best course of action has so far been to use my authority to organize a transformation of authority, step by step.

In short, I cannot act as if I have no authority, am not an authority, and cannot use authority fairly and democratically; and I cannot act as if they are ready to assume authority. I bring authority into the room as a veteran professor, a white person, and as a tall man. Further, I am an authority on a few things that matter, such as some social issues of serious concern, some bodies of knowledge worth knowing, some learning methods for a critical curriculum, some life experiences in and out of school that are worth sharing, some ways of learning to write and use writing, and some deep feelings about knowledge and culture related to social justice. So, I must acknowledge and establish my various kinds of authority while distributing some power by inviting students to negotiate the curriculum. The power that uses power to share and transform power is the power I am seeking.

The Power to Transform Power: Authority Moves to Siberia

In search of transformative power relations, faced early and often with the Siberian Syndrome, I followed an instinct not to lecture from the front of the room when I first began teaching at the College in 1971. Back then, I witnessed the Siberian Syndrome in my classes and was awestruck at the force of student resistance. What to do? I danced to every tune my pedagogical imagination devised and borrowed whatever I could from colleagues with whom I was building a remedial program. Some interventions helped, some didn't. Then, intuition and desperation led me to move to Siberia itself, the stronghold of student exile and resistance. I went to Siberia to deal with its obstacle to learning. Apparently lost in my first years at this low-budget college, unnerved by and unhappy with student alienation, I rejected lecturing from the front and began teaching dialogically from the back of the room.

Seated in dreaded Siberia, I found myself among the students who wanted least to sit near me. This choice provoked some disturbing and hilarious moments. Our mutual discomfort was visceral. They grimaced. I sweated. Once in their territory, I spoke tentatively with them and they grudgingly with me. They leaned back or to the side in their adjacent seats to open up more space between us. During class dialogue, I posed questions directly to them, close up, which made it hard for me to write them off as "illiterate" students or as cultural "deficits" or as "common" people; it also made it harder for them to write me off as an "irrelevant" or "talky" teacher with a superior "attitude." We were too close physically to objectify each other. Face to face, it also became awkward for students to remain silent. Yet it was also difficult for them to speak, because the traditional, restrictive discourses known as teacher-talk and monosyllabic student response were not appropriate for our close-up encounters.

This repositioning of my body from the front to Siberia thus resulted in some interesting disturbances in both of our behaviors. The students had to decide whether to move away from me and migrate to the other side of Siberia or to relocate themselves toward the front of the room where I wasn't, or to stay put and respond to me or to just keep quiet (which I mentioned is hard to do when the teacher is sitting a foot away and talking to you). Some students re-established the distant relationship between us by moving away from me, resisting my disruption of seating protocols by repositioning themselves. They moved to the front which I had evacuated or to the side of Siberia where I wasn't seated.

When they went to the front, they were pioneering a "New Siberia" in an area supposedly belonging to the teacher. Students in the front rows faced another problem of body positioning. They had to decide whether to keep their seats facing the front I had evacuated or to turn their necks or seats around to face me at the rear, where I had resettled. Moving into discussion circles eased the neck problem. Still, that part of the circle that touched the front desk maintained a residual aura as "the front of the room." On the other hand, wherever I was sitting in the circle was also "the front of the room" simply because my white male professor's body was there with its socially-vested authority. In these complex reconfigurations, there were varying degrees of change from class to class, with unavoidable growing pains associated with questioning a powerful protocol—the didactic teacher at the front lecturing students on subject matter in academic discourse. Yet, despite the tensions, I found something exhilarating and even comic in these rearrangements, challenging old habits and relationships, undermining protocols, reinventing a small but apparently powerful tradition of who sits where, practicing a little of the democracy and equality we hear so much about in schools, media, and the speeches of politicians. With my body in Siberia, it became simply harder for us to construct our traditional relations at such close range. Their habits of half-attention to the talking teacher or of sabotaging the lesson plan and rejecting their own potentials for learning, and my habitual training in teacher-centered discourse, are helped along by the traditional architecture of classroom seating. By moving to Siberia I stumbled on one small way to question habitual power relations.

In considering my move to Siberia as an attempt to overcome teacher-student alienation, I'm reminded of Lev Vygotsky's (1962) discussion of the "Law of Awareness," which suggested that a break in a routine or an impediment to an automatic activity raises awareness of the activity and routine. When a routine is broken, we then have a chance to notice it, question it and consider alternatives. We can use critical-democratic discourse to transform the relations we begin with. In this way, discourse is a material force able to mediate transformation, which takes place through a cognitive relationship Vygotsky named "the zone of proximal development," to indicate what people can learn with one another which they are not capable of learning alone. Mary Louise Pratt's (1991) definition of "the contact zone," which I've referred to before, is an advanced version of Vygotsky's "zone of proximal development," because Pratt enumerates specific rhetorical and pedagogical arts which can make the zone critical, democratic, and transformative instead of unequal, colonizing, and oppressive. The key difference here, emphasized by Pratt, is disturbing the routinely "asymmetrical" power relations through which we rhetorically, pedagogically, and socially construct unequal selves.

Every curriculum is a zone of one kind of development or another depending on the power relations and subject matters undertaken in it. Traditional classrooms provide the status quo with educational contact zones that normalize inequality and authoritarian relations. A break in the routine provides an alternative zone in which to question our participation in the status quo. My move to Siberia had some of that altering effect, of dislocating a familiar habit through which students constitute themselves as subordinate "outsiders" and the teacher constructs herself/himself as the authoritative "insider." Critical-democratic pedagogy, then, as a "contact zone" or as a "zone of proximal development," becomes a laboratory for the counter-hegemonic reconstruction of the social self.

Disturbing the students' perception of "the front of the room" was one way I tried to question hegemonic authority. Later on, year by year, I discovered that moving around the room worked better than simply sitting in the rear to disturb the habitual exile of students and my habitual training to be a lecturer. My mobile position in the room also disturbed the emergence of "New Siberias" when students relocated to parts of the room where I wasn't. When I speak at campuses or conferences, I sometimes leave the podium and move to the rear, especially when there are students avoiding the front rows and congregating in the back. Public forums are structured like classrooms, in terms of the expert authority being positioned at the front, higher up, far away, with wary audiences keeping their distance, especially students from classes required to attend my talk (for their own good, of course). I find myself unable to give a formal talk in lecture halls whose Siberian corners are packed with uninvolved students avoiding the empty space in front of the lectern, so I usually evacuate the podium and move to Siberia where I begin a dialogue with the alienated students about their education.

Perhaps the larger connection of the Siberian Syndrome to power in society is obvious by now. We develop in a society with a democratic story about itself that is so enveloping and sentimental that it is hard to notice how authoritarian and oligarchic power actually is, at work, in school, in government, in business, in the media, etc. Power in society is like power in schools, colleges, and classrooms—unilateral, unelected, top-down, hierarchical, patriarchal, not democratic. Just imagine if schools were run democratically; students would participate in policy-making at the classroom, departmental, and institutional levels, thus becoming socialized as active, critical citizens who took the initiative in framing their own purposes (to use Dewey's formulation of democratic society), who didn't wait for authorities and the media to tell them what to think about and what things mean. Thus, when I moved to Siberia in my early years of teaching, I was disturbing more than seat preferences. An architecture of social power sits down with us.

The Seat of Power: Authority and the Body

Crossing the grand cultural canyon between teacher and students by going to Siberia was intuitive for me, but it was not an easy thing to do. I've hinted along the way at a few things that made it easier back then: my tall white male body, my youthful exuberance and democratic dreams, and my good luck to begin teaching in activist times when hope and social change were ideas whose time had come. I was simply tall enough, confident in my white male physicality and my professorship, and animated by Utopian desires in an insurgent age, to draw on the authority of my gender, my color, and the activist times to take some risks. Different bodies, skin colors, and genders carry unequal authority into the room. The gendered nature of authority, for example, has been examined in many feminist readings of pedagogy (Culley and Portuges 1985; Ellsworth 1989; Bauer 1990; Luke and Gore 1992; Gore 1993, to name some). The issue of presumed authority and the gendered body was discussed by Don Dippo and Steven Gelb like this:

> We initially saw the "problem of empowerment" as one of simply rene-gotiating the distribution of power with students. Yet the ability to do so presumes that students, at least at the outset, recognize some measure of authority and expertise on the part of faculty . . . [W]e have come to appreciate the inappropriateness of generalized calls to share power for other faculty members whose authority and expertise are continually threatened or dismissed. As men, working in early childhood, primary, and junior education where the majority of students are women, we rarely, if ever, even hear about let alone have to face the aggressive/abusive challenges to authority which many women faculty members must confront on a regular basis. (1991: 85–86)

Masculinity does privilege my right to assume authority in a patriar-chal society, but maleness by itself is not a lock on power, not if a male teacher of color is addressing white students, and sometimes not for white men at some schools and colleges. Unlike Dippo's and Gelb's apparently pacific classroom experiences, I have faced aggressive challenges despite my authority as a tall, white, male professor, especially when dealing with tough young white men from the working class, a few of whom threatened me directly over the years, and, during one term, two of whom required the chief of security to get their aggression under control. Yet, from colleague's reports, I understand that the situation is worse for female educators and for those of color.

A teacher's authority to question the status quo also varies with the changing tides of politics. Different eras have different political climates, encouraging or repressing democratic activism. In what I have called the "conservative restoration" following the activist sixties—the reactionary period from Nixon through Gingrich—it became increasingly harder for me to pursue experiments, as students, colleagues, and administrators pulled in their sails, in tune with the declining social movements and the rising reactionary politics of these decades. In such times, teachers and students feel less secure about questioning the status quo, so the deeply rooted Siberian Syndrome is harder to disturb.

Disturbing Authority: Human Agency and Siberian Alienation

A progressive climate in society is a refreshing support for teachers and students who choose to question the status quo. But, in any era, the Siberian Syndrome will be a contradictory act of resistance and accommodation, as I mentioned earlier. Such complex human agency is not mere passivity and not mere withdrawal from academic work. Seeing Siberia one-dimensionally as simply withdrawal distorts its active reality. As Foucault suggested in his description of how power busily circulates at the site of institutional discipline, Siberia is a complex way to construct oneself socially in relation to authority; it can at times be more engaging than front-row participation in the official syllabus. There are subtleties which make Siberian resistance a textured instance of the human power to act on experience despite a dominating process. For many students, Siberia is an attractive alternative to a non-negotiated syllabus delivered in uninspiring teacher-talk. Posed as a site of resistant agency, Siberia functions for students as a means to cope with and to undermine the official culture of schooling and the authority of the teacher.

Put simply, it is easier for students to resist authority from the cor-

ners than from the front of the room. Siberia is thus a partially protected staging area for culture war in the classroom, separated from the
base of operations established by the teacher from her or his fortress
at the front. At the margins of a classroom, students have more opportunities to resist. This is one example of the postmodern recognition
of marginalized sites becoming spaces of empowerment.

Students avoid the front because it's the center of disempowering
authority, the headquarters of alien power, I might say. The front
broadcasts official knowledge and is the governing seat of teacher authority. Being at the front instead of in Siberia puts students nearer
the center of formal power, close to the narrating voice and judgmental
gaze of the teacher. What this means in terms of the school experience
is that sitting near the front places students under the most demanding
discipline (surveillance) in the classroom. Sitting near the front requires
attention to bookish work (an approved syllabus) and to a top-down
alien discourse (teacher-talk). The closer to the front you get, the more
likely it is that the teacher will ask you questions about remote material
and will observe your behavior with greater care. Students sitting at
the front have to be more alert, more involved, and more engaged in eye
contact with the teacher. This alertness and involvement are physically,
intellectually, and emotionally demanding, especially when the curricular contents are low and when the teacher speaks a strange discourse.
In the back of the room, students can more easily evade questions from
the teacher while also avoiding eye contact. In Siberia, students can
relax their eyes and necks by paying attention to less. They can also
perform some services and distractions for each other.

What are the active if fugitive services Siberians perform for each
other? For one thing, as the teacher lectures or asks questions, they can
quietly consult with each other about what the teacher is saying to them
and asking from them, whispering translations of the teacher's academic
idiom into words they can understand. They can also feed each other
whispered answers to the teacher's questions, so that they can answer
decently when called upon. If tired, they can more easily take a nap in
the back of the room. If they are falling behind, they can copy someone
else's homework or seatwork, do homework for this class or another, or
read a textbook chapter for a test later on in this or another course. Further, they can have whispered social conversations (schmoozin' and crui-
sin') or play games (I once discovered two Brooklyn guys playing poker
in Siberia while a remedial writing class was underway) or get something
off their chests (I came across two white guys in the Utopia class using
Siberia to badmouth New York's flamboyant black activist Reverend Al

Sharpton, instead of doing the group work for the day) or read illicit material like the sports pages of the daily paper or the schedule of classes for next semester (whose byzantine inscriptions they must decipher in time to make some decisions at upcoming registration). When the course material is remote, the teacher incomprehensible, or their time too short in the stressed-out byways of everyday life, for many students Siberia is the easier place to be while class is in progress, for both alienated men and alienated women. As I mentioned above, these micropolitics make Siberia a site of human agency, a lived experience, not a mere passive withdrawal. Such anti-authoritarian agency also disrupts the start and functioning of critical classes because a dominant pattern stays in place until a counterhegemonic process dislodges it and wins over a critical mass for transformation.

Needless to say, old habits die hard. Student resistance to my dialogic invitations, including my physical arrival in Siberia, persists and varies from class to class. In some venues, my interventions are more welcomed than others. Years of socialization have led us to internalize the unilateral authority of the teacher as the normal, "commonsense" way to do education (Mayher 1990). To be in school means to be enveloped in didactic teacher-talk. A real class is one where the teacher does most of the talking, we learn. Students have little to teach each other, it seems, so why listen to your peers when they speak? In this way, traditional authority produces the Siberian Syndrome through the "pouring in," "banking," "deficit-filling," and "pharmaceutical dosage" methods of instruction (to use Dewey's, Freire's, Bruner's, and Boomer's metaphors of depositing prefixed parcels of knowledge into allegedly empty student minds). To say these are socially constructed practices is to say the obvious, because education is a social institution which evolved historically to teach students what kind of people to become, how to see society, and how to fit into the status quo.

By moving as far as they can from the "the front of the room," then, students resist official discipline while also accommodating to its reign. They don't displace or transform the teacher or the syllabus, but neither do they embrace the teacher's language and curriculum or allow it to function effectively. Such a compromise with power cannot be changed by simply moving my teacher's body to the rear. That was a useful start that needed more. My disruptive action had to be followed by a critical learning process involving more than the relocation of the teacher's body. It concerns how we choose and study subject matter, how the class is governed, researched, and evaluated, and how differences in the room get expressed and negotiated.

Back to the Basement Utopia: Can the Classroom Become a "Constitutional Convention"?

We are the metaphors we learn and live by. "The Siberian Syndrome" is a metaphor I use to dramatize the architecture of control and the anti-intellectual results of traditional power relations. Routine habits need dramatizing because they tend to fade into the background and become experienced as unchangeable nature rather than as transformable culture.

In the everyday culture of the classroom, students do not invent Siberia on a whim. They head for the distant corners because the learning process constructs that position as an appropriate option. They are more or less driven to their corners year by year; eventually, they help the process along by preferring the distant seats before a new teacher has even opened his or her mouth on the first day of class. Witnessing this disturbing student preference for the corners, I decided to study and disturb it. As I said earlier, the bizarre spectacle of most students preferring to sit as far from me as possible is a condition I never got used to and still refuse to accept.

Still crazy after all these years, I want to believe that critical thought, democratic authority, congenial relations, and humane social policies have a future even in windowless classrooms. Imagine an ideal setting to discourage intellectual work and Utopian dreams, and room B-34 will appear in your thoughts, with thirty-five students facing the front in silent rows. By negotiating the curriculum rather than by legislating from the front of the room, I hoped to change the basement Siberia into a "constitutional convention" where we shared authority, cogoverned, and codeveloped the syllabus. The strange thing about the story I will tell is that some students liked power-sharing all too well, embracing it in ways that nearly ended the class before it began.

Return now with me to B-34. With the Siberian Syndrome fully in place as the Utopia class began, I looked out on thirty-five faces waiting for me to do education to them as the next authority in their long school lives. In the cinderblock room, on the verge of yet another reach for a Utopia course, I saw the students spread out from deep Siberia forward. They watched me with impatient eyes. I turned to them with dubious hope.

TWO

Sharing Power, Democratizing Authority, and Mediating Resistance

Negotiating Cultural Conflict: Shared Authority Joins Critical Pedagogy

"Why are you taking this course?" I asked the Utopia students on a sign-in questionnaire on the first day, while I thought to myself, "Why am I teaching this course?"

To build a pedagogy situated in student conditions, I needed to learn many things, including their reasons for being in room B-34, our basement tunnel to Utopia. My education in this peculiar place began with interrogating my motives and goals before class and then moved to learning their situation as soon as we met. Their role in this room at the bottom of the school universe included educating the teacher on the first day of class.

Now, if basements can give birth to Utopia, then surely pigs can fly. To soar boldly with *les trois petites cochons*, to invent through critical pedagogy some bacon on the wing, I can also say that it helps to turn teacher-centered rhetoric on its head. Not simple, the power-sharing project begins by democratizing discourse. Transforming traditional classroom discourse involves what Nan Elsasser and Patricia Irvine called *"new speech communities . . .* where teachers and students work to promote educational equity and cultural diversity" (1992, p. 32). Rules for speaking in this new setting not only "consciously contravene the accepted norms of school discourse" but they also differ from the discourses prevalent in the teacher's and students' home communities.

Elsasser and Irvine identified four characteristics common to the construction of a new speech community in class:

- Language Choice: Students have the opportunity to read, write, and speak their own language variety as well as the standard.
- Generative Content: The curriculum is chosen by students and teachers to address issues they consider important.
- New Knowledge: Students and teachers produce knowledge for themselves and others.
- Action: Students and teachers initiate and/or support actions which challenge inequitable power relations in and out of the classroom. (p. 32)

One way to inaugurate a new speech community on Day One of class is to invite students to take the most active role while the teacher restrains her or his verbal profile. On the first day and after, students should talk a lot and produce a variety of texts which educate the teacher about their interests, levels of development, idiomatic diversity, cultural backgrounds, and thematic preferences vis-à-vis the syllabus. Their initial discourse replaces the routine of the teacher's pre-emptive lecture on what things mean and what will be covered. This is the function of the initial questionnaire I handed out, which includes the query, "Why are you here?," thus inviting students to inform me about their choices at the same time that it helps reduce my discursive profile.

On the first day, if I had enacted traditional rhetoric as a unilateral authority, I would have begun by narrating the syllabus ("reading the riot act") and by lecturing on the course material (the pre-emptive didactic presentation). Doing these things, I would have followed the expected script and fulfilled my antipodal role in the Siberian Syndrome. That is, I would have behaved as the polar opposite to the Siberianized students, who expect me to address them in one-way teacher-talk. In anticipation of my dominating discourse, they automatically gravitate to the back of the room before my remarks even begin; in so doing, they construct me as well as themselves on the first day of class. I try to resist their habitual expectation/construction of a unilateral teacher at the front by not handing out a syllabus and by not lecturing. By resisting their expectations for a syllabus and a lecture, I hope to align the rhetoric of this class against the unilateral discourse that called Siberia into being in the first place. So, instead of making a teacherly presentation, I invite students to explain what brought them to this emboweled chamber for a study of Utopia and to reply to some other questions I'll enumerate shortly.

From their answers on the sign-in sheets, I discover that some students are indeed interested in Utopia as a subject, and a few have even been advised by friends to take my course, but most have never heard of me and don't have any special interest in the material. Most students do not come looking for me, for critical pedagogy, for Utopia, or for power-sharing. They do not bring alternative or New Age agendas into the catacombs of B-Building. Most are simply trying to get through college. Education itself has reduced their expectations to a point below the threshold of expecting a deep intellectual experience. All in all, to their credit, they made it this far against the odds, and they plan to keep going past me and the Utopia course, which is listed during registration time as one section of a generic sophomore/junior English elective called "Literature and Humanities."

Typically, the several sections of this elective are each based on a different teacher-selected theme. Whichever teacher offers a section gets to pick her or his own theme. This is an empowering arrangement for the teachers, who don't have to follow a standard syllabus or use a required text. But, what about empowering democracy for the students?

As a routine feature of formal education, there are no democratic mechanisms for students to propose their own courses, themes, or syllabi. They have no institutional power to plan courses; curriculum is made for them by others, by teachers and academics who often love knowledge and have the best interests of the students in mind. Nevertheless, when people are not consulted about policy and process in their experience, they are denied citizen status as members of a democracy, as Dewey warned many decades ago. When it came to democratic education, Dewey was clear about student involvement:

> There is, I think, no point in the philosophy of progressive education which is sounder than its emphasis upon the importance of the participation of the learner in the formation of the purposes which direct his activities in the learning process, just as there is no defect in traditional education greater than its failure to secure the active cooperation of the pupil in construction of the purposes involved in his studying. (*Experience and Education*, p. 67)

Dewey saw collaboration as essential to democracy. Without formal participation in decision-making, students develop as authority-dependent subordinates, not as independent citizens. Still, there is nothing unusual about the absence of democracy, though it is unusual for America's patron saint of education to remain ignored so many decades after he first criticized traditional schooling for rejecting student participation. The denial of student authority is the invisible business-as-usual of schools and colleges, which are run by professionals and administrators. Here is how governance responsibility was stated by one college in 1994 in a policy paper on the professional duties of teachers:

> Faculty are responsible for providing a clear syllabus that sets forth class policies and goals. The syllabus must also include faculty office hours, absence policy and procedures, and an explanation of the grading system. Faculty are also responsible for giving timely notice to students of any substantial deviation from the syllabus during the course of the semester.

Such a statement could be read as a professional standard or control, a code to monitor the delivery of professional service by the faculty to the students. But are teachers' merely delivery systems for preset rules and knowledge? This is the notorious "banking method" of education. Faculty alone are given control of knowledge-making. But, the above code does go on to indicate that "Students shall have an opportunity to evaluate their courses," perhaps at the end, perhaps at midterm, even if they do not have authority to negotiate it. Such unilateral authority is standard practice, a friendly fit with the lack of democracy and with the dominance of hierarchy in all social institutions. Of course, in the face of undemocratic practices, students do assert themselves, informally and subversively, by telling the teacher what they like and don't like, by disrupting class, by resistant nonparticipation (Siberia), by faking interest, by breaking the rules (cheating on tests, buying term papers, copying someone else's homework, reading Cliff's Notes instead of books), by cleverly "playing the angles" to "beat the system" (like manipulating the teacher to get by with a grade or conning an advisor to get into a closed course or for some financial aid), and sometimes by protest actions like walkouts, sit-ins, rallies, marches, newspaper campaigns, petitions, or lawsuits. But, formal authority is invested unilaterally in administrators first and most, teachers next, and students rarely (some places do have student delegates on standing committees).

This political structure is so old and routine that it is barely perceived or questioned (see Nieto [1994a] for a deep argument on the benefits of including students in curriculum planning, and Hopfenberg and Levin [1993] for a report on how the Accelerated Schools Project works to democratize decision-making). Students come of age without exercising the democratic arts needed to negotiate authority in diverse settings (Lappe and Dubois 1994). Not developing democratic habits, they lack experience in governing public affairs, in taking responsibility for policy-making, in what could be thought of as trying on civic authority for size (Isaac 1992). Here is how one of my female students (a 30-year-old white education major who went to technical college in Germany) described her awkwardness when I invited her and others to negotiate a learning contract with me for their final grades: "I feel unease judging the learning contract proposal. In the last twenty-five years, nobody ever asked me for my opinion on this topic. (I certainly complained to my classmates about the structure in the classroom.)" She had lived in two nations describing themselves as democracies, yet it seems she was never a constituent of her own education, only a recipient of it who complained privately to peers.

To question the absence of democratic practice and other politics of the status quo, I was attracted to the theme of Utopia in the 1970s when I first taught a Utopia course (and wrote about it in *Critical Teaching and Everyday Life*). Later on, in the more conservative 1980s and 1990s, I saw the new multisection "Literature and Humanities" elective in the English Department as a chance to renew the Utopia course, which had been canceled during one of the endless rounds of budget cuts. Renewing the Utopia pedagogy was meaningful to me as one small way to resist the growing reactionary climate. So, I listed "Utopias" as the theme of a section, where I hoped to merge civics with literature and democratic process with critical pedagogy, all the while wondering if I was going too far in an age of peanut dreams and cloudy skies.

Transforming Expectations: Can Power-Sharing Change Human Development?

At frantic registration time, students see a short menu of the sections available in the "Literature and Humanities" course, with my "Utopias" listed among them. Regarding registration, one determined student, Denise, an older woman returning to school, wrote that "Every time I register for classes, I want to drop out of college . . . Students shouldn't have to waste so much time getting signatures, going from office to office because classes conflict." Another student, Maureen, a busy 20-year-old dietary clerk for a retirement home, added, "I feel that the college has cut so many academic courses. They cancel classes and all the students have to try and find another course which is important for their majors. Then you squeeze about 50–55 people in a classroom and everyone is so uncomfortable." More than a decade before, the poet and Open Admissions teacher Adrienne Rich recognized the educational damage done by this depressing encounter with college, where students endure "a many hours' wait in line at registration, which only reveals that the courses they have been advised or wanted to take are filled, or conflict in hours with a needed job" (1979, p. 61). She didn't treat registration as a ho-hum cliché but saw it as a dehumanizing obstacle thrown in front of working students who were claiming some chance for higher education. Registration is especially discouraging to those who have the hardest time getting into college, staying there, and graduating. After registration, Rich went on to write, the students fall into "a semester in courses which they never chose, or in which the pace and allusions of a lecturer are daunting" (p. 61). Rich pointed to the students' restricted sense of agency. Their dispiriting experiences with registration, with physical discomfort, and with academic lectures machine-gunned at them, interfere with their intellectual development. In such a dehumanizing process, many simply become too alienated or exhausted to take intellectual life seriously. One student, Maria, a 19-year-old bank teller, wrote on the opening day that "Whatever classes I want are closed. It's very frustrating. I think if we all get the classes we want we would actually see what we think is interesting and possibly follow the subject up with a job." Another Utopia student, Stephen, a young and ambitious part-time chef, summed it up like this: "This school has become dilapidated, and is unconcerned with practical education, too. Most of the classes I've taken reflect the inability of this school's teachers to inspire my deepest interests in school subjects. To put it more directly, I haven't gotten a helluva lot out of the college experience (so far)." I read the parenthetical "so far" as a challenge to me, the next teacher in his life, to make this semester different from the others. Thus, apparently silent or uninvolved students have a lot to say when the rhetorical setting opens to them.

With negative feelings smoldering from the Siberian corners forward, how much performance can we expect from Stephen the chef or the others if we pretend their alienation isn't there or that disempowerment is not an issue? Schools, colleges, and classrooms (as well as workplaces) do not function as "cultural forums" where meaning is negotiated (as Bruner [1986] would phrase it) or as democratic associations where purposes and policies are communally framed (as Dewey [1966] would pose it). To establish the learning process as a cultural forum or public sphere for the negotiation of meanings, it helps to get students' thoughts and feelings into the open as soon as possible. Thus, I have routinely asked students why they took the course, what they want to get out of it, and what suggestions they have to make education work better for them here. These initial questions involve the students as reflective constituents who are consulted in the making of their education. The absence of such democratic discourse depresses their intellectual involvement as well as their development as citizens.

Not only depressing, undemocratic curricula can also be deceptive. For example, the elective status of my Literature and Humanities "Utopias" course is truly a fiction. For a liberal arts degree, students have to fulfill compulsory distribution requirements from a list of sections that is shrinking due to budget cuts. At registration, they sign up for whatever courses are open, to accumulate credits by any means necessary. Their "free choice" has been narrowed by the fiscal impoverishment imposed on our college by state and corporate pressures to cut social services like education in the public sector. In addition, working-class commuter students have little open time in their week to choose widely among courses. They have to fit schooling in between jobs, commuting, and family lives. Always on the run, they pick classes that blend with their crowded schedules. The nominal elective status of the Utopia course thus belies its compulsory nature given economic policies in society and given the conflicting demands of education, family, and wage labor in their lives. They arrive at my Utopia class more or less driven into it, by their need to hold down jobs, by commuting, by the budget crisis transferring wealth from public to private areas, and by the time demands of family life. The stressed-out lives of multiple-job holders drew this front-page attention in *The New York Times*:

> When Robin Thornburgh lost her job as a $25,000-a- year paralegal, she was scared. Her husband, David, an office clerk made barely enough to cover the groceries and the rent in their $700-a-month apartment in Arlington, Va. So, she is trying to make up the lost income by working two jobs—as a full-time clerk for a loan company and a part-time book-keeper for a company that rents out bodyguards.
>
> "It kind of stinks, the two of us having so many jobs," said Mrs. Thornburgh, who earns $600 a week, more than matching her former pay, but must work 55 hours to do it. "You argue about money and about hours and on top of everything, we are both trying to get through college. We go different ways too much." (Uchitelle 1994b, p. A1)

Commuting to college in the "New World Order" of the 1990s, she and her husband were likely to be taught by part-time adjuncts who commuted between teaching jobs on several campuses, just as students also drove to multiple employments to make ends meet, in an age when the "middle-class" was in decline.[1]

Commuter students could of course solve part of their problem by choosing *not* to go to college. This is a free country and the world's largest free market, we are told. The Thornburghs and other working students, like Stephen and Maureen above, are free to consume something else besides college with their time and tuition dollars or to consume nothing at all and just spend more hours at home, at work, on the streets, in political groups organizing against budget cuts, or simply in each other's loving arms. But, the free market is not really free. People like the Thornburghs don't control the job market, the housing market, the money market, the food market, the insurance market, the car market, etc. In reality, they are jockeying for position, couple-by-couple, person-by-person, in a society where wealth and power lie in corporate hands. If a working person doesn't go to college, she or he will fall behind her or his peers in the race for a degree that might open the door to the few better-paying jobs available, which might allow one or both Thornburghs to quit a low-paying job, so that they could see each other more and have a relationship not overwhelmed by corporate "mergers," "globalization," "restructuring," and "downsizing." Dropping out of college could free up some of their time and money, but at the price of a college credential which may help them find but cannot guarantee better employment. All the college degree guarantees, economically speaking, is the chance to compete in a job market where corporations are moving North American jobs to cheap-labor havens like Mexico, Poland, and Brazil. College credentials may help an individual compete with her or his U.S. peers, but what about the cheap college-trained labor in Mexico City, Warsaw, São Paulo, Dublin, and Bombay (where skilled computer engineers were paid about $1,000 *a month* in 1996 compared with the same workers earning three to six times that amount in the United States)? Economic "globalization" is ideal for big business but bad news for working people in the United States, who are running faster merely to stay in place or to slow the decline in their standard of living. Thus, the free choice of going to college and the free market are about as fictional as the elective status of my Utopia course.

Knowing the unfavorable economic context in which I teach and in

---

1. See Uchitelle (1990, 1991, 1994b), Lohr (1988), Holusha (1993), Bryant (1994), Kagay (1994), Cassidy (1995), and Sheehan (1995) for reports on the declining U.S. labor market in the 1990s; and Freeman (1976) and Schor (1991) for scholarly background.

which students take the Utopia class helps me avoid blaming them for "lack of motivation" and for career anxiety which limits their interest in humanities and experimental learning. As John Kenneth Galbraith wrote some time ago: "It is the vanity of educators that they shape the education system to their preferred image. They may not be without influence, but the decisive force is the economic system" (1967, p. 238). More recently, Stephanie Coontz wrote that "recent research negates the one factor that might possibly be blamed on either family or teacher inadequacies: workers' alleged inability to keep up with the shift to high-skill jobs" (1995, p. k20). Coontz reported that "there has been no significant increase in the proportion of high-skill jobs during the past few years. The striking fact is that real wages have declined among youths whose reading skills and high school graduation rates have been *improving* for the past 20 years" (p. k20, emphasis in original). David Berliner and Bruce Biddle (1995) have also debunked the myths which blame schools, students, and workers for the national underemployment problem. How is it that educational achievement goes up while real wages go down? Because it is as Galbraith said—the economy and not the schools dominate the fate of educational credentials in the job market, and because, as David Howell (1994) asserted, employers have been able to undermine labor unions, negotiated benefits, minimum wage protections, and full-time work with part-time and temporary workers known as "contingent labor" ("adjuncts" in higher education). Under these conditions, Coontz concluded, "Increasingly, and with good reason, youngsters wonder what is the point of playing by the rules" (p. k12).

Can a transformative pedagogy come to grips with the political fictions disguising social realities? The fictional elective status of my Utopia class is a social constraint I work under. Add to this the absence of student authority in choosing the topic for this or any other course. Still other conditions limited my critical-democratic pedagogy in that Utopia class. As I said, we had one of the worst rooms at the College: in the basement, without windows, under the cafeteria and gym. This low-budget College was so overenrolled and undercapitalized that too many students were stuffed into courses that met in every available space. Unforgettable B-34, a narrow room, bordered by dirty beige cinderblock walls, washed in dull florescent light, had a ventilation system in the ceiling which hissed. We had to talk above the sound of the ceiling vents. Imagine the determination it took to hold a conversation in a room like this. The students had to talk louder than they are comfortable doing in classrooms. Talking loud attracts attention to yourself, requiring confidence in your appearance, your voice, and your remarks. Loud talk in a classroom thus involves risk and exposure which white men are more likely to handle than women or minorities. And the vents were good at producing noise but not at venting the room. The air weakened as the class rolled on, with the room losing its oxygen and becoming steamy. (We did have a second classroom assigned for one session a week, but that room was unheated and was adjacent to the expressway and the daycare center, so that roaring trucks and yelling kids became our new noise companions while we sat with our coats on in winter.)

Besides the problem with noisy ceiling vents in the basement room, we had other hurdles peculiar to a low-budget college for working students. As Maureen the dietary assistant suggested above in referring to class size, there weren't enough chairs. Students do not merely compete for the choice Siberian corner seats; they compete for seats, period. As course offerings shrunk and enrollments grew, classes kept getting larger. Some rooms ran out of seats. A few students arriving late had to forage outside for chairs and carry them back to our chamber. I gave up my unique leatherette teacher's chair under these conditions and sat on the handsome formica desk. It's also hard to form discussion circles and peer groups in a room so crowded with people. Such was the picturesque scene of urban mass higher education in New York, touted by some as the new Career Palace for working people and by others as the historic democratization of the academy, here in the richest city in the wealthiest society in the world. And so, somewhere under the rainbow, I began the Utopia course in the basement, like a canary in a coal mine inhaling vapors of a cadaverous age and singing for my subterranean life, in a scoundrel time when distant powers defunded education while demanding world-class achievement from students and teachers they cared little about. No sky, no windows, one steel door as the only escape, too few chairs, cinderblock walls in need of fresh paint, a floor littered variously with styrofoam cups, soda cans, juice jars, candy-bar wrappers, white take-out sandwich bags, and occasional sticky spills of coke, with hissing air vents above, and a curious black hole on the wall where a clock once hung but now contained only errant wires pointed carelessly in all directions, reminding me that time is not merely flying by but has indeed already flown. In this august setting, there was only one appropriate thing to say to the students tightly packed from the corners of deep Siberia to the edge of my professorial toes: "Welcome to Utopia."

A Rainbow in the Cave: Beginning with the Theme of Change

With "Utopian" anything unlikely in such a degenerate time and place, I indeed welcomed the students to the course called "Utopias," told them my name, and encouraged a few late arrivals to find chairs outside and hurry back. Then, I distributed the sign-in sheet I mentioned earlier, with its questions, some of which helped me learn the students' personal situations on and off campus: their names, addresses, phones, ages, employment and hours worked each week, number of credits taken this term, family life (raising children), daily newspaper, and favorite TV shows. The sign-in sheet also posed four substantive issues, the first of which I discussed before:

1. Why did you take this course?
2. If you could change one thing for the better about this College and your education here, what would it be?
3. If you could change one thing for the better in New York City, what would it be?
4. Do you want any class time spent on the war with Iraq?

In addition I verbally asked them to write on two questions about "Utopia":

5. What does "Utopia" mean to you?
6. What questions do you have about "Utopia"?

About question 1, students were frank: fifteen admitted outright that they took the course because it fulfilled a requirement or fit into their busy schedules; eight wrote various weak versions of "sounded interesting," which I read as weak commitment or as self-protective euphemisms for little interest in Utopia; four announced that a friend or teacher recommended me or the course to them; two wanted an English class to help improve their writing; two wrote that they wanted to learn about "people and places"; and four specifically mentioned the theme of "Utopia" in explaining their reason for taking the course. On the whole, then, I learned from them that only four students out of thirty-five arrived in B-34 because of their interest in the subject matter.

The fourth question above, on Iraq, was something I added because that class began during the Gulf War of 1991. In the Utopia class of the previous term, the buildup to war worried students, so they wanted to discuss the crisis. In the new semester, I took the initiative and offered the option if these students felt such a discussion should be on the agenda. This subject was not compulsory because students could reject the topic outright. I exercised my right to propose and the students had the right to dispose, which meant I did not impose. Although a teacher-initiated topic in the Utopia class, the Gulf War was not merely a theme from my agenda because some students from the previous term had generated it for class discussion. This makes it partially a Freirean "generative theme" emerging from student suggestions, experiences, conditions, and expressions. As it turned out, twenty-nine of thirty-five students wrote that they wanted to discuss the Gulf War, which suggested strong interest. Later, I'll explain how this topic was taken up by that Utopia class, which handled it differently from a resistant journalism class I taught the same term, showing me once again that each class is a distinct gathering of individuals presenting different limits and possibilities. No matter how well I get to know students in general, they aren't stereotypes I can take for granted with a standard syllabus that will work in every course.

Besides the Gulf War, there were two questions on the sign-in sheet about what students wanted changed at the College and in the City. These questions introduced social criticism and the imagination of change, which I consider appropriate for the study of Utopia. I hoped to begin a critical discourse right away, in their words, not mine, as the foundation of the syllabus and the learning process. I counted on them having grievances about the College and the City as well as thoughts for improving both (see Williams, 1993, for a school-improvement project similar to this at the secondary level). Further, this invitation to "critical thinking" was not an abstract exercise in logical skills (induction, deduction, fallacious reasoning, etc.), or in rhetorical models (comparison-contrast, seriation, summarizing, narration, etc.), or in decontextualized mental puzzles; rather, it was context-based and student-centered, rooted in subject matter familiar to them, thus making it more likely they could perform critically and "metacognitively" (Bruer 1993). In this pedagogy, then, I define "critical thinking" in a classroom as a literate social performance enabled in an experientially and linguistically meaningful context, enacted in the language students possess, inside a purposeful, negotiated process which encourages them to question the cultural assumptions of society and to imagine alternatives to the status quo (see Brookfield 1987a; Scribner and Cole 1981).

On Day One, by asking questions rather than by lecturing, I practiced an alternative rhetoric through a reversal I mentioned before: frontloading student discourse and backloading the teacher's commentary. The rationale and method for frontloading student expression were items I also discussed in some detail in *Empowering Education* (1992b), so I won't repeat those arguments here. What I will reiterate is the need to restrain the teacher's didactic voice so as to generate student expression as the foundational discourse. Problem-posing dialogue begins with questions for writing and discussion, in which I restrain my authoritative academic voice by saying as little as necessary in the early going, so that I can listen to as much student expression as possible, from which I draw out further problems to pose and into which I eventually backload my own commentary. I try to discipline myself to follow the students rather than disciplining the students to follow the teacher's pre-emptive lecture. This practical method of frontloading student discourse is what Freire would call a "praxis" of dialogue and which Dewey would call an "agency" of democratic education—that is, practical means to put theory into action. Backloaded teacher commentary will have less of a dominating effect on the dialogue, since it enters late and in a form integral to previous student remarks, after students have had a chance to articulate their positions. The teacher's authority does not dissolve in such a rhetorical setting but rather enters dialogically according to the shape of the students' own discourse.

By posing questions on the Utopia sign-in sheet, I sought the least amount of teacherly discourse to get the most amount of student activity underway. Still, it's not easy to come to the first class without a formal syllabus and without a pre-emptive lecture. These two mechanisms of control are reassuring comforts, especially to younger teachers, and to those whose authority is socially undermined by such things as race and gender. In my very first year at the College, as a new and inexperienced teacher, I leaned on detailed syllabi for reassurance. More recently, though, I've seen awesome syllabi from two veteran male professors who specify what will be covered on each class day as well as non-negotiable rules for attendance, lateness, and grading, with impressive reading lists and due dates for all papers and exams. The two professors' syllabi began with statements from them summarizing the meaning of the subject matter. These frontloaded words filled one-third of the first page of each syllabus, single-space. The syllabi themselves reflected the teachers' pre-emptive lectures through print, supporting the professors' authority when they began speaking from the front of the room.

As an alternative democratic rhetoric, to invite students to become negotiators and critical thinkers on the fateful opening day of the Utopia class, I posed questions about changing one thing for the better in New York and one at the College, and, asked "What does the word 'Utopia' mean to you?" and "What questions do you have about Utopia?" Then, I gave them time to write in class, while I wrote also, trying to be patient with a dialogic process that I had to lead and follow at the same time.

Leading and Following: A "Pedagogy of Questions"

The Utopia course thus began with what Paulo Freire and Antonio Faundez (1989) called a "pedagogy of questions." I assumed an interrogative rather than a declarative posture in the rhetorical setting. Saying as little as needed to get a process underway, and posing questions more than making comments, I attempted to legitimize my authority while restraining my authority, profiling myself as the teacher while keeping my teacher's profile low. I would *not* say that this is easy. Patience, patience, patience, I say to myself in class—don't overreact, don't speak too soon or too long—ask yet another question, listen some more before you speak . . . And sometimes it works. When it does, the results are intriguing. Even deep Siberians have a lot to say once they decide to talk up. "Talking up" (not the same as "talking back") is not easy for students in most classrooms, where they fear saying the wrong thing or fear ridicule/disapproval from other students or from the teacher for speaking in nonstandard dialects/nonacademic styles, or fear censure from fellow students for being too cooperative with the teacher ("ass-kissing," "brown-nosing"), or where the subject matters seem too foreign or irrelevant to inspire participation. As long-term exiles in classroom discourse, students generally need time and a reason to speak up and some will not manage to do so inside the confines of one semester.

Like the students who wrote on the sign-in sheet their preferred changes in City and College life, I too have criticisms of where we live and where we study, some of which are similar to theirs, some different. The departures between us are that I grew up seeking public forums for my social criticisms and that I research my grievances, while they do not. I write books, go around the country giving talks and workshops, speak to colleagues in committees, offices, faculty meetings, and conferences, teach graduate and undergraduate classes where I raise critical issues, sign petitions, send letters to officials, join and donate money to various groups, consult with some activist formations, go on marches, attend rallies and demonstrations, etc. They rarely take their critical voices into public spheres. Some do work in voluntary organizations—the network of charitable, religious, fraternal, union, and community associations found all over the country. Some do write letters to the editors of their local newspapers. A few write for the campus paper or have a hand in student government. Now and then, older students attend local school boards and community boards in their neighborhoods. Some of them are politically involved with local conservative politicians. One unusual student in the Utopia class, Jeremy, actually worked with the Democratic Socialists. For the most part, though, activism is foreign to them and social criticism is limited to casual complaining in private conversation, where it is often said that talk is cheap.

I thus opened the Utopia class as a cultural forum for their critical discourse, inviting them on the first day to write about the City, the College, and the meaning of Utopia. They used this opening to raise a number of issues. To be concrete about the material frontloaded by students, I will offer here the items they wanted changed in their education at the College of Staten Island (CSI) and in their lives in New York. The following two agendas are in their own unedited words, written on the first day in answer to my questions. I collated and synthesized their responses and handed out in the next class a sheet summarizing the key issues they raised (the number of times any item was mentioned is indicated in parentheses):

Changing CSI for the Better
1. "Parking—too crowded and not enough security." (7)
2. "Open more sections to reduce class size and make classes more personal. Some classes don't have enough chairs. Too many classes have been cut back." (7)
3. "Improve registration/advisement—it's bureaucratic, frustrating, and panicky; advisors don't know what they're talking about and don't seem that interested in helping students." (6)
4. "More interesting subjects to choose from; more inspiring teachers who stimulate student interest." (3)
5. "Attendance requirements should change." (2)
6. "Two- or three-hour courses need a break in between." (2)
7. "There should be different requirements for older students returning to school." (1)
8. "When a professor is not doing a good job, something should be done about this." (1)
9. "Students should have a bigger voice because we often aren't heard." (1)

10. "Combine the St. George and Sunyside campuses." (1) [NOTE: From 1976 to 1993, the College operated awkwardly on two far-apart campuses connected by a slow shuttle bus.]

11. "Mix lab classes with theory classes in the electrical department, because material covered in both tend not to coincide." (1)

12. "This school is dilapidated; better facilities and more interesting student activities needed." (1) [NOTE: The College moved to a new campus in 1993, but, unfortunately, budget cuts prevented hiring enough groundskeepers to adequately maintain the sprawling campus. Lack of sufficient parking space remained an unsolved problem after the move, also.]

13. "SLS courses should be just education courses." (1) [NOTE: SLS (Science, Letters, and Society) is the name of the undergraduate teacher education program, a liberal arts-oriented curriculum based in the Education Department. One student apparently opposed the liberal arts requirements and wanted only to focus on education, which is a complaint of some working students who feel that liberal arts requirements delay their graduation, costing them more tuition, slowing down their careers.]

14. "Build dorms to offer students an experience of living on their own." (1)

15. "Stricter oral tests for foreign teachers so they could communicate better with students." (1)

16. "Books are way too expensive; we need a book exchange." (1)

17. "All classes should be available at night for students who work full time." (1)

18. "Teachers shouldn't lower their standards or expectations to what they think students can do; teachers should not teach down to students." (1)

Making NYC Better

1. "Programs to deal with homelessness and poverty; homes, hospitals are needed for low-income people; refurbish abandoned buildings." (11)

2. "Reduce crime; more police on patrol; reinstate the death penalty." (9)

3. "Racial harmony; racism is a huge problem in NYC; people in other states criticize us for it." (4)

4. "Change Mayor Dinkins; get rid of bad city managers." (4) [NOTE: In item 3, four white students criticized racism in the City. In this next item, four other white students called for the removal of the first African-American Mayor of New York, David Dinkins, who faced growing hostility in some white neighborhoods while in office. Apparently, students don't have one position on the race issue, even though the antiracist side

is less vocal in class, as I discussed previously in *Empowering Education.* Democrat Dinkins narrowly defeated Republican Rudolph Giuliani in 1989 but then lost narrowly to Giuliani in 1993. The white, ultra-conservative borough of Staten Island voted overwhelmingly (3 to 1) for Giuliani both times. If Staten Island's vote was left out, Dinkins would have won re-election. Historically conservative, Staten Island was a Tory stronghold during the Revolutionary War, was one of the last counties in the North to abolish slavery in 1828, and was a significant pro-George Wallace site in 1968. The Island is home to many "white-flight" urban refugees who moved across the Verrazano Bridge from Brooklyn. Yet, four white students criticized racism in New York. This is one example of how frontloading student discourse can educate the teacher about the ideological profiles and conflicts among students.]

5. "Less pollution on our streets and air; control the Fresh Kills landfill to reduce the garbage there." (4) [NOTE: As I mentioned in chapter 1, the Fresh Kills Landfill on Staten Island is the largest dump in the world, sending out noxious odors, scheduled to close by the year 2000 without ample provision to replace it, leading to official calls for a garbage inciner-ator which will burn trash and add more effluents to the City's already polluted air.]

6. "City training programs should be set up for those on welfare. Im-prove the welfare system to encourage people to find jobs." (4)

7. "Deal with the drug problem." (3)

8. "Taxes are way too high." (2)

9. "Change people's nasty attitudes; make people more friendly." (2) [NOTE: This emotional criticism was raised by two male students, who expressed sincere interest in "an ethic of care" (Larrabee 1993), without using such a concept.]

10. "Honesty." (1)

11. "Improve the economy and create more jobs; too many layoffs." (1)

These were their starting agendas for writing, reading, and discussion. From them, I learned the students' priorities and perceptions, which became the opening points and raw materials for constructing the dis-course and syllabus. Agendas like these are also documents for my classroom research into their ways of seeing the world, so that I can understand them a little better each year.

In their City agendas, homelessness, crime, poverty, racism, and pol-lution stand out, which may surprise some who think that students of the 1990s ignore social problems. To the extent they care, the method of frontloading student discourse in a problem-posing dialogue gives students a chance to voice their concerns. At the campus level, tuition is going up while the quality of education is going down. Understandably, this equation works against students, who feel it in their wallets, in their crowded classes, and in the frustrating registration process. A shortage of classes and an increased use of adjunct teachers leave many students unhappy. They don't like taking courses from overworked or uninspiring teachers, whether professors or part-timers, and they don't like foraging for chairs due to overcrowded classes. They want seats in class to be waiting for them (a reasonable expectation) and they want well-trained teachers excited about their subjects (also reasonable). These items indicate they have critical thoughts about the quality of their education. A syllabus or institution that ignores student conflict with education sends a signal that intellectual life is hostile to student concerns. How, then, can we expect students to work hard under these conditions? In terms of simple convenience, students expect a place to park their cars. In terms of power relations, only one or two explicitly raised governance issues (students having more say, firing bad teachers). Significantly and typically, no one asked for critical pedagogy or for authority to negotiate the curriculum; such conceptual frameworks belong to my discourse, not theirs. In their own discourse, the above agendas are the terms in which they actually question the status quo, from sometimes contradictory positions (like on racism). How I, the teacher, question the status quo or how other academics debate the issues is not what counts at this moment. What matters are the themes that appear most often on their pages, in their own idioms, relating to their experiences and needs.

In their agendas, the items that appeared most became "generative themes" chosen by students for project groups, which I asked them to form voluntarily. These self-selected issues are "generative themes," in a Freirean sense, because they were generated out of student experience and writing, based on their perceptions of their social lives, good for generating critical discussion about larger issues. This method of discovering generative themes answers one key question of critical pedagogy—"Where does subject matter come from?" The generative themes emerging from the frontloaded discourses of students offer an alternative to themes unilaterally designated by teachers in a preset syllabus (which is the problem, I think, with Gerald Graff's method of "teaching the conflicts"). When students generate themes for the syllabus, their participation becomes more organic and their withdrawal into Siberia less necessary. After facing the thematic question of

"Where does subject matter come from?" the next issue involves the learning process: "What do we do with it?"

Where Does Subject Matter Come From? And What Do We Do With It?

Part of the answer of what to do with subject matter was offered just above, in my mention of the project committees students formed from their self-selected themes, which is familiar in education as student-centered, collaborative learning (Bruffee 1984, 1993; Schniedewind and Davidson 1987). In the ensuing chapters, I will present what happened to these projects. For now, to continue with the issues of where subject matter comes from and what we do with it, I want to stay with the story of the first day, which included my questions, "What does Utopia mean to you?" and "What questions do you have about Utopia?" I wanted students to establish their initial understandings of the course's theme so as to pass some ownership of defining the subject matter to them. I had unilaterally chosen the subject of Utopia, so I tried to balance that action first by asking them to develop generative themes like the ones above on the City and the College and, secondly, by posing the course title as a problem for the students to define and question.

When they finished writing about what Utopia meant to them and what questions they had about Utopia, I first asked them to read their individual texts out loud in chorus for some immediate revision of their writing (an exercise I call "voicing," which is discussed in detail in *Critical Teaching and Everyday Life*). Vocalizing their written work helps students gain a more intimate relation to their own discourse. After they recited in unison, I asked students to make any changes or additions they wanted in their texts, followed by reading them in peer groups to discuss their agreements and disagreements and finally choosing one consensual or synthesized text (if they agreed) or conflicting texts (if they disagreed) to read to the whole class, thus drawing again on the pedagogy of frontloading student expression and student-based conflicts (if conflicts emerge) rather than beginning with teaching the conflicts among academics. This approach also began collaborative and participatory learning from the first day, helping to build a process that might reach out to the deep Siberians by giving everyone something interactive to do. The most withdrawn Siberians as well as the others need to be involved as soon as possible.

This initial collaborative exercise enables students to develop their

positions on Utopia in dialogue with each other, without my professorial discourse pre-empting their understandings and without a requirement that they reach consensus. While students are working together,
I keep my ears posted to the sound of the room but I do not micro-
manage the individual groups. The declining hum of conversation tells
me that they have finished their work. Sometimes, a few groups will
go off task and start socializing, using the conversational hum as a cover
for cruising or for animated talk on last night's Knicks, Rangers, or
Giants game. When I sense this happening, I approach the group and
direct their attention back to the material by asking to see what they
wrote, if they mostly agreed or disagreed, who will read, and will they
want to be the group that reads first when we reconvene, etc. This is
not a permissive pedagogy which allows students to do whatever they
want with class time.

In this exercise, I wanted to take advantage of a democratizing structure in collaborative learning, that is, its creation of students-only
groups which exclude teacher-talk and thus can develop student discourse relatively distant from the teacher's idiom and values. This use
of collaborative groups as a students-only developmental space in the
classroom, as a means to restrain the influence of my positions on their
discourse, is especially valuable in the early going, when students produce the texts and themes to be frontloaded. It creates something of
the "safe house" effect which Mary Louise Pratt (1991) proposed as
essential for disempowered groups to construct a critical discourse in
situations of unequal authority. Later in the process, I sometimes circulate among the groups, to hear how they talk among themselves and
if their talk changes to suit my presence or follows its own logic. My
arrival in a group changes the dynamics, sometimes for the better in
nonperforming groups, sometimes for the worse in groups that want
to mimic what the teacher thinks in order to please me and get a good
grade.

When the groups completed discussion of their Utopia texts, I called
them back into whole-class session for reporting one by one. I sat taking
notes on their statements, asking questions of the designated readers
to draw out their meanings further. My habit of taking notes focuses
my concentration on what is happening in the dialogue while also providing me with a written record of the class, which I study at home
before the next class. Taking notes also sends a signal to the students
of my attentiveness and interest. I am listening carefully to them, displaying a habit of respectful concern for their ideas. If they see themselves as people with important things to say in the presence of a

teacher who listens carefully to their words, the process has a better chance of establishing a dialogic discourse. Generally, they are startled to find me taking their words seriously, reading back their own statements from my notes, and making references to their utterances a week or a month later in other contexts. "Being listened to" means that they count in the rhetorical setting. If they feel that they count, the students will be encouraged to participate as constituents of a speech community. So, my attentiveness to their words and my subsequent quoting of their remarks helps authorize them as stakeholders in and creators of the learning process. In this instance, I use my authority as the teacher to credit their remarks.

Their texts on what Utopia meant to them included the following statements:

1. "A place considered to have every luxury for people and having few problems and seeing to it that every person's problem is taken care of. A place where people have equal opportunity. A place where there is peace and lack of tension that would cause war."

2. "My idea of a utopia would be a perfect world. Everyone would be treated equally, regardless of race, sex, or other reasons. There would be no poverty, because everyone would have the same income. People would not be afraid to walk and speak to anyone. Of course, war would not exist."

3. "Utopia is an ideal world where everyone gets along. This ideal world would function smoothly. Hate and envy would not exist. War would not be in our vocabulary. We would live in the 'Garden of Eden' before the apple fell."

4. "Communities where people conform with others who have similar lifestyles, beliefs, customs, and needs. These individuals tend to isolate themselves from the mass population, trying to create a perfect society."

5. "I think that utopia is supposed to mean a perfect society, but a perfect society to who? What is perfect to one person may not be perfect to another. I don't think that there is perfection. Everything has its flaws. Any society will have problems because any group of people living together cannot possibly be compatible in every aspect."

These texts were decently written and "correct" in one way or another. They were good starting points for dialogue. As a composite, they comprise what Bill Bigelow (1990) and Linda Christensen (1990) call "the collective text," or a discourse characterizing group thought and feelings inside the language of the group itself.

Noticing a high profile of themes related to conflict, affluence, and equality in their statements, I drew these issues to their attention, naming them aloud, asking them to confirm my perceptions of their perceptions. If they hear their discourse differently than I do, I need to know. We don't have to reach agreement or consensus on what the texts mean, but we do have to inform each other as to how we are reading our words and our worlds. My interpretations do carry more weight because of my position as the teacher; but then, this exercise is not an exam with one correct answer for each question. By initiating an activity of multiple interpretation, I hope to set a working style in class of long-term inquiry from diverse perspectives through which knowledge is constructed in a dialogue of competing explanations.

Specifically, in this initial discussion of what Utopia means to them, the last text, no. 5 above, the one concerned with human conflict interfering with Utopian community, raised several issues that I posed back to the class one at a time, by asking, for example, "How compatible do we have to be to make a Utopian community or even a classroom work? What kinds of incompatible conflicts could wreck a community? How could a community manage conflict so that it isn't destructive?" But this discussion floundered due, I think, to the abstract nature of the issues and to the first day of class being the most cautious time for students. To make it easier for them to respond, I rephrased the material into an impromptu example that made the issues more concrete. I said, "A member of a Utopian community is not doing the work he or she is responsible for. How would the group deal with this?" This formulation got more response, but mostly from the students at the front, which left me still needing to animate the mid and deep Siberians. The front-row students brainstormed a gamut of replies, ranging from various punishments like loss of pay, less vacation time, or fewer privileges to use facilities, to individual counseling for behavioral change, to outright expulsion from the group. What did not emerge was the question about why the person was performing badly in the first place. Could there be something wrong with the community's organization of work? Did their system need review? Unfortunately, the discussion evaded this issue, so I raised it in my backloaded comments. Then, another question about Utopia emerged, namely, one text's contention that "every solution creates new problems." In some ways I agree, but I don't experience the new problems as necessarily setbacks, as the text suggested. Some other students, more optimistic, I suppose, did chime in with the feeling that a Utopian process is organized to solve problems as they come up rather than being overwhelmed by unexpected problems due to piecemeal answers. One student, Stephen, the ambitious young chef, put it this way, "To me, a utopia is a place where real solutions can be found, not just quick-fixes or patch-work."

I also noticed that a number of the student texts made explicit reference to war (see numbers 1 through 4 above). I believe this shows the power of teacher authority and suggestion, even in a backloaded, dialogic pedagogy where I avoided a pre-emptive opening lecture. I mentioned the Gulf War in the sign-in/question sheet I handed out, signaling my interest in and approval of this topic. Only a few words from me, even in printed question form, were suggestive and authoritative enough to orient their thought in a specific direction. Now, this doesn't mean that students will easily or automatically accept my suggestions or believe my dissenting view of that War; they don't easily adopt dissident opinions; besides, I didn't lecture to them about the War. But, it does mean that if I express an interest or position, the students don't relate to it necessarily as "right" or "wrong" but rather as authoritative, and whatever authority is interested in can become a door to bad or good grades, depending on how they deal with the subject. Many have learned to manipulate the teacher for a good grade by mimicking the teacher's opinions. They may not agree but they copy the teacher's positions to win the approval of authority (a higher grade, some slack for late papers or for an extra absence, etc.) This reminded me again how my authority can create unauthentic discourse, what I call *faux learning*, a kind of theater of manipulative discourse where students play at postures they think will help them get by. I want to limit their need and opportunities for theatrical manipulation and my exposure to it, so I try to speak with great restraint in the early going, to lessen the tilt of the discourse away from their real values and toward my perceptions, to lessen the chance that they will mimic my words merely to win approval. That danger always exists in the unequal power zone of the classroom. I am, after all, the teacher, the one assigned by the institution to do education to them, the only person in the room with the power to give grades. Undemocratic authority, then, creates the conditions for the faux learning often underway in classrooms.

Because students learn that the most conflict-free way to deal with schooling is to mimic the teacher, the teacher's words weigh in like stones and like feathers *at the same time*, weighty and weightless simultaneously because of their privileged position. Teacher-talk is weighty like a stone because of its institutional and disciplinary authority, with the teacher as grade-giver and as designated expert in a body of knowledge. Concurrently, institutionally weighty teacher-talk is feather-light, first because it is culturally isolated from the community idioms, everyday themes, work conditions, and subjective perceptions of the students and, secondly, because it is part of a unilateral process which drives students into the Siberian Syndrome. Students can fake interest to make the teacher's words seem more influential than they are. Meanwhile, their real intellectual energy will be saved for subjectively meaningful encounters elsewhere. This strange *pas de deux* between teacher and student utterances produces a lot of sound and fury signifying *not nothing*, but rather showing the contradictions of unequal authority which power-sharing hopes to overcome.

Breaking the Stalemate: Utopian Problem Posing

So far, the students in the Utopia class were defining their notions of Utopia and their questions about this subject. My primary task at this point was to draw out the issues raised by their texts, from which we could identify the next level of issues suggested by the current level of discourse, which is how a problem-posing process evolves organically, cycle by cycle. In this process, one student, Maureen, the young and earnest dietary clerk who had written frankly on her sign-in sheet that she wanted Mayor Dinkins out of office and that she took the course to fulfill a requirement, wrote the following: "As I was growing up I heard the word utopia every now and then whether in school, home, etc. I always understood it to mean a "perfect" land to live in peace and harmony with everyone and everybody . . . As I stand now, a utopia for me is just to succeed in a career I choose, hopefully have a good marriage, and just get through life as happy as possible." For Maureen and many others in the room, Utopia meant a happy life, which, to them, is raising a traditional family and having a normal career, inside the status quo. However, some students did express more transformative notions.

For example, the chef I mentioned above, Stephen, a genial young white man with dark curly hair and an easy smile, who listed "Hockey" and "The Simpsons" as his favorite TV shows, wrote a different response than Maureen the diet clerk: "I believe to achieve [Utopia] we must become one as people. We must think for the best of the American people instead of for the best for ourselves. I believe we need a leader like FDR or MLK to lead us. To show everyone the way to a society free of fear and full of oneness." His communal perspective was unusual for that class, shared by few, and I wondered if he was putting me on, saying hyperbolic things he thought would please me, to get a good grade. He was a bright, likeable guy, not a deep Siberian, but one who sat in the middle rows. Yet, my suspicions grew as the term wore on, because while he called for a moral Utopia in our society, he apparently had no plans to take part in building one. A few weeks after the discussion on what is Utopia, Stephen wrote his vision of "the good life," to him a private dream of personal success more specific than the vision mentioned by Maureen above. He didn't covet "fancy cars or planes," as he put it, but he hoped "to own my own business or become wealthy in the service industry . . . I would look to own my own house in Northern California and be married to someone I really love . . ." In a runaway consumer culture like ours, other students became even more specific than Stephen, describing the kinds of cars, mansions, pools, clothing, and vacations they wanted for their "good life," an exercise spun off from reading Skinner's *Walden II*, which I'll return to later on.

Still, some students resisted delirious consumerism more than others. For example, a small minority in class suggested alternative visions of the "good life." One young woman, Stephanie, an elite college-transfer student who worked with retarded kids, wrote "I'd like a little cabin in the field where the sun comes through the windows. I'd like to feel that I am valuable to society in some capacity." Another student I mentioned before, Jeremy, a soft-spoken, thin young man who was the only one in class with experience in radical groups, said that Utopia is where "Everyone would be treated equally, regardless of race, sex, or other reasons. There would be no poverty, because everyone would have the same income. People would not be afraid to walk up, and speak to anyone. Of course war would not exist." Stephanie and Jeremy were two students who displayed, during the term, some substantial commitment to alternative values, unlike Stephen, the affable but hyperbolic chef-to-be.

Not knowing what to make of Stephen, I pondered the texts written by Stephanie and Jeremy and wondered if I'd be able to mobilize these two students in class as allies to question the mainstream values expressed by most of the students. If I could enlist students to debate their differences, then I'd avoid becoming the lone voice questioning the status quo. As I said earlier, I hope to discover student conflicts to bring into constructive dialogue with each other, to avoid my becoming the only one questioning mainstream beliefs and traditional points of view. But, identifying students with some socially critical values is only half the battle; getting them to articulate their values in class is even harder. The students have been generally reluctant to voice progressive ideas and thus risk strong disapproval from the conservative majority of their peers. The few critical students in my classes, like some dissident teachers, often self-censor their speech, avoiding public exposure and the unpredictable consequences of vocally questioning the status quo. I ask students to maintain a civil environment in class for the dialogue, but their lives together extend outside of the cinderblock walls of the basement room, so I can't monitor their civility in other classes, in the cafeteria, in the parking lot, in the gym, etc. The risks they take in our class can have spillover effects inhibiting the freedom of some to speak up, especially the more vulnerable, like people of color, homosexuals, women, and students left of center.

As I mentioned, I also asked the students to write down their opening questions about Utopia. To frontload the classroom discourse as much as possible in their idiom, they need to ask questions as well as to make comments. They too must be questioners and problem-posers, not only me, because questioning is the epistemic stance of critical learners and citizens. Here are some questions students raised that first day:

1. "Is everyone's definition of Utopia the same? Who determines what Utopia is? Why don't we acknowledge the subjectiveness of utopianism?"
2. "If Utopia is so unattainable, what is the purpose? Why are we so concerned with it if it's unattainable?"
3. "Do you think it's reasonable for people to think we can achieve utopia? If it's unrealistic, why do so many communities try to achieve this?"
4. "Can any individual society live as a utopia or must it include the entire world? Is utopia possible on a small scale?"
5. "How can we make utopia happen? What would it be like? How would we live? Where do we start to obtain a utopian lifestyle? Is it a desirable goal? Would it get boring? Would we still have goals and aspirations? Can we attain a utopia within our own selves?"
6. "Where does the word utopia come from if it doesn't exist? What can we be taught about it?"

There is a healthy skeptical edge in these texts. Students expressed doubts about the idea and purpose of Utopia, even the study of it! These questions had an attitude about them, which is good because the students were emerging into the material, not memorizing or mimicking my take on it. They were challenging me to prove that Utopia was of human value and curricular value. That's a worthy challenge for students to pose to their teachers on the first day of class, not taking the material for granted, not easing back into Siberia and waiting to be told what to think.

In class, I didn't comment on their questions one by one in mini-lecture style. That would convert the dialogue into a press conference, where I respond to questions posed by the group. Instead, I asked the students to choose which question to begin with, to authorize them in codeveloping what is usually thought of as "the teacher's lesson plan." They chose number 5, "How can we make Utopia happen? What would it be like? How would we live? etc." But, there were too many global issues to get through in one discussion. Number 5 really required the whole course to address. As this dialogue went on, question no. 6 came up in the exchanges, "Where does the word Utopia come from?" a simpler issue on a number of minds, at which point I intuited an appropriate moment to raise my profile. At this late point in the session, I offered some structured comments on Utopia, backloading remarks into a dialogue based in their thoughts, writings, and spoken comments. They had already spoken and written more words than I had. Here are the notes I rework each term from which I deliver what I called in *Empowering Education* a backloaded "dialogic lecture" (as distinct from a traditionally frontloaded "didactic lecture"):

UTOPIA: Utopia means "no place" in Greek: 3 Traditions
A. Literature: Utopian → Thomas More, *Utopia*, 1516; *Looking Backward*, 1888; *Herland*, 1902; *Walden II*, 1948, *Ecotopia*, 1974.
     Dystopian → *Brave New World*, 1934; *1984*, 1949.
B. Communities: set apart from mainstream life
     1. Religious → Shaker, Oneida, The Farm
     2. Nonreligious (secular) → Twin Oaks, Los Horcones
C. Social Action: campaigns, projects to deal with social problems with "alternative" or nontraditional ideas: boycott tuna to save dolphins, what to do about garbage, book: *50 Things You Can Do to Save the Earth*.

I spoke about the origins of the word Utopia in Thomas More's book of that name. I mentioned that I would ask students to read about various Utopian traditions, about literary texts that often served as social criticism and tracts, about reports of Utopian communities, and about social action in society itself. (Later, I will return to "the reading list" to criticize my own inadequate handling of it, because I failed here to structure it in a democratic manner, leaving it controlled by me alone.) My orientation to Utopia presented this subject along a continuum of change-agency and did not teach Utopia as exclusively visionary or literary events related only to novels and separatist communities. That is, I wanted students to see Utopian ideas and action along a broad continuum of human agency, a broad human interest in critical thought and social change. In thought, writing, and action some people have attempted social criticism and change of which Utopia is part.

Of course, there is nothing inevitable or obligatory about this way of presenting Utopia. It emerges from my political understanding of Utopia in history. This way of thinking about and teaching Utopia is a choice I make as an educator, just as every syllabus and learning process represents political choices by teachers, departments, faculties, institutions, school districts, or state education agencies. When I stipulate my understanding of Utopia and how to teach it, I am not claiming a neutral or universal stance on knowledge. Philosophically and politically, I state my definitions and try to be consistent and self-critical, to be explicit about the political investments I (and all teachers) bring to teaching and learning, and how close I come to enacting them. No knowledge or teaching can be neutral because all emerge from some ideological position in society and all influence the development of students in one direction or another. To influence human development is to make political choices about what kind of people and society we should be. In essence, all formal education is politically oriented learning that is organized and directed by one kind of authority or another. The teacher, the subject matter, the learning process, and the institutional practices are the developmental forces. In the critical pedagogy I have been defining here and elsewhere, teachers don't stop being authorities or academic experts, but they deploy their power and knowledge as *democratic authorities* who question the status quo and negotiate the curriculum rather than as authoritarian educators who unilaterally make the rules and lecture on preset subject matter.

Still, there is no getting around the fact that a socially critical version of "Utopia" represented *my* stance toward the topic and *not* the students' desires or understandings. After they had defined and questioned Utopia, I represented it from my perspective as change-agency and social-historical critique. This is something I take responsibility for as a critical teacher. At least I backloaded this position in a discourse heavily weighted toward student expression as the foundation. Students can and do reject my position without punishment. For example, some of the Utopia students objected to my focus on change-agency and civics; some criticized my politics directly to me and openly in class, as well as in written course evaluations to me and to the College Administration. One student in particular, Stephanie, bright and articulate, let me know often that she preferred more writing and reading in literary works and less attention to social applications, which I will document in a later part of this book. Of course, I wish they all agreed with my orientation of the course, but some didn't and were not silenced. I felt the democratic process succeeded when Stephanie and others felt secure enough to criticize me. That was the democratic authority I was seeking in class. In that Utopia group, I posed Stephanie's objections to the other students and found the majority preference was for the civics orientation because most wanted to know what was wrong in society, what can be done about it, and how Utopia related to their lives. But, the class was significantly divided, which is hardly surprising. Those divisions stayed vocal all semester, so I will be reporting them in more detail. For now, I want to mention that the democratic side of a critical pedagogy means not ignoring, silencing, or punishing unhappy students but rather inviting them to make their criticisms public for deliberation. By bringing conflict and alienation out into the open, I hope to interfere with the formation of Siberia.

Whose Utopia Is This? Metacognitive Frameworks for Analysis

After my dialogic lecture above, I then offered some conceptual handles for studying Utopian thought, literature, communities, and action. I wrote on the board a metacognitive framework for an interdisciplinary, change-oriented approach to the subject:

Some Basic Utopian Ideas:
1. Futurism
2. Questioning the Status Quo
3. Social engineering
4. Decision-making

I explained these ideas as follows:

1. Futurism—hope, invention, experimentation, imagining and designing a better way to run society in the future, launching experimental projects and attitudes.
2. Questioning the Status Quo—looking critically at problems in society, not accepting the ways things are as final, fixed, or the best we can hope for, assuming that the way things are can be questioned and changed for the better, recognizing that real and deep problems exist for which we can find answers in politics, economics, education, media, relationships, etc.

3. Social Engineering—human beings are products of society while society is the product of human thought and action; individuals are the results of their social experience and society is created by what we do together; change society and everyday experience and you can create the conditions for changes in human behavior; re-engineer the system we live with and new conditions for human behavior and societal development will come into play.

4. Decision-making—How do policies, rules, laws get made? Who makes them? Who has authority? Who gives orders? Who takes orders? What are the structures for making decisions? Are they democratic?

I later changed this framework to a five-part structure because of the weak analysis in the students' writing and questioning. I intuited a need for a fifth concept I called "systemic thinking," as a critical means to emphasize the larger social connection of single items, to locate individual situations in their larger historical context as part of a social system.

I introduced the term "systemic thinking" because I intuited its place in a process where students often came up with solutions that fit too comfortably into the status quo. For example, in regard to the often-repeated problem of too little parking, the students suggested building an even bigger parking lot that would require cutting down as many trees as necessary on campus to accomplish this. A few years later, on the new campus, with parking unsolved, the students in a journalism class also proposed the same solution, cutting down trees, paving lawns, and building more parking lots. They also failed to make systemic critiques of "Homelessness in NYC," not connecting the immediate issue to a larger context in society or to Utopian reconstructions. In the case of the homeless, I asked systemically, "What policies have produced homelessness? Why are there so many homeless today while there were so few visible on the streets only ten years ago?" In addition, I brought in readings relevant to the theme of homelessness which focused on urban housing policies in the 1970s and 1980s. I'll return to these issues and this problem of systemic thinking in a later chapter that reports in-depth on the students' project committees.

Having raised my academic profile by backloading the Utopian concepts into the discussion, I asked students to use them as analytic tools. In exploring the Utopian character of any novel, community, or project we studied, I urged them to observe how much questioning of the status quo was evident, how much social engineering of new economic and personal relationships, how much the local or personal problems were situated in a context of the larger society, how much imagining of a future time when we live on different terms than now, and how different were the ways of group decision-making. This framework was hard for students, so they asked me to explain it more than once. They don't have much experience with such conceptual thought, which should surprise no one.

(Surprisingly) Critical Students: Utopian Action on the Class Itself, a Near-Death Experience

In presenting a method for critical thought on Utopia, I mentioned to the students that the "system" is also in our classroom. We might begin questioning and experimenting with the status quo right here, the way we relate as teacher and students. I named an experimental alternative to traditional education—"negotiating the curriculum"—for which I also used synonyms like "power-sharing," "shared authority," and "cogovernance," to indicate collaborative decision-making, democratic deliberation over policy, and codevelopment of the syllabus.[2]

When I proposed "negotiating the curriculum" to the Utopia class, I assumed that the students had heard the words "negotiating" and "curriculum" before, but had never heard the two together in a single phrase. When I asked, I found out that no one, including the elite-college transfer-student Stephanie and three women students who were paraprofessionals in the City's public schools, had ever seen or practiced "negotiation" or "power-sharing" in any classroom. So, my proposal that we negotiate the curriculum was greeted with sturdy silence and eyes of wary wonderment. Understandably, the students reacted cautiously and curiously to my invitation that we go where no man or woman has gone before, into the enticing but risky space of power-sharing. The practice of democracy in education was as familiar to these all-American students as was the Japanese tea ceremony.

Noncommittal about my proposal to share power, the students were self-protective until they could hear more about this strange practice of negotiating the syllabus. Their ears awaited specifics, including ears

2. For thoughtful reflection on "negotiating the curriculum," see the instructive book of that name by Boomer and colleagues (1992). For other good discussions and examples of shared authority at different levels of education, see Geri Kirkwood and Colin Kirkwood (1989), Christine Sutphin (1992), Helen Woodward (1994), Amber Dahlin (1994), Elaine Garan (1994), Barbara Brodhagen (1995), Scott Greenwood (1995), and Gail Tayko and Jonathan Tassoni (1996). Also, Elsasser, Irvine, and others (in Shor 1987b) have used the Freirean "generative theme" method to negotiate the syllabus with students.

alert in deep Siberia, but time ran out on our first class, for which I was very grateful. After two dense hours in the basement chamber, I was exhausted. I needed sunlight, oxygen, ginseng tea, chocolate ice cream, a shower, and early retirement at full pay. I didn't have the energy to negotiate a sprout salad right then and was lucky that I didn't have to. But, the next class was only forty-eight hours away. In two days, the negotiation process would begin in earnest, surprising me with an unexpected torrent of student desires.

Some years back, I had written humorously about "the withering away of the teacher" in a self-directing critical process (see *Critical Teaching and Everyday Life*), but I didn't imagine "the abandonment of the teacher" and the stampeding dissolution of the process itself. Now, in this course, some Utopia students would propose that we by-pass withering and go to instant evaporation of me and the class. Prior classes had taken control of different parts of the coursework, but none had ever proposed ending the class! And I was responsible for this situation, because I had been inviting negotiation more and more each year, until it reached the point where I faced negotiating myself out of existence. The upcoming class session would have the makings of a pedagogical Bastille Day from the students' point of view, freeing themselves from jail with keys provided by the teacher-jailer himself, which left me in a pickle of my own persuasions, about to be deep-sixed like the ancien régime, wondering what to do next.

THREE

Escaping Siberia: Students Ask, "Why Come to Class?"

Utopia and Siberia in One Basement: Teacher-Talk, Student Exile, and Shared Authority

How much power-sharing is possible if Siberianized students and professionalized teachers have known only unilateral authority? How much alternative thought is possible in lives crowded with distractions and work but not with critical learning or dissident culture? If school and society offer little practice in democratic participation, how much transforming action is possible in one windowless Utopia class?

Perhaps the previous sentences are merely rhetorical questions which answer themselves. They do simultaneously question and answer the difficulty of transformation in the grotesque conditions of the Utopia basement, in a conservative age and in a downsizing economy. On the other hand, these questions are not simply rhetorical mirrors that reflect on themselves. They are also *experimental issues* which do more than cross-dress moot conclusions as questions. They more than wink rhetorically at the reader, I would say, because questioning the status quo is an unpredictable adventure that interrupts routine behaviors, expectations, and relationships. Power-sharing challenges business-as-usual, which can lead to an instructive something or to an instructive nothing.

Now, while trying to change an undemocratic status quo is bound to be instructive, who can deny that something is surely better than nothing? Still, an instructive experience is enhancing by itself, as

Dewey (1966) suggested, when he defined "culture" as the ability to make meaning from one's social experience and "education" as a social experience that increases one's ability to make such meaning, so that we go forward more intellectually armed to understand and to act in society. Well-armed or not, trying to change school and society will feel quixotic in certain times and places. Yet, when dominant paradigms are called into question, the outcomes cannot be dismissed or predicted in advance. As Myles Horton and Paulo Freire (1990) put it, "we make the road by walking," which means we discover what can be done by doing, despite our beliefs that little can get done at a certain moment, and despite our theories about what should happen compared to what actually does. This is an experimental and reflective attitude toward practice which John Dewey (1933) and D. A. Schon (1983) might approve, which Stephen Brookfield (1987a; 1987b) posed as the essence of critical thinking applied to all arenas of adult experience, and which reminds me of Antonio Gramsci's (1971a; 1971b) phrase about the "pessimism of the intellect meeting the optimism of the will," or what I think of as getting something done despite all I know about the obstacles against getting anything done, perhaps like dancing to a song with constantly changing rhythms.

An experiment in shared authority—what I call cogovernance or power-sharing or shared authority in a negotiated curriculum—can certainly produce surprising and discomforting outcomes, like the moment I faced losing the Utopia class, which I will describe in this chapter and the next. Negotiating the syllabus offers students and teachers alternative social development, alternative ways of being, knowing, speaking, relating, and feeling, beyond and against traditional classroom arrangements. For obvious reasons, alternatives are both alluring and threatening, promising hope, novelty, validation, and relief, as well as conflict, loss, risk, responsibility, and the vagaries of the unknown.

The status quo has an inertial strength carrying along many people who actually resent the system, especially in times of diminished dreams and rising insecurity. Further, every society has its carrots and sticks for buying into or out of its norms. Like employees everywhere, many teachers find it safer and simpler to nest in traditional methods than to risk official punishment and professional isolation by experimenting for critical change. Students can also find it easier to settle for the known ruts of Siberia than to take chances reinventing their social selves. Yet, a resilient interest in self and social change peculiarly remains, leaving the status quo constantly but unpredictably vulnerable, not only because so many people are uninspired and unsatisfied with the way things are, but also because society and people are never finished developing, both being far too complex for total control. Human society, everyday experience, and individuality are filled with unused potentials, unexpected anomalies, undeveloped critiques, unmet dreams, unresolved contradictions, and unsupervisable moments. Always *in progress*, never finally under control, the self-in-society is continually constructed by what we do and say and by what is done and said to us. Critical-democratic pedagogy intervenes in this ongoing process of development to question the traditional construction of self and society. For interrupting the routine ways we learn, talk, and develop, Utopia is a theme with some promise and surprise.

Alternative Development of Self-in-Society: The Rhetorical Setting

With Siberia in place as the Utopia course began, I opened the second class session with a serious run at negotiating the curriculum. Day One had begun a dialogic, participatory, and critical process based in student discourse, with some students participating more than others. In the second class session, I made power-sharing explicit by asking students to consult with me on a number of issues, big and small. Uncertain about their openness to the unfamiliar practice of negotiation, I planned to ease into it through simpler questions first—like classroom seating and hand-raising—hoping that the deliberations would not drop at my feet like a slippery bottle of milk.

On the first day, as I mentioned, I didn't hand out a detailed syllabus, even though some students asked for one and such teacherly practice is customary. Anxious to know what they are up against with each new teacher, students understandably want an official syllabus as soon as possible. I meet this anxiety in a minimalist fashion by mentioning a few books to read, some writing assignments, a project, and telling students I want to include their choices in the syllabus—which helps me stall for time so that I can introduce negotiation at an appropriate moment. Thus, instead of reading the riot act on Day One, I frontloaded student discourse in an exercise that posed the course title as a problem while also asking students to reflect on changes they wanted in the City and the College. Into this discourse I then situated a conceptual framework for Utopia—futurism, social engineering, experimentalism, alternative decision making (and later) systemic thought—which I explained before.

On Day Two, I suggested that we might practice these Utopian concepts right here in class, by experimenting with and re-engineering the learning process, especially with regard to decision-making authority, class rules, and the syllabus. To begin the experiment in negotiation, I proposed that we could treat our class itself as a small social system for experimental change. To make this concrete, I began with the two simple, exemplary issues I mentioned above. First, I asked students to think about how they preferred to arrange the chairs in the room. Did they want to sit in rows facing the front or in a circle? Second, I asked them to make the rules for speaking in class. Did they want to raise hands and have me call on them, or did they want to regulate the discussion on their own?

First, let me review the negotiations on seating arrangements, the apparent simplicity of which actually includes questioning the Siberian Syndrome itself—to stay in rows that sustain the boundaries of the front and back of the room or to move into a circle that questions these relationships.

For a number of years, sitting in a circle has been a cliché of student-centered education. The discussion circle which displaces rows has understandably lost the freshness it had in the 1960s and 1970s, when it captured the imagination of many educators. Still, despite its familiarity, circle seating has not taken education by storm, just as Progressive Education in its Deweyan heyday of the 1920s and 1930s never took American schools by storm (Cuban 1984). The students in my classes report that their English teachers at the College and in high school have often asked them to sit in circles but that this practice is not common in other disciplines. For the most part, they report a traditional rhetorical setting still in place—students sitting in rows facing a teacher at the front who lectures, who asks them to buy expensive commercial textbooks and memorize fragmented information, who gives short-answer exams with little classroom dialogue. As one young white student named George said later on, comparing his other classes with our negotiation process, "I'm a nursing student, so for me this is culture shock! In my other courses, I'm handed 2,000 pages of information and expected to spit it back—that's what science is all about." George rose to the occasion by embracing the new process, but raising the issue of seating in one class did not change what the Nursing Department or science courses do. Rather, it offered an opportunity to reflect on the power relations of learning, especially the architecture of control represented by furniture and the location of bodies in the room.

For some teachers, sitting in discussion circles rather than in rows automatically makes a classroom "empowering" and "dialogic." But, I would argue that this is too simple an answer to building a transformative curriculum. Discussion circles are "tools for convivial learning," as Ivan Illich (1973) put it, more egalitarian than rows of students facing the teacher at the front. Yet, a circle is not enough by itself to constitute a counterhegemonic, critical-democratic pedagogy, just as relocating my teacher's body to Siberia and evacuating the front of the room was not enough by itself to sustain a transformative syllabus, as I discussed earlier. Singular practices like seating must be situated in an overall critical-democratic curriculum oriented toward change. Defining circle seating as empowerment by itself is simply too easy and too "utopian" (in the sense of being uncritically detached from power relations in the system as a whole). It misses the complex strategies and resistances involved in the transformation of students and teachers in the rhetorical setting of a classroom.

Central to this transformation is what I have been referring to as "the rhetorical setting," which concerns the social relations of discourse at a specific site of communication. "The rhetorical setting" (see Dowst 1980; Berlin 1987; Lindemann 1995) traditionally includes several interactive elements: one or more rhetors or encoders (speakers/authors/presenters), one or more receivers or decoders (audience/class of students/viewers/readers), a mediating language (appropriate register, dialect, discourse, and protocols for communicating), a subject matter (themes, texts, images, topics, events, etc.), and a situation, setting, or noetic field (the reality of the communications exchange). I would add to this model of the rhetorical setting another element called "the political climate," which I define as the environment of power relations in and around the site of communication which influences the shape of discourse, primarily centered in social identities and cultural conflicts of gender, race, class, caste, and sexual orientation. The metaphor of "the political climate" refers to the interface of global, local, and personal realities, to the ways in which the "temper of the times" and the regimens of local institutions interact with individual identities at a site of discourse. Put simply, "the political climate" affects the discourse possible in any specific time and place.

"The political climate" thus speaks about the power circulating in any context of communication. Besides the obvious impact of Foucault on this analysis, important contributions to understanding the political climate in rhetoric have also been made by feminists (Annas 1985; Belenky et al. 1986; Brodkey 1989 and 1994; Bauer 1990; McCracken and Appleby 1992); multiculturalists (Smitherman 1993 [1977]; Anzaldua 1987; Darder 1991; Banks 1992; Nieto 1994b; Baker 1993a and 1993b); and by critical theorists such as James Sledd (1969), Richard Ohmann

(1976; 1987), Harvey Graff (1987), James Berlin (1988; 1994), Gerald Graff (1992), and Donald Lazere (1992b). Ohmann's class-based close readings of literacy, technology, and the troubled history of freshman composition have been especially valuable, as have been Berlin's discussions of the converging agendas of rhetoric, composition, postmodernism, and cultural studies. Earlier, Kenneth Burke had focused attention on the social context of communication by suggesting that discourse embedded "attitudes towards history," in his words. In *A Grammar of Motives* (1969), Burke proposed five elements for examining this rhetorical setting, including the "scene" or setting in which communication occurs; the "act" that names what happened; the "agent" that names who did it; the "agency" that names how it was done; and the "purpose" that names why it was done. "Rhetoric," originally an oratorical art of persuasion in civic affairs, was collapsed and quarantined into freshman composition in the late nineteenth-century American university (Ohmann 1976; Berlin 1984; Miller 1991) and is now recovering broadly as the pluralistic "new rhetorics" (Brown and Enos 1993) concerned with a wide range of cognitive, expressive, and social issues. Among the rhetorics especially interested in the "political climate" of discourse, there is social-epistemic rhetoric (named by Berlin [1988]), concerned with "critical literacy" (Shor 1992; McLaren and Lankshear 1993) and with the historical and ideological setting in which we undertake the production (composition), distribution (delivery systems), reception (reader/audience-response), and interpretation (critique and deconstruction) of linguistic (oral/printed) and nonlinguistic texts (images, ads, relationships, film, folkways, political structures, etc.) (Hurlbert and Totten 1992; Berlin and Vivion 1993; DeJoy 1994a).

Rhetoric includes the analysis of discourse relations. It asks, "Who is addressing whom in what setting, at what time, in what kind of language, for what reason and purpose, and with what result?" By analyzing the kinds of knowledge, relationships, and power any discourse displays, we can read the political climate of that setting. This involves asking further questions, such as: "What are the rules or protocols for speaking? How are they made and enforced? Who do they authorize as speakers and who do they silence? How are the discourse and learning process gendered, racialized, and class-based? What varieties of discourse and dialect are observable and how is each expressed, used, and valorized? Where does subject matter come from and what is being done with it? How does the subject matter relate to personal contexts and to the larger social context? Are those relations of power made explicit, are they dismissed, or are they left unexamined? To what extent does the discourse question or confirm the status quo in school and society? To what extent are institutional requirements and dominant discourses influencing the syllabus and discussion in class?"

In terms of changing the political climate and the rhetorical setting of the classroom, circle seating can help disturb the unilateral authority of teacher-talk. It can also disturb Siberian withdrawal, with the downside of invading a certain privacy some students seek from sitting in rows (see Gore 1993). Circle seating does make a classroom less private, but it also helps restructure discourse from one-way lecturing to multilateral dialogue. This is democratically valuable, because the way we sit and speak with one another teaches us stances toward authority, knowledge-making, and society. But, the transformative potential of a circle should not be oversold because it needs to work inside a whole curriculum questioning power relations.

We Are Where We Sit: The Dialectics of Circles and Rows

The actual negotiation over seating in the Utopia class began when I asked students to discuss with a partner how they'd like to sit in class, in a circle or in rows, and then the whole class would debate and vote. As it turned out, that class preferred a circle, which is the choice of perhaps half of the students of the courses I teach. My current undergraduate courses both chose circles in the desire for more discussion with more people involved.

But, some classes prefer to sit in rows where Siberia and privacy are easier to maintain and where less participation is expected from them. Some feel safer in rows, less exposed to public eyes and to the teacher's gaze. Some prefer rows because they would rather listen to teacher-talk than to student-talk; they consider the teacher a knowledgeable authority for whose wisdom they are paying good money; some also consider their peers boring, uninformed, or just plain dumb (one upwardly mobile foreign student wrote the following unedited note to me anonymously: "DO NOT let students participate when they have nothing good to say. The most of them are just being STUPID, and what is even worse is that you think you have to applause them. Please, show some respect to our standards and intelligence."); lastly, those students who prefer teacher-talk can also view talkative students as self-serving dominators of discussion (an issue I will return to shortly).

Students come to class expecting the teacher to do most of the talking, because that's the way education has been done to them so far. Education, they have learned, means being talked at, and many are simply used to being enknowledged with the teacher firmly in command. Thus, if sitting in rows is what students want after debate and voting, that is the way we do it.

After the vote in the Utopia class in favor of a circle, the students rearranged their seats, which is not easy to do in an overcrowded room. Once the chairs started moving into a wandering curve, another issue went into motion for me—where do I sit? If there aren't enough chairs for everyone, I stay seated on the small gray steel/formica desk that is the frontal shrine of teacher authority (my low-budget omphalos at Delphi). Often, if a chair is available, I go off-center and move one way or the other and sometimes to the residual Siberia clinging to the back walls where the putative circle swerves to the corners. By choice, the deep Siberians are usually the last to embrace the negotiating process. So, while they went along with the group vote on circle-seating, they barely edged out from the corners to form a wavy line at the rear. In that tight classroom there wasn't much room for them to move toward the front, which seemed to suit them just fine. More than a circle is needed to lure deep exiles from their distant nests.

About seating, what interests me is recovering active student subjectivity to replace their learned withdrawal. This is a Deweyan goal for democracy as a community of franchised members with each having authority and responsibility for framing rules, meanings, and purposes. The seating debate represented a public forum for discussion of a previously undiscussed, non-negotiated experience. Once legislated unilaterally by authority, seating is now being negotiated democratically. This is a small but notable moment in the classroom, when authority-based routines are put on the table for scrutiny and reformation. When "seating" becomes a public issue, so does authority, flushed out from its own inertial nest.

The Experience of Making Experience: Raising Hands and Mutual Consent

Besides sitting in rows, another classroom practice taken for granted is the students' raising of hands whenever they want to speak. Unexamined is the teacher's authority to call on the next speaker. I wanted to discuss this routine behavior also, as a second small way to introduce negotiation and to question power relations. After we moved into the odd-shaped "circle" permitted by the crowded room and the Siberian clingers, I asked students to decide if they wanted to raise hands during discussion and have me call on them or if they preferred to speak by self-regulating mutual consent. Of course, they wanted to know what I meant by "self-regulating mutual consent," which I explained as follows: "When you want to speak, you start talking, without raising your hand, and if others speak at the same time, you look around at each other's faces and regulate yourselves without waiting for the teacher to decide who should speak in what order; you do this by deferring to each other, by looking around and asking yourself if it's your turn to speak or if someone else should go ahead of you." I mentioned that it's a good idea to give the floor to someone who has not yet spoken in class or has spoken the least so far, to get as many people involved as possible. Through self-regulation, students mutually establish the order of speakers, instead of it being done by the teacher. Self-regulation means that they share responsibility for maintaining the dialogue, I added. When we reach a silence, a conflict, or a blockage, the students help us get through it and don't wait for the teacher to take charge.

It should be obvious that mutual consent is a far more advanced democratic practice than sitting in a circle. Self-regulation is an elegant and complex architecture for democratic discourse. It requires attentiveness, patience, generosity, and cooperation. It is also fraught with gender, race, class, and caste issues: the patriarchal habit of men who interrupt women at will, the reluctance of students of color to speak up in a white-dominant setting, the discomfort of working-class students of all colors and of foreign students with having to speak in the standard English and academic discourse of the classroom, and the student-to-student competitiveness for grades in an entrepreneurial economy with limited access to good jobs (dividing students against each other into certain castes, like "go-getters" and "climbers" versus "slackers" and "losers"). In a lively discussion class, many students dislike peers who talk over others. They see these peers as rude or as sucking up to the teacher for a grade. While teachers tend to reward talkative students who respond to questions, society also rewards tough guys, operators, and empire-builders. As verbal bullies and discursive entrepreneurs, some talky students don't mind being impolite or aggressively competitive. In class, at work, and in daily life, men especially behave in the caste of "rising stars, "big shots," or self-impressed "honchos." The more aggressive male types tend to take over conversations, push their way to the top, or push people around. Others with something to say, who are less aggressive, less rude, less safe in public exposure, or less confident, like many female students and those of color in a white institution, will simply find it harder in a macho climate to take the floor if they have to start speaking without raising hands. Still, this is not the whole story. Older women tend to be more assertive in class than younger women or younger men. And then, some student talkers of both sexes speak a lot for the right reasons—they are enamored of learning and they know that discourse is a way to propel their education. As the teacher, I need to acknowledge the expressive gifts of those in class eager to converse about the material for reasons beyond merely getting a good grade.

Given this mixed situation, it should come as no surprise that widespread disapproval greeted my proposal for mutual consent. The students voted for raising hands rather than for self-regulation. I could have suggested that we try mutual consent for two weeks and then decide to keep it or not, but my teacher's intuition told me not to push on this point then. In their rejection of mutual consent, they expressed legitimate worries that a few self-serving people would dominate discussion and talk too much if I didn't regulate them. One young woman student, Marguerite, put it this way, "I don't like the way some people monopolize discussions. I think you should call on some of the shyer students for input in a discussion." In an earlier class that had chosen mutual consent, an adult African-American woman, Rose, complained: "I did not like the fact that people always felt the need to dominate class discussion. I did not like the fact that we didn't have to raise our hands because I am not a rude person and if someone is talking I don't like to butt in. If we were to raise our hands more people may get a chance to talk." Yet, still another Utopia class had voted *for* mutual consent and it proved workable there. Choices and outcomes are apparently situated and localized, group-specific, not uniform or universal.

Thus, my Utopian proposal for mutual consent, which I thought distributed authority more democratically, appeared threatening and less democratic to this group of students because it portended a classroom dominated by a few talkers and a weak teacher authority. I believe they intuited the difference here between freedom and license, between democratic structure and domineering chaos. They preferred a strong but fair central authority in class as the best guarantor of open discussion. This negotiation about a routine practice—raising hands—had once again foregrounded an issue of power in the classroom. Negotiating authority in this manner at least activated students as thinkers about their educational experience. Whichever way the choice goes, the important thing is to question a routine behavior so that the teacher's authority to call on people and their responsibility to raise hands is mutually agreed on, not taken-for-granted. My power to regulate the discussion was not *assumed* by me *ex officio* but was *assigned* to me by the constitutional assembly underway in class. If students assign authority to me, they are becoming policymakers in the rhetorical setting.

With these first and simpler deliberations behind us, I then cleared my throat to get ready for the big enchilada—"contract grading."

South of the Border, Down Utopia Way: Crossing into Contract Land

Learning contracts are not unfamiliar in education. Often, they are used in adult environments where faculty serve as facilitators for self-directed, mature students. These students typically design their own study programs in consultation with a faculty mentor or a committee of sponsors. Some notable efforts in this direction have been offered by the City University of New York's special intercampus B.A. Program, the University Without Walls, the Union Institute with its non-traditional doctoral studies, Empire State College for adult learners, and the Fielding Institute, among others. In public schools, some alternative high schools like New Trier (Illinois) in the 1970s and Scarsdale (New York) in the 1980s began experimenting with student-teacher negotiation. One ongoing experiment in negotiation at a public secondary school began at Ithaca's Alternative Community School with 60 students in the 1970s and grew to 260 twenty years later (see Lappé and Dubois 1994, chap. 9). The Ithaca school organizes democratic decision making through a weekly "All-School Meeting" (students and staff), an "Advisory Board" (four representatives each from students, staff, parents, and community), student committees (fifteen groups delegated to handle such things as discipline and serving lunch), and a weekly "Staff Meeting" of teachers and administrators. At the classroom level, students do not decide their grades, but "The teacher presents the plan of what she or he wants to accomplish in the course, then asks the students, 'What do *you* want? How will we evaluate ourselves?'" (Lappé and Dubois 1994, p. 209). For another example of negotiation without formal contract learning in a U.S. public school, the pedagogy of Barbara Brodhagen (1995) is helpful: her Wisconsin 12- and 13-year-olds write a class "Constitution" (see the Appendix to this chapter) and deliberate with the teacher on curriculum planning. Middle-school teacher Scott Greenwood (1995) deploys a series of learning contracts for his students, with successively more student choice built into them as the term progresses and as they gain familiarity with the process.

The most extensive experiments in classroom negotiation appear to have come out of public schools in South Australia, as recorded in a thoughtful text I referred to earlier, *Negotiating the Curriculum* (Boomer et al. 1992). The Australian experiments emphasized *collaborative group contracts* rather than *individual documents*. The classes deliberated as a whole on four essential curricular questions about studying any subject matter (here represented as "*x*"):

1. What do we know about x?
2. What do we need to learn about x that we don't already know?
3. How are we going to learn it?
4. How are we going to show or exhibit to others what we have learned about x?

Then, the students and teacher discuss a document called a "work-required assessment" as a means of determining what readings, papers, projects, class participation, etc. would be required for a grade (see chapter 4, by Susan Hyde, and chapter 11, by Nancy Lester, in *Negotiating the Curriculum*). Despite being limited by traditional syllabi, textbooks, and testing, the Australian teachers recorded some dramatic changes from their democratic negotiations with the students. In these early experiments, critical questioning of knowledge and power in society had a low profile compared with the emphasis on student-centered democratic process, a shortcoming noted by American educators Nancy Lester and Cynthia Onore, who contributed to the volume. Merging democratic process with critical thought on knowledge, power, and society was my interest in the Utopia class which I am reporting in this book. In another effort toward merging shared authority with critical thought, Nan Elsasser, Kyle Fiore, and Patricia Irvine (see Shor 1987b) adapted Freire's "generative theme" method to Caribbean language courses so as to negotiate the syllabus with the students, resulting in some very rich examples of situated pedagogy. Instructive efforts to negotiate the curriculum in some college courses have also been recorded in a new volume by Gail Tayko and Jonathan Tassoni (*Shared Pedagogies* [1996]).

In my own college classes, I introduce collaborative group contracting to academically uncertain adult working students spanning a wide range in age and maturity, who have come to class not expecting to negotiate, and who have little or no experience in self-directed learning. With them, I attempt to negotiate a classwide document codifying our agreement about what academic work is required for what final grade. The contracts developed in my classes, which I will detail below, propose requirements for reading, writing, lateness, absence, and class participation, in distinct levels of work corresponding to different grades, A, B, or C, with successively less work negotiated at each lower grade, something apparently not done in the Australian model or in the learning contracts utilized by Greenwood or in college by Peter Elbow (see the Appendix to this chapter for a copy of Elbow's contract). However, Amber Dahlin (1994) does encourage her college "writing-about-literature" class to construct a syllabus where grades of A to F are awarded according to the number of outcomes achieved by any student from the following negotiated list:

Outcomes: By the end of the semester we will have:
1. Read a wide variety of literature and comprehended it.
2. Learned the common vocabulary of literature.
3. Learned to write better.
4. Written three formal essays analyzing literature and completed work in a genre of choice.
5. Done a project of some sort on the reading.
6. Explored different kinds of literary criticism.
7. Shared responses and explored how reading affects people differently. Further, we will have shown respect for the opinions and interpretations of others in class discussions, writing, and small groups. [Note the "rules for class discussion" aspect of this item and the next one.]
8. Structured this course, monitored its progress, and contributed to its successful completion by speaking our minds, thinking about goals, and solving problems as they arose. (p. 31)

Completing all eight outcomes earns an A, seven a B, six a C, five a D, four or fewer an F. Dahlin reports that when she asked the class on the first day to write lists of "things you'll like to be able to do or have done by term's end" and "thoughts about grading, attendance, and assignments," three of the seventeen students immediately left the room rather than negotiate the syllabus, while those who remained "approached the task with varying degrees of enthusiasm." By the end, though, "Without exception students felt that the process had been worthwhile," Dahlin writes (p. 29).

In the Australian model, adapted by Nancy Lester for graduate teacher education in the United States, the required syllabus of any school, department, or state agency is considered a necessary "constraint" on student-teacher negotiations, that is, mandated material that must be covered and can't be negotiated, though it can be studied critically. In my college classes, I have the authority to set the subject matter and don't have a mandated syllabus or reading list. This gives me more freedom to negotiate a contract with the students. More free to negotiate, I also choose to raise two sets of questions not included in the four basic issues noted above in the Australian model. The first set of my additional questions are important to ask *before* beginning the formal study of any subject matter ("*x*"): *Why are we studying* x? *Where did* x *come from? Why must we read and write and talk about this subject matter? Who has required it for what reasons?* These initial issues would encourage a critical stance toward authority and education rather than a routine acceptance of the standard syllabus. Another set of critical questions can be asked *after* the Australians' last item above (how to display what has been learned): *How has the study of* x *changed us? How can we use what we have learned to continue changing ourselves as well as to change school and society?* I will come back to this final question in the last chapter, to show some actual responses from the Utopia students.

With an expanded agenda of six questions instead of four, questioning x in a negotiated curriculum will be more critical of power relations, thus coming closer to merging student-centered process with social critique. But, still, the critical-democratic character of such pedagogy is limited by the institutional authority I bring to class and by the institutional setting which frames our work (such as the requirement that I give letter grades). My teacherly authority to grade them keeps some students wary of the negotiating process, fearing the consequences of crossing me—so they either join in merely because I seem to want it, or they stay out of it because they don't know how to protect their interests in this new arrangement.

The authority I bring to class has to unbalance the democratic process. I could describe the imbalance this way: As the teacher, I am *inviting and allowing* the students to practice democracy rather than they having won this right *for themselves.* The experiment in negotiation is the result of my political initiative, not theirs, representing my long-term social development into such an agenda, not theirs. This makes power-sharing and social critique risky Utopian leaps for them, greater than the steps ahead I am taking with shared authority.

Because students are not *self-authorized* to share power but rather are *teacher-authorized* in this situation (I authorize them instead of them authorizing themselves) the Utopia course represents a cultural exercise or laboratory, not a social movement of broad change in school and society. Had the students democratized the classroom at their initiative, an entirely different counterhegemonic politics would be represented here. They, ahead of me, would have brought to class the intention to reconstruct authority in favor of cultural democracy. As it is, I am inviting them into a critical stance toward knowledge, knowledge-making, and power. If they had invited me to teach that kind of class, it would mean that they had previously developed this intention through various social experiences in class and out. Under those circumstances, we would all be situated in a very different history than the one described in this book. That history would represent a grassroots, mass constituency contending for authority from below, at this site and others.

Still, without having authored this exercise themselves, the students can gain something useful from being authorized by a critical teacher. With permission for negotiation, they can experience the class as a laboratory for alternative self-development, which is a political opening afforded by an alternative teacher to develop the students' (and teacher's) democratic arts and critical thought. Even within these obvious limits and contradictions, once a process goes in motion by whatever means, it can take on an unpredictable life of its own, which is exactly what happened in this Utopia class. This teacher-authorized negotiation took a dramatic student-centered turn that threatened to dissolve the class, which I will detail below.

In class, to launch the contract phase of negotiations, I mentioned to the students that I had brought learning contracts and asked if anyone had done this before. No one raised a hand. None of them had any experience with this process. So, I explained that it related to the Utopian ideas of questioning the status quo, experimenting with new relationships, and socially engineering a new process for decision making. Part of the status quo in education is the teacher's sole right to make the syllabus, to set the assignments and deadlines, and to evaluate students with grades. In this Utopian experiment with contracts, I proposed, the teacher would no longer set all of the rules, decide the grading policies on his own, do all of the evaluation, and be the only one announcing requirements. Students would make important decisions and evaluations about their work. The curriculum would be mutually discussed. I added that this was one way to question the status quo because students did not now have the right to decide such things. I told them that I thought education works best when students set goals for themselves, clarify their purposes, deliberate with others on the rules, evaluate themselves, their peers, the process, and the teacher, and not wait to be told what to do and what things mean. When you have intentions, power, responsibilities, and purposes, you are more connected to what you do and focus more intelligence on your experience (once again a Deweyan concept of democratic education).

After making this explanation, I looked around and saw some interested faces, some bored ones, some perplexed, and some lost. I expect a certain number of glazed eyes whenever I talk at any length in class about anything. I simply cannot involve everyone in my discourse no matter how plainly, humorously, or appropriately I craft my speech with them in mind. Those in far Siberia are usually the ones to pay least mind to what I say. Some looks of confusion are also common when I ask students to take part in unfamiliar practices. They simply don't know what they are expected to do or what they are getting into and are not sure they trust me or their own competence. I can't imagine a class like this in a place like this at a time like this eagerly embracing my proposed learning contracts; if it did, I would probably fall dead from cardiac amazement and expect to wake up at the gates of pedagogical Paradise. Besides, this was not the first road to democracy littered with shards of doubt, so I pushed ahead and handed out the sample contracts with my proposals for earning grades at three levels, A, B, and C. I asked students to read over the sheet, write on it any questions they had, discuss the details with a nearby partner or two, and see if they wanted to suggest any changes today in class. I mentioned that after today's discussion on the contracts, students would have a week to decide one of three options:

1. Sign up for one of the grade levels and the work required in my proposals (as amended in class debate), or
2. Sign up for the contract negotiated in class with personal amendments fitting your special interests or needs, or
3. Throw my proposals and student amendments out the window [so to speak—something hard to do in a windowless basement!], write your own document instead, and sign up for your own personal contract negotiated individually with me.

I offer the third individual option for writing your own contract to accommodate those students who want to go their own way. The third option allows them to make the negotiations as individual as they want. A few do write their own contracts. A few amend the class document with their personal clauses. In addition, a small number of students don't sign the negotiated contract and don't negotiate their own agendas privately with me. They take the Siberian Express straight out of this Utopian territory, ignoring the process out of protest, weariness, boredom, absentmindedness, or disorientation. They want me to teach them and grade them the old-fashioned way. Fortunately, only a few spontaneously choose to ignore the whole shebang. I accept these students buying out of the process and forcing me into a traditional position because, frankly, I don't know what else to do with them. Students cannot be compelled to be nontraditional; they can only be invited and if they choose not, they have the right to compel me to be traditional toward them. As I said, a controlling principle of critical-democratic practice is that the teacher's right to propose goes only as far as the students' right to dispose.

The contract sheet I prepared before class and handed out to students proposed the following work required at each grade level, with attached notes:

CONTRACT GRADING
For an 'A' Grade:
- 1 absence
- 1 lateness to class
- no leaving class early
- 'A' quality on written work
- all work handed in on time
- be a leader in class discussion
- write 1,000 words on each of three assigned books
- Do two Utopia projects, one on changing the College and one on changing NYC; make class presentations on each and hand in a written report (1,000 words) on each.

For a 'B' Grade:
- 2 absences
- 1 lateness to class
- no leaving class early
- 'B' quality on written work
- 1 paper late
- participate regularly in class discussion
- write 750 words on each of three assigned books
- Do two projects, one on changing the college and one on changing NYC, and hand in a written report (750 words) on each.

For a 'C' Grade:
- 3 absences
- 1 lateness to class
- no leaving class early
- 'C' quality on written work
- 1 paper late
- participate sometimes in class discussion
- write 500 words on each of three assigned books
- Do one Utopia project and hand in a written report (500) words on it.

NOTES:

1. Papers handed in on time can be rewritten for a higher grade as long as you hand in the rewrite one week after you get it back from me. You can rewrite papers as often as you like for a higher grade as long as each rewrite is handed back in one week.

2. There will be a midterm and a final exam in class with questions designated for different grade levels.

After handing out this sheet, I gave students time to discuss it among themselves to encourage them to take stances. This in-class time for peer discussion is crucial. It affords students a chance to think out loud among themselves without the teacher's supervision so that they can develop their own positions in language familiar to them. If the class is to become a cultural forum for debating meanings (as Bruner [1986] suggests it should), I have to strengthen their discursive authority in relation to mine. To feel more authoritative, students need time to think through the material. They generally are not allowed this opportunity in the traditional "question-response-evaluation" discourse dominating teacher-centered classrooms (Heath 1978). In what often passes for classroom "discussion," students usually have only a few seconds to respond to the teacher's questions. Further, when they are asked to think in speech or in writing, they feel pressured to guess the right answer or ideal text on the teacher's mind (Knoblauch and Brannon 1984) and to perform in the academic idiom of the teacher, which is awkward and inhibiting rather than organic to their linguistic habits of thought, thus producing depressed academic performance. It's not easy for students to think on their feet in class, especially when presented with unfamiliar subject matter in an alien academic idiom. The rhetorical setting of traditional classrooms partly maintains unequal power relations by its failure to give students ample time for constructing their stances through writing, reading, and speaking in their own idiom.

Rhetorical Reinventions: Contracts Against the Status Quo

With the learning contracts in hand, the students talked at length in groups of two or three as I waited for them to be ready for whole-class negotiation. When I reconvened the class, I asked for questions, amendments, and comments on my original proposals. For a moment, no one said anything as I looked slowly around the room nodding at one student or another to encourage some response. Ten seconds of silence in a classroom always feels like ten hours of nada. My nerves were edgy, but I did what I could to maintain a level manner. Finally, one student (bless him) said his group wanted to know why tests were required. He meant the midterm and final exam I had listed in the notes to my original contract proposals. As a dialogic practice, I try not to answer a student question the first time I hear it, but rather ask the questioner or others to speak about the issue. This allows students more time to develop their positions before I give my response. It also gives me a chance to hear more remarks from students so that I can better understand their intentions. So, I asked him to explain his objection. He said that people in his group didn't like tests. I asked why. He hesitated. I waited. After a brief silence, he didn't know how to go on, so I turned to others in his group. One of his partners said he didn't like the surprises of exams. Another said she thought too much was riding on a one-shot preparation. I asked the class generally why they thought teachers gave tests. Someone said that it was to make sure they did the work and learned the stuff. I then asked how could I be sure they were doing their work and learning the stuff if I didn't give tests? They said I should be able to know what people in class knew. But how?, I insisted, how can I know? A student responded that I should listen to them when they talk and learn from the things they write. Was everyday classwork a better indication of a student's performance than a test?, I asked. Heads nodded. They seemed to think so.

For the most part in school, tests are yes-no, fill-in-the-blank, factoid-obsessed melodramas, memory olympics, and commercial short-answer standardized regimens that come and go without a context. I did well on these dreadful tests, but I despised taking them when I was a student. They disregard reflective intelligence by being artificially timed short-answer exercises; they deny writing as a knowledge-making recursive process of invention and revision; they rule out collaborative learning; they prevent students from consulting sources when they need to know something, which goes against the genuine habits of scholarly work. Further, standardized short-answer tests are also prejudiced generally against female students who are socialized to think in complexes rather than simplexes, to work collaboratively rather than individualistically (Belenky et al. 1986). Patriarchal culture develops males primarily with the habits for simplistic, self-centered assertiveness useful in test-taking. Standardized test scores also correlate with race and with family income, being biased against students from working, poor, and non-white homes (Meier 1989). Thus, I give exams rarely and prefer giving open-book essay tests and take-home exams which ask students to think through substantive issues. I also consult with students in designing the essay exam in order to get them to devise some of the questions. Further, there are collaborative questions on my exams which allow students to think and write together during test-time. Yet, in the Utopia class, I was not wedded to the need for exams. It was a soft position in my own plans for the course, so it was easy for me to give ground. I told the students that I'd put off testing.

A student then wanted to know more about the rewrite policy, where students can revise any paper handed in on time for a higher grade. He asked if only the highest grade counted in a series of rewrites, a question that comes up virtually every semester in every class. I said yes, only the best grade counts. Understandably, he and other students liked this proposal. I offer it to encourage students to write more, to keep up with class work, and to take revising seriously. A rubric of contemporary composition theory is the crucial role of revision in the development of writing and understanding (see Perl 1980; 1994a; 1994b). So, I told students that I would help them rewrite for a higher grade by explaining on their papers how to improve them. I announced that I was available outside of class to work with anyone on improving her or his writing.

The rewrite issue pleased a good number of students, but then the negotiations went into a deep spin around a question asked by a 20-year-old student, Annette, an accounting major working twenty hours a week as a hostess/floor manager. Annette, who would later argue strenuously with me about her paper grades, asked what it meant for me to require A or B *quality* on written work. How did I know what A and B quality were?, she said. This was a fair question, but at the moment I drew a blank. In the past, students had occasionally asked what I looked for in papers, but none had ever explicitly questioned me on how I knew an A from a B from a C. Perhaps this issue came up now and not before simply because Annette was prepared to ask it, unlike most students who shy away from directly challenging the teacher on her or his judgment. Annette was a middle-row type, not a deep Siberian. She was more assertive than the back-corner students and more likely to be one to take risks by interrogating the teacher in a course that invited questioning. A few students have such boldness. Then again, perhaps the issue came up explicitly just then because the Utopia class crossed a certain threshold of negotiation. That is, student authority to question the teacher is conditioned by the teacher's posture of negotiation, which I was elevating year by year, until my negotiating stance perhaps became high enough to authorize students into more assertive questioning. Since that Utopia class, explicit questions on my grading standards have occurred again, but not as strenuously as in Annette's case, and not uniformly in all courses, so the presence of an opinion-leading student in class apparently influences the extent of negotiations, once again making this a situated pedagogy.

Faced with a new situation, I had no comfortable reply ready to explain my qualitative grading standards. I had to think out loud, on the spot, and I was thrust into the same position as the students who were responding spontaneously to my questions and contract proposals. I wondered to myself, how *did* I know what an A or B paper was? I knew it would sound bad if I confessed that the whole grading process was merely subjective on my part—how would that credit my authority? In giving grades, I apparently took my experience, judgment, and fairness for granted, so maybe I should just fall back on what rhetoricians call *ethos*, my sincerity, my ethical posture, my identity as a dead-serious teacher, my face and voice radiating fairness, competence, good intentions, and so on. But, that's an infantilizing "trust-me" attitude, which is another way to maintain my authority by giving a paternal, mysterious response to a reasonable, direct student query about what deserves an A, B, or less. Politically, unilateral authority benefits from infantilizing the students; if a traditional teacher talk downs to them as if they are children, then that makes the teacher papa, the boss. This personalizes the power relations in a patriarchal way. Now, students hate to be patronized, commanded, or manipulated, which is what paternal vagueness about grading does, by mystifying the power relations of the classroom into unspoken subjective standards of judgment exercised by an elder whose authority must not be questioned. To authorize the students as adult constituents of the process, I had to be always open to questions and always explicit, especially about grading standards, but my brain was stuck!

I wanted this class to *demystify* the education process, not to fall back on mystery. This kind of difficult moment in the negotiating process has a name I gave it in the first chapter—*the discomforts of democracy*—when previously unexamined and unquestioned authority is called upon to explain and justify itself publicly in response to student interventions.

Well, I had to say something, so, on the spot, I began by saying that after twenty years of teaching English and reading papers, I try to be open, fair, and careful when I give grades. I said that I comment a lot on student papers, responding to their thoughts and to their writing, to make my evaluation a meaningful exchange, not just a simplistic giving of a grade or a rushed correction of errors. I told them that I look to see if the student met the minimum number of words for A or B level and then I judge quality in terms of serious and organized thought—writing which shows a deep attempt to explain the issues that concern you, carefully probing your own thoughts in words that give your ideas shape, using illustrations that justify a point of view, not just throwing words on paper, not just throwing a paper at me. Because I write a lot of notes on their papers, I added, they can count on advice about rewriting for a higher grade. (In an effort to demystify grading, Peter Elbow emphasized "effort," "thinking," and "substance" as his standards for giving a "B"—see the Appendix to this chapter for his definitions of these qualities.) Were my remarks enough to settle the issue? No. It still sounded squishy and subjective, appealing to my authority as a veteran teacher and my ethos of good intentions and high expectations. I felt the weakness of my response dripping to the floor. So, I said more, which I'll report in a moment, following a brief reflection on grading, to get a handle on what's involved in this conundrum.

To say that grading troubles many teachers (and students) is to understate the obvious. Here is how Australian teacher Susan Hyde discussed grading in the Boomer volume on negotiating the curriculum:

> Without changes to what is valued and how we evaluate, negotiation regimes will be constrained and undermined . . . There is a good deal of literature that demonstrates that grading in schools, while being supposedly unbiased, is based on a value system that advantages more privileged students and, therefore, perpetuates inequalities in class, race, and gender

. . . It encourages and legitimizes competition as a way of sorting out what is seen as success and failure and, indeed, is an important ideological factor which underpins the way society and its economic structure is organized . . . I am convinced that collaborative learning cannot be developed in classrooms that revolve around competitive grading . . . If a teacher believes in sharing power in the classroom, then she needs to seek ways to include non-competitive assessment in her practice. (1992, pp. 69, 71)

Hyde acknowledges that abandoning competitive grading will put many teachers at risk in traditional schools. In her situation, she was able to hold a class meeting at the end of the term where students collaborated in generating the criteria for grading, something which I do in the beginning of my courses through the contract proposals.

Grading also troubles many students, some more than others, and my Utopia class expressed more concern than most. For example, Annette also questioned me on the quantitative minimums, saying that some students will just write extra sentences to get in their A-level word count, meaning that the shorter paper is really the better one, while the longer one is just stuffed with filler. (I hear this claim from students virtually every term.) I asked the class if some students will write "filler" just to meet the word minimum, and heads nodded in agreement. So, I said they were right—putting empty words on paper is not A-level work and won't receive an A even if it reaches the minimum words required for an A. I proposed then that if they write a well thought-out paper but run short of the minimum word count for A-level, I'd read the paper and make suggestions how to expand on something meaningful, so that the student could rewrite and still get the A. This proposal of mine met with mixed reactions, perhaps because it meant that I was standing firm on minimum lengths for papers and not giving in to reducing the word count, which would mean less work for students if I did give in. I suspected that students here were bargaining for a lighter work load, not just questioning the terms of my grading judgments. It's reasonable for working students to want a lighter load, so I was open to negotiating the work required as well as my grading standards, but I wanted them to offer a specific proposal regarding paper size for each level. No one in that Utopia class made such a proposal, although students in some later classes did, leading, in those other courses, to reduced minimums for written assignments at different grade levels.

Overall, how should I rethink grading? Consider, in the first place, that in negotiating the contract, when I proposed "A quality on written work," I had signaled that there were some *qualitative* standards in my judgment of "good writing" (which I inadequately explained above and will try again below). The other contract provisions dealt with *quantitative* issues—number of absences and latenesses, number of papers, minimum number of words on each paper, etc. These parts focused on countable items, not subjective or professional value judgments. To get closer to grading, let me pick up where Susan Hyde above left off, to review the politics of *quantitative* grading before finishing my discussion of Annette's question of how I know what A or B *quality* is on written work.

Quantitative grading based on *the amount of work done* tends to reward those students more interested in the course (English or communications majors like me, most likely) and more in control of their time and money (those fully employed and better-paid, again like me). Grading by *amount of work done* privileges those who earn better than average pay and who don't have to moonlight on a second job, or those whose tuition is paid by an employer, agency, parent or spouse, or those who don't have to work outside of the home because they are supported by someone else's wealth or income, or those who don't have to raise kids, or those who live near work and school and have less commuting to do, or those who don't have to take a heavy course load each term. These are some (but not all) of the factors influencing a commuting student's *quantitative* commitment of time and attention to writing papers for a course. These factors affect the academic success of many working students in higher education (over 5 million now attend some 1,200 community colleges in the United States, with many others enrolled on four-year campuses (see Cross 1971; Cohen and Brawer 1982; Karabel and Brint 1989; Pincus and Archer 1989; Dougherty 1991, 1994). I have students who take a full program of courses while working full-time and raising children; other students in class are single, childless, and living at home, supported by a spouse or by mom and dad. Can one grading standard be fair for such wildly different circumstances? Should grading be based on individual social conditions, then? Should it be structured first around the already unequal situations among working-class students of different genders, colors, and family situations, and structured secondly around the economic inequality between worldly students and those from wealthy backgrounds? A gross inequality exists in the money spent on the education of students from different social classes at all levels of education (Karabel 1972; Kozol 1991). With unequal resources invested in different groups' development, should students be graded differentially, perhaps on a point system that takes into account time demands as well as social prejudice against their class, gender, color, and life circumstances? For example, going to school in property-poor districts is an immense obstacle to academic success, with only about 10 percent of students from the bottom income brackets making it through college by age 24, compared with better than 60 percent of those from upper-income homes (Mortenson 1993–94). Can teachers in an unequal society pretend that there is a universal student for whom single standards are fair? Should students continue to be graded on academic performances dissociated from social factors like race and class, as if we live in a fair meritocracy? Is it equitable to treat all people the same when they have inequitable relations to power and resources in school and society? Raising kids, commuting, and receiving lower wages are handicaps to academic work which affect working women and minorities disproportionately because working-class mothers are expected to take care of children, keep house, and earn money while they go to college, and because minorities are paid less than whites in the job market and have twice the unemployment rate, in good times and in bad, despite the major advances in educational achievement they have attained as a group in the past decades (Pincus 1995). But, how can I give grades based on nonacademic factors like hours per week changing diapers or helping a 10-year-old with homework or serving burgers part-time at McDonald's for an indecent minimum wage or being paid less as a gas attendant because you are African-American or Hispanic, or coming from a New York City high school which spends about half as much on its students as do the wealthy districts in the suburbs? Perhaps these issues matter less on elite, residential campuses, where the students tend to be younger, from higher-income households able to invest family funds in their children's needs (like state-of-the-art computers), with few students raising children or holding down full-time jobs, and with little commuting to take away from study time. Mass higher education is a working-class phenomenon, an ordeal and a dead-end for the majority who drop out, an adventure or pleasure or irritation for others who get through, and an economic ladder for some (Pincus 1980).

Grading, then, quantitative or qualitative, is especially troublesome in a low-budget college because it is blatantly involved with social inequality. The working student is basically handled and judged by someone alien to her or his social class and community while being processed in an underfunded institution whose political purpose was identified decades ago by Burton Clark (1960) as "the cooling-out function in higher education." These conflicts are easy enough to see in mass higher education; they severely undermine the egalitarian image created by the enterprise (Dougherty 1994). They affect the fairness of grading, whether I focus on quantity or quality of a student's work. Given these circumstances, what is "A quality writing" in a course like this, for students like this, in a college like this, at a time like this, in a society like this?

This paragraph cannot simply answer the complex question ending the last one, because I don't have an easy answer. Peter Elbow (1986) chiseled at the granite of grading and positioned himself as coach, lawyer, and judge, trying to straddle the contradictory roles of being a student advocate and an institutional/professional enforcer at the same time, accepting the contrary postures of promoting and sorting out students. He embraced the contraries of his unilateral authority as a "gatekeeper" who graded students as long as he helped them learn how to perform well enough to jump over the academic gates set for them by non-negotiable authorities. His honesty is admirable in facing the responsibility of helping students meet non-negotiable standards. But, the social critique of grading and inequality which I offered above still beckons, unanswered and unforgiving. The hard answer taken up at some places (like Evergreen State College) is to abolish letter-grading and to keep narrative evaluation, which Elbow participated in earlier in his career and speaks well of.

Until grading can be abolished at my College or is abolished generally, what am I to do? Organize students for a campaign against grading? I like this option, but I doubt that students would embrace it in the first week of class. It would be too imposing and too much my agenda, especially in an age of "conservative restoration" (as I have called recent decades, in my *Culture Wars*). Another way is to present the social context of grading to the students, as I presented it in the previous paragraphs, and to let them struggle out their scheme of fairness under these conditions. Such a presentation on my part might frontload the discourse with too much of my words and ways of seeing, thus unbalancing the process early on and silencing the students; then again, it might appropriately include them in the dilemma and deliberation; it's risky for a professor to talk a lot in the early going if a course is supposed to be dialogic. Still another option would be to convene a student group in class to hammer out a grading proposal based on their perceptions of fairness. The whole class could then debate the proposal of their peers along with my input. This option appeals to me because it would generate a student-based text to compete with my own. That would be a good exercise in democratic rhetoric and Utopian reconstruction, but would it exhaust the class with a marathon debate on process? We would have to set limits on the time devoted to the constitutional assembly of the course, which is something I already keep in mind as I negotiate. Another option is to use outside teachers for portfolio grading, which is a more complex solution to relieving a classroom teacher of sole responsibility for grades, but excludes the students themselves from the deliberation (see Belanoff and Dickson 1991).

None of these options came to me at the moment I was on the spot in the Utopia class on the second day and needing to defend my grading judgments. So, I fell back *faute de mieux* on my ethos, my face of good intentions—experience, openness, fairness—jury-rigged with standards of serious thought I look for in student writing, coupled to ways for students to contest my decisions and to rewrite for higher grades. I said to the Utopia students that I'd been grading papers for twenty years at this College. I told them that I read student papers slowly, carefully, and in depth, making lots of marginal notes, not just slapping on a grade and a one-sentence missive at the end. I then went on to say that I opposed grading because it separates students from teachers (witness the Siberian Syndrome) and students from each other (witness the front-row scholasticons), dividing people into competitive grade-seekers when they should be collaborating. But I did not have the power to abolish this requirement now, which meant it was a limit I couldn't avoid. All I could offer was my commitment to be fair and open-minded and to give them the option to rewrite for a higher grade. After many years of teaching writing and grading student papers at this College, my standards for "good writing" were formed by learning what students can do. I told them that if any student thinks I gave an unfair grade on a paper, he or she can talk to me after class about why the work deserves a higher grade. I promised to listen and explain what it would take to rewrite for a higher grade . . . And, as it happened, some students like Annette did complain aggressively after class, and sometimes I did raise their grades. Their right to complain was established as well as the teacher's obligation to listen and defend his judgment. My authority was not unquestionable. In the course, I also asked students to evaluate themselves and to evaluate each other, so that I got various inputs.

For the moment that day, in regard to grades, we had apparently worn each other out, because the students didn't pursue the issue further, for which I was grateful. Through this discussion, my teacherly right to grade them unilaterally was not taken for granted just as my right to require students to raise hands and wait for me to call on them in discussion was also not taken for granted. The process was brought out into the light of day (actually, into the gray florescent light of our windowless room). Eventually, one of the older women in class, Tina, a good writer herself and a paraprofessional in the public schools, spontaneously decided to serve as a "peer rewrite tutor" whose special project would be to work with any student who wanted help rewriting for a higher grade. Her voluntary service was credited as part of her individualized "A" contract. To my surprise, I had a peer tutor for the class at a time when no budget existed for such a thing at the College, though she did come at a price to me, which I would estimate at about a thousand dollars of democratic discomfort.

The Price of Democratic Change: Debating Class Participation

After my impromptu defense of my fairness and experience in grading papers, a student then asked about my proposed requirement that A-level students had to be "leaders" in class discussion. I explained that discussion leaders took part often in the dialogue and did more than just talk. Such leaders listened to what people said, asked questions of their peers, engaged in student-to-student cross-talk without waiting for the teacher to respond to each comment, and took responsibility for picking up the dialogue when we hit silences or points of disagreement. They also noticed when we were going off track and helped refocus the issue, I concluded.

Now, this level of responsibility for discussion is far and away more than students ever assume. Can students learn in a few weeks how to be skilled dialogic leaders? No. Neither can teachers learn dialogic skills that quickly. But, they can begin practicing new discourse habits that point in a democratic direction, which is what matters. Becoming a good discussion leader takes years of reflective practice (Cochran-Smith 1991; Auerbach 1992; Carter and Curtis 1994). To develop dialogic talent, a teacher needs institutional support and student cooperation to run a seminarlike discussion rather than a traditional lecture class. Many school districts and academic departments mandate certain texts to be read and material to be covered in sequence. At this level of outside management of the classroom, the teacher cannot easily close the door and ignore the authorities. Lecturing machine-gun style then becomes a political compulsion restricting dialogue. Under these limits, the teacher is compelled to become a verbal delivery system covering the official syllabus in nonstop teacher-talk. Other obstacles to dialogue include the teacher's professional status, gender, and race, because new teachers and adjuncts, women, and teachers of color bring less authority to the classroom than do veteran, white, male, full-time instructors. As I argued earlier, authority is gendered, racialized, and age-based. With differential authority attaching to skin color, sex, age, and faculty status, teachers have unequal positions from which to attempt dialogue. Given these social pressures against *teachers* enacting dialogue in class, I know it is a lot to ask students to participate in leading discussion.

Like students every semester since, some in the Utopia class objected to the provision requiring participation. One young woman, Sandy, was unhappy with requiring A-level students to be discussion leaders because she said that these students might begin talking too long and too often, just to get in their A-quota of words. (We were back to the earlier issue of macho talkers, verbal entrepreneurs, and high-achieving stars overspeaking others.) Even when they had little to say, some students might talk just to qualify for an A, she added. I had to agree that this was a danger. There is limited air time in class. So, what to do? How could I give up participation as a contractual goal when I agree with Dewey that it is the number one educational value (and so listed on the agenda I developed in *Empowering Education*)?

I wanted a provision signaling students that they should construct the class with their words and not wait for me to fill the time and space with teacher-talk. So, I posed this problem back to the students: "What could we do to encourage and reward participation while not setting up students to out-talk each other?" They mulled it over, but no one had a clue. (In a woman's course at a Southern college, "Groundrule 22" reads, "We have the right to talk and not to talk on individual class days, so that an individual is not pressured to respond to every issue." See the Appendix to this chapter for a copy of the class rules agreed to by the students and teacher there.) This Utopia class wanted to reduce the requirements for A and B contracts when it came to leading discussion. I complained that too much responsibility for discussion-maintenance was left on me. But, the students felt that is exactly where such responsibility belongs. So, faced with strong resistance here, I withdrew the provision requiring high-level participation for A and B contracts and suggested instead that we leave it informally that the higher the grade level, the more class participation students would take on. If some A or B students hogged air time in discussion, I'd talk to each privately about giving others a chance. The students were willing to live with this for the time being. But, the truth is that it's hard to monitor participation unless a student hardly talks or talks a great deal, which makes his or her level of participation obvious. I would have to say that "participation" is mostly a qualitative performance. My intuition is that our negotiation over this at least sent a message to students how important I think discussion is in the learning process, but I did have to retreat on the proposal.

In general, when negotiating the curriculum, I feel out how much authority or work students will take on, nudging them to reach the limit. Authority is a moving target from term to term and even week to week within a term. It changes as the semester develops. For example, in a previous Utopia class, students exercised authority by writing an explicit agenda for my role as the teacher, as part of their code of classroom rules: "The teacher shouldn't make you read your papers out loud in class if you don't want to. The teacher should become part of the class by giving his point of view, expressing his opinions, and being a leader, and not being an outsider or just okay whatever students say. The teacher should be a referee when the discussion gets too heated. If someone is monopolizing the conversation, then the teacher should cut in and stop it. The teacher should be understanding and cooperative when it comes to students' personal problems that affect their work." The students wrote, debated, and voted in these provisions, making explicit what they expected from me, including the above provision that I should not become an "outsider." Apparently, the negotiating process made some worry that my profile would be too low in class. I was being advised to raise my profile here, to be more present as a commentator and authority who kept order, a reasonable student request given the classrooms many have experienced in high school. They want authority to be fair and flexible, but competent and in charge. This agenda also included the final sentence's proviso that I take a social attitude toward grading, that is, consider a student's personal problems as factors in the grade she or he earns. I now wish I had pursued that opening further, to pose the social questions I mentioned above, concerning grading and inequality.

We Are What We Read: Power in the Choosing of the Texts

After compromising on class participation for A and B contracts, I was asked about the books I had in mind for them to read, which I announced as *50 Simple Things You Can Do to Save the Earth*, *Walden II*, and *Ecotopia*. The first is a very readable, "green" perspective on practical consumer actions to reduce waste and pollution. The second is the most famous Utopian novel, well-known in academic corners but unknown to my students. The last is a Utopian novel by Ernest Callenbach that was very popular in the 1970s when it first appeared. Faced with unfamiliar texts, the students had no opinion on these readings. Traditionally, teacher-selected reading lists are part of the machinery of control. The "required readings" comprise a teacher's or an institution's unilateral action. For most of my students, school books have been boring, and, in college, often very expensive. They can't afford $60 worth of textbooks, but they are sometimes obliged to buy them. Not having a choice in reading matter only compounds the anti-democratic experience of education, with predictable anti-intellectual results. If the teacher says read these books, students resign themselves to reading them or skimming them, getting by on papers and exams, and forgetting the material before the next semester even begins. I, too, had unilaterally assigned the reading list. This was not good, I thought to myself. I did not do this part of the process well. I took the readings for granted when I should have structured them into the deliberation itself. Here is how Christine Sutphin reflected on her same mistake in teaching a college "Women and Literature" course:

> I had certainly never intended to "domesticate" students, a particularly telling metaphor considering that the majority of students in this class would be women. But the fact that I had not included them in the process of choosing made me realize how closely I had been bound by the old models even when I thought I was committed to the interactive classroom. In my classes, students participate in presentations, discussions, and workshops and are encouraged to come up with their own ideas for papers. But I had never asked them to be responsible for choosing what we read, just as none of my teachers had ever asked that I take on that responsibility. (1992, p. 31)

Sutphin reports that she changed her practice so that "The first few weeks of class we read material I assign while the students meet in groups to decide what work each group would like the class to read." She puts several anthologies on reserve in the library for students to consult, but they are free to choose material elsewhere. The students not only select readings but also lead class discussion on their choices, a method I have been using recently and will discuss below. Overall, Sutphin says the students prefer this new way of doing the reading list and would like it extended to other courses.

In the Utopia class, I should have provided a longer reading list, say eight books, and asked students to choose the ones they wanted to read and in what order, as well as having the right to add their own books to the list. Let's say that I bring to class copies of the eight books in the first week or two and have students browse through them for an hour or more, reading some pages inside the books, discussing them with peers, and then voting for three books and the order of studying them, based on whatever principles they choose. I would ask each student to write her or his reasons for choosing a book so that I and they can learn their standards, and I would not be surprised if they chose the shortest and the cheapest books, for obvious reasons. Following their selections, I would then feel free to add another book or two of my own choice, because I am allowed to make selections in a mutual process. Once I knew which books we had negotiated for the reading list, I would then get on the phone, call the publishers, use my credit card, order them immediately, and expect them to arrive at my office over the next few weeks, some sooner than others. In class, I would pass around an envelope and ask students to reimburse me for the cost of the books. Like Sutphin, I would bring some reading selections to class that were available immediately for discussion until the student-selected materials arrived. I did a version of this negotiated reading list in a recent class and it worked out well. The selection and sequencing of reading matter is something students can undertake as part of the constitutional convention of the course, in public school as well as in college (see Hyde, chap. 4 in Boomer et al. 1992 for a report on school children who rewrote their required math textbook and selected their own sequencing of its chapters). In the Utopia class, I failed to negotiate "the reading list" because I was too nonchalantly the professor when it came to texts. I was too focused on *my* academic relation to books, not on the role of books and reading lists in their experience.

The students' nonreaction to the reading list was followed by a dramatic turn of events when it came to discussing the contract's *attendance requirements*. I was next given a major-league lesson in the creative and unpredictable moments in a critical-democratic process.

Utopian Rules: No Attendance Required! Class Dismissed!

The initiator of the big lesson in power-sharing was the student named Angela, who was 21, a media studies major, with piercing dark eyes and a demanding gaze that grabbed your attention when she looked at you. She had long brown hair surrounding a thin face, was about 5'2", white, bright, and full of fight. Articulate, unintimidated by a professor, Angela was no Siberian and no brown-nose. She sat near the front, a scholasticon of her own design. On her sign-in sheet, Angela wrote that she took the course because it was a requirement that "seemed interesting." She also penned an idealistic definition of Utopia on the first day of class: "Utopia, in my opinion, is a society where there is no conflict, greed, jealousy, hate, or any other negative influence. There is love, of everything and anyone. There are no problems to work out of any sort. Everything is perfect."

Students like Angela at the front of the room have a variety of characters. They can be scholastic high-achievers, the fraction of students comfortable with academic discourse in its various forms. Contending with the stiff idioms and institutional rituals of schooling, they are students who adapt to the academic code, have a metalinguistic aptitude, and are oriented toward the abstract thought common in higher education. On the one hand, they can become the teacher's right-hand women and men (a/k/a "teacher's pets") to whom the teacher gratefully turns for student responses in those awkward moments of silence following the teacher's asking a question in class. On the other hand, those students who choose the front can be allies of the deep Siberians, not of the teacher, serving their more distant peers by asking pointed questions to the teacher which other students are reluctant to pose, to get the teacher to repeat her or his remarks, especially about unclear assignments, complex instructions, excessive homework, and confusing subject matter. Speaking for and identifying with the students instead of with the teacher, front-seaters can make teacher-talk easier to cope with for those behind them at varying depths of Siberia. How the front-row scholasticons handle their position influences the attitude of students and teacher to them.

Some back-row students do see the scholastic stars as stuck-up social climbers, self-impressed class traitors, and ass-kissers hungry for a grade. Not Angela. She was smart and ambitious but no teacher's pet. She bargained for concessions that many students found attractive and kept me dancing to a fast fiddle. As it happened, she sat next to another front-seater who played a good second fiddle—Doug, the tallest student I had ever had, 6'6", strapping, handsome, dark hair and moustache, 25, a bio major/pre-med hopeful from the ethnic neighborhoods of Brooklyn. He was an effective complement to Angela, whom he towered over. Like Angela, Doug said that he took the course because it was a requirement. About changing the College, he wrote (unedited),

"When a proffessor is not doing a good job and all of the evidence points to this, get rid of the teacher!" Concerning New York, he added, "Improve race relations and get rid of all the assholes who think they are doing a good job of running the city (very poor management)." Doug had voted to discuss the Gulf War in class and later wrote a very interesting paper on it, while Angela had voted against a war discussion.

In the negotiation, Angela's special complaint was about attendance. She objected to the part of the contract that limited absences. I had proposed one absence for A level, two for B level, and three for C. This was totally unacceptable to her. Directly, firmly, unapologetically, she proposed having no attendance requirement at all. An attentive silence filled the room as she made her proposal; the deep Siberians were listening. Angela offered an amendment to the contracts: Coming to class should be completely voluntary for all grade levels. Students could miss as many classes as they wanted. In fact, according to her, students could miss ALL classes and still qualify for an A, B, or C. She asserted that students really didn't need to come to this class or any other and they'd still be able to do work that qualified for an A. I looked around and noticed increasing student attention to her.

Her proposal for no required attendance left me uncertain. I intuitively didn't agree, but I had no counterproposal, and all in all, was unsure of how to present my position. After she spoke, the students stared at me, waiting for my reply. I heard the ceiling vents whooshing above my head. This was going to be a tough sell—why students should be required to come to class. I had to sell a curriculum they had hardly seen; they barely knew me as a teacher; they wanted more free time and less class time to take care of their own studies, jobs, and personal lives. Slow to speak, I imagined escaping through the vents. If only the suction were strong enough to lift me up and deposit me outside, so I could enjoy the diesel exhaust from garbage trucks on their way to the dump.

I suppose that the student dislike of classes and attendance can easily be mistaken as mere anti-intellectualism, or as plain resistance to a required course, or as simple laziness. Some of these conditions no doubt exist. But, there is also a power issue here—the control of time, space, and motion in life. Will the teacher control their time in this class or will they control their own time? The stressed-out schedules they follow with jobs, family, commuting, coming to class, and doing homework run many of them off their feet. Angela and Doug both reported working about twenty hours a week at jobs off campus.

Stephen the chef put in twenty-eight hours a week while going to college full-time. Bobby, the deepest Siberian in class, did thirty-two hours in a pizzeria. Eleanor was a receptionist on the job thirty hours. Doris, a young psychology major, had two jobs, as a bartender and as a clerk, for a total of forty hours a week. Overall, with no required attendance, they would have more control over their lives and needs. Angela's bold proposal promised one less class to attend, without punishment.

Further, there is a latent critique of education embedded in their desire to avoid attending class, which Angela made more explicit. She also judged the appeal, relevance, and value of classroom learning to their lives. Before reporting Angela's remarks on this, I want to end this chapter with comments from a very bright graduate student in one of my seminars—Donald, a 30-year-old gay white fellow who grew up poor and worked nights on Wall Street to pay his own way through college. He read about Angela's proposal and wrote to me that "I immediately aligned myself with her and could sense my own resistance to your argument in favor of classroom attendance. The irony is that, although a usually active classroom participant, I by and large hate attending class. And while I have rarely missed classes throughout my college 'career,' I have attended them less and less the further I get into my graduate studies. The classroom's irrelevancy has become increasingly apparent to me . . . as an adult, I should not have to come to class. I would grant the same privilege to my own students: I think I would rather have people who wanted to be in class than people who didn't." Can you see how he seizes the moral high ground in his final comment? His rhetorical feet are firmly planted in the ethical territory I want to occupy—voluntary participation instead of compulsory attendance—but he took over this ground from a position opposite to mine, so where could I stand? He is apparently a working-class winner/ survivor in the academy, the fatherless son of a cleaning woman who pulled himself up by his own bootstraps through graduate school, so this was not sour grapes or the voice of a slacker or an anti-intellectual loser who resented required attendance. Neither was Angela a loser or a slacker—so we teachers must face the unpleasant fact that formal education and everyday conditions in society are such that some of the brightest students do not want to come to class.

Well, the ball was in my court after Angela's intervention. The students on the edge of their seats smelled victory in the death of required attendance. The Siberians were alert, and every teacher knows that when Siberians rise for the hunt, something big is in the offing. I wondered how to deal with the expectations raised by Angela's amendment. Just imagine—they could get A's without having to come to class—this was truly Utopia! Instant Utopia in one classroom! No required attendance was within their reach, like getting paid without having to go to work, promising free time to make life a little more civilized and a little more under their control. Intuition nagged at me and said I couldn't agree to this and still keep a dialogic process. But, how could I deny their delicious Utopian dream, their desire for greater control in education and in life? How could I compel their attendance in a supposedly democratic process? That seemed impossible, and so did agreeing to let the class vanish out the door, perhaps never to return, leaving me alone in airless B-34 to ponder the virtues of critical pedagogy and power-sharing.

APPENDIX

A. "Class Constitution" negotiated in Barbara Brodhagen's 7th-grade class, Georgia O'Keeffe Middle School, Madison, Wisconsin:

1. We appreciate our individual differences. We recognize that each person is unique.
2. All individuals will be treated with respect and dignity. There is no room for put-downs in our room.
3. We will be honest with one another in order to build trust.
4. We will learn to resolve conflicts, which may involve learning to live with nonresolution.
5. Each person will truly listen to every other person.
6. We will cooperate and collaborate with each other.
7. Learning will be meaningful.
8. We recognize that people learn in different ways.
9. Assignments, field trips, hands-on experiences will be varied so that everyone can and will learn. If everyone tries, we ALL will succeed.
10. Having fun will naturally become part of our experiences.
11. All individuals will be organized and on time.
12. We will respect the right to pass (not take a turn).

Brodhagen adds that her school "has a culturally diverse enrollment of about 600 students, many of whom are eligible for free or reduced-price lunches. Classes are heterogeneously grouped, and students labeled as needing special education are integrated into all classes . . . During the two years from which this story is told, as many as 56 heterogeneously grouped students were assigned to two teachers who had responsibility for math/science and language arts/social studies. They were joined by a special education teacher who had been assigned to work with students labeled 'learning disabled.' " Brodhagen reports that "For many years, I worked with children identified as having a learning disability . . . Rarely did I see students in any of those classrooms participate in determining what they were to learn or how they would learn it . . . I began talking to colleagues and friends, trying to create another view of school. We talked of designing school experiences that involve students in all aspects of classroom life, including curriculum planning" (from "The Situation Made Us Special," in *Democratic Schools*, edited by Michael W. Apple and James A. Beane [Alexandria, VA: Association for Supervision and Curriculum Development, 1995], pp. 83–100).

B. "Class Groundrules" written by students at a college in Georgia, reportedly adapted from *Critical Teaching and Everyday Life*, in a "Wymyn and Religion" course, Spring 1994:

1. Everyone must be allowed to finish her thoughts unhampered.

2. Be aware of the time when you're speaking; don't go on and on; think before you speak.

3. Try to evenly distribute the conversation among all of us, so it's not just the teacher and the more assertive talkers who speak.

4. Welcome each other to make mistakes; it is only through making mistakes that we move beyond them.

5. When we disagree with each other, don't attack; don't be predatory (but it's okay to be aggressive on an intellectual level); avoid being negative when expressing an opposing opinion.

6. Don't take or give disagreements personally; don't bring in personal statements as a means of slamming someone's statement; refrain from name-calling and personal attacks.

7. When possible, resolve conflicts before leaving class.

8. Let what's discussed in this class remain in this class.

9. Create a class environment that allows for freedom of expression and freedom of opinion.

10. When giving opinions, back them up; ground all dialogue in constructive efforts and studies.

11. Do away with an "intellectual hierarchy" so that everyone's knowledge base is respected.

12. Ask the teacher to give her personal opinions when you want to hear them.

13. Create an atmosphere where there is no fear of reprisal for not being "politically correct" (whatever that is!).

14. Allow each other to speak without interruption or intimidation.

15. Do not attack another's beliefs—differences can be discussed without purely emotional outbreaks.

16. Respect each other as wymyn and as individuals with personal viewpoints, whatever those views may be.

17. Remember that we have a sense of humor and we don't have to be cruel to get a point across.

18. Whatever is being said does not necessarily have to be accepted, but we need to be open to other's insights.

19. Develop a level of comfort in the class so that we can all express ourselves honestly.

20. Agree to disagree.

21. Open discussion with specific structure, and experiment with different pedagogical methods, such as, fishbowls, 2 index cards for speaking used up before the end of class, rotating moderators, etc.

22. We have the right to talk and not to talk on individual class days, so that an individual is not pressured to respond to every issue.

23. No one person must be allowed to overtake the discussion.

24. Work throughout the semester on developing our listening skills; respect others and listen to what they are saying and then *think* about it *before* responding.

25. Practice patience (or be "patiently impatient"—Paulo Freire).

26. We must work to make the classroom space anti-racist/anti-oppressive.

C. "A Contract Grading Method," by Peter Elbow, University of Massachusetts—Amherst (for a freshman writing course)

About Grading

Imagine that this were not a course in school but just a group of people who freely decided to work with me on writing. We would have a workshop. No official grading, just working and feedback. Notice how different that is from what we have here—where many of you are not here by choice and I have no choice but to give an official grade. Nevertheless I will try to *approximate* those workshop conditions in this course.

That is, I will try to create a *culture of support:* a culture where you and I function as allies rather than adversaries and where you cooperate with classmates rather than compete with them. I find that conventional grading often leads students to think more about grades than about writing; to worry more about pleasing me or psyching me out than about figuring out what you really want to say or how you want to say it; to be reluctant to take risks with your writing; sometimes even to feel you are working *against* me or having to hide part of yourself from me. (I taught for nine years at a college where we gave no grades at all—just written comments. It was a much better system.)

Therefore I will use a kind of "contract" grading system. It might look artificial at first, but there's nothing natural about regular grading. It may sound legalistic as I explain it here, but I want to make sure there are no misunderstandings.

You are guaranteed a B for your final grade:

- if you meet the course requirements on lateness and attendance (read it carefully);
- if you hand in your assignments on time—including "process memo" and all notes and previous drafts stapled or strongly attached (one lateness allowed);
- if your mid-process drafts are really mid-process (with first drafts attached)—not just first drafts;
- if your final versions represent real revising or changing, not just correcting or touching up (they don't need to be *better* but they need to be *different*);
- if your final versions are well copy-edited, i.e., free from almost all the mistakes in spelling and grammar; obviously it's okay to get help on this; please type final drafts;
- if all your assignments show two crucial ingredients—*effort* and *thinking*;
- if you hand in your journal writings on time (one lateness allowed)
- if you show me that you are giving good feedback to others in the class—supportive yet thoughtful too.

Your final grade will fall rapidly below a B if you don't do all these things.

About effort and thinking. When I first tried this system, I didn't specify effort and thinking and I sometimes got writing that was just going through the motions. I'm *not* demanding "excellent" writing for a B because I don't want you to worry about whether your writing conforms to my idea of "excellence"; but I am demanding what is perhaps the most important quality of all in good writing: trying hard and getting some genuine thinking in there.

What do I mean by effort? Well, you don't have to *suffer* for a B; it's okay if you are having fun with your writing, even fooling around sometimes. But you do have to *work*. And what do I mean by *thinking*? Your writing doesn't have to be true or logical; it's okay if your ideas are odd or if I disagree violently with them; you don't even necessarily have to have *fully understood* what you are writing about (that's asking the impossible). But you do have to *make the mental and intellectual gears turn*. You have to get some hard thinking in there—some struggle to figure things out. Thinking, by the way, is the main thing that's needed for "college" or "academic" writing. In one sense, then, I'm not pushing you; but in another sense I clearly am. That is, you don't have to worry about quality in one sense of the word (true excellence—whatever that is), but you do have to worry about "quality" in another sense (substance).

If you want an A/B or an A for the course, you must (in addition to meeting all the conditions for a B) get most of your writing up to what I consider an A/B or A level. I will try to be fair about this: I will count later writing more than early writing—thus give more weight to where you end up than to where you start out. And I will consult with other 112 teachers in determining A/B and A standards. But I should warn you that there are usually few A/Bs or As because the Writing Program has tough standards. Besides, B is an honors grade. Frankly, I hope that you will just meet the contract for a B and take this as a chance to *forget about grades* for the whole semester.

I hope you like this system. It will let you experiment and take chances in your writing and you can't lose (as long as you come through with effort and thinking). I will give you honest feedback and tell you where your writing seems strong or weak or doesn't work for me, but that will be feedback not grading. You can experience me as coach and ally rather than someone to psych out or try to con, because my criticism will not count against you. You can *learn* and *benefit* from any criticism I give you without feeling threatened by it.

But you don't have to like it. Some students don't. You will probably have to work harder for a B here than in certain other courses—where if you are good at the subject you can get an A for just showing up at the exams. But I'm not asking for any more work here than I asked for when I graded in the regular way—and no more work than other ENG 112 teachers ask. We in the Writing Program see no reason why this course should be less demanding than, say, math or physics. After all writing is probably more important in its payoff than math or physics since writing has been demonstrated to be the major ability that correlates with success in college. In other words, even though I'm wanting this to be, in a way, a "nice" system, I'm not pretending to wield less power or authority than if I graded conventionally. The point is that I am trying to *use* that authority and *focus* that power in a more productive way.

Attendance policy. As in all 112 sections, you are allowed one week's worth of class absences during the semester, no questions asked. Each additional absence will pull down your final grade. If you come without your assignment on a day it is due, that's an absence. (Because this is an 8 A.M. class, you'll probably have to work at being on time.) If you miss class, you are still responsible for the material and content of the class. Set up a buddy system today—so you can always find out what you missed.

Final Word. What is driving me in teaching this course? What are my highest priorities, goals, hungers? I care most about two things: (1) that you should all learn to *like* writing and learn to use it as part of your lives—not just for academic duties; (2) that you should use writing to help you with hard think-ing—stretch your minds, wonder and question and try to figure things out.

[NOTE: At the bottom of this hand-out, Elbow writes to readers, "Feel free to copy or adapt. Please give credit if convenient." There is no date on this document.]

F O U R

Power-Sharing
and the Birth of
the "After-Class
Group"

Angela Against Attendance: Negotiating Control
of Time and Bodies

Angela provoked the most Utopian expectations so far by proposing no required attendance. In doing so, she asserted her authority
to question power relations. At the root, she challenged the right of
the teacher to control her time, her attention, and her body (where she
must go).

Angela was bargaining for the minimum contact with authority necessary to get an A grade. In this negotiation, she didn't question the
academic contents of the Utopia course. She took a position against
constraints on her time rather than a critical posture toward the subject
matter. Her proposal was essentially a radical administrative reform
which would put students more in control of their time and motion,
but not in control of such things as the reading list, for example. This
is all the more reason why my routine imposition of the reading list
was a mistake, as I mentioned in the last chapter. Precisely because
control of "content" has such a low profile in student intentions, subject
matter needs to be emphatically negotiated. Angela's desire for no required attendance was thus not a struggle over who owns the subject
matter that helps develop her mind. "Subject matter" apparently began
as a nonissue to her and the others, something they were resigned to,
though that would change when we began studying some of the texts
I had imposed, as I'll report later on.

Knowing Angela and the resilient other students, I would have to say that they began the course feeling in control of their minds and strong enough to resist me and school's contents. This is why I humorously referred to them earlier as "waterproof veterans of schooling," because they have learned how to resist the information torrents of the official syllabus as well as the tides of teacher-talk. It's the control of time that has eluded them and that matters most, not the control of ideas. They simply don't feel intellectually dominated by the status quo, which is an interesting conflict with my point of view, given that I bring to class theories of "hegemony" and the social construction of the self (see Williams 1977). Unlike my perspective on how dominant or hegemonic forces influence individual development, through such mechanisms as schooling and mass media, the students don't see themselves constructed intellectually and emotionally by the "system" and its machinery. It sometimes feels to me like we are living in two different worlds, theirs blithely ignoring hegemony and mine ferociously foregrounding it, theirs a place of autonomous individuality and self-creation while my world is a place of the socially constructed self. They focus on individualism and self-reliance, two hegemonic values deeply embedded in a corporate society, but which they experience contradictorily as values through which to resist "the system." Perhaps everyday life is too complex for critical theory to explain it or for critical pedagogy to transform it. But, it should surprise no one reading this book when I say that I still prefer my way of seeing reality to theirs.

Hegemony usually works best when it hides its own operation, and it does appear that my students generally feel freely in control of their "real selves" while not freely in control of their time, bodies, or money, because of schooling, work, commuting, family, the cost of living, etc. This helps explain why Angela's hard bargaining for some freedom of time struck a responsive chord in the other students. Their notion of "liberation" is more time and disposable income, not an intense critical inquiry into the status quo. I already have more time and income than they do, so given their lesser class position, it makes sense for them to desire the extra hours and extra cash that would open up more options for their "real selves."

In her desire for more control of time, Angela was apparently authorized by the negotiating process to question required attendance, just as earlier the process had authorized Annette to question my assumed authority in grading. The "cultural forum" aspect of negotiation (Bruner 1986) functioned in these instances to produce a constitutional assembly in class, which brought teacher-student conflicts out into the open. First Annette's questions about grading and then Angela's amendment against attendance put power issues on the table and pushed the consequences of negotiation to a higher level. Assertive students like Angela, Annette, and tall Doug, take the lead in showing what can be done with the new authority made available to students by a critical-democratic teacher. A class blessed with a critical mass of leading students can evolve more quickly into a constitutional assembly, which will then function unpredictably (the discomforts of democracy), requiring teacher and students to be flexible, patient, and imaginative.

Not the least difficulty is my teacherly desire for the comforts of control, which compete with my desire to let go and share authority. I simply wasn't prepared for Angela's proposal. Nevertheless, being without ready answers to Angela was healthy for me and the process (if also uneasy for me) because it disrupted my assumed authority and obliged me to meet students on their terms. A process which asks teachers to teach by the seat of their pants transfers some momentum to the students, thus shifting the rhetorical center of gravity and partially leveling the playing field.

With the field of negotiation uncertain beneath my feet, I felt in my heart and head that I couldn't agree to Angela's proposal of no required attendance. It meant giving up more control than I was prepared to risk at that moment, I am sorry to say. I couldn't imagine being a critical teacher without a class, surrendering my small amount of constructive contact with working students, which has been the laboratory where I work as a social-change agent and from which I grow and write as an educator. But, how could I argue this awkward position, that they had to stay in class because I needed them more than they needed me? That I needed them to test my theories of transformational pedagogy, which they had little or no interest in? What right did this give me to require attendance, to compel it in a supposedly democratic process? Why, indeed, should students be required to attend class? Just because I want them there to fulfill my dreams of self and social change? This was an impossible corner I found myself in.

Why should there be a limited number of absences? Some colleges here and in Europe have no required attendance. Why should I insist on it? In the crowded basement classroom, in the middle of contract negotiations, once again I had to examine the ethics of my pedagogy. Was I maintaining them as a captive audience who now saw the chance to break free? How many schooldays in the past had they celebrated the absence of their regular teacher as an instant holiday and a divine break from the dreary routines of mass education? How often had they driven their substitute teachers crazy and nearly run them out of the room on those festive days? Now, Angela was proposing what could become a permanent break in the routine, a potential nonstop holiday from this Utopia class. For me, the allegedly critical and democratic teacher, the ironies were unsettling, especially since I penned in 1980 the humorous metaphor of "the withering away of the teacher," as I mentioned before (see *Critical Teaching and Everyday Life*). Too many chickens were coming home to roost. Utopia threatened to be born in the airless basement if only I would get out of the way and let it happen, let go, and agree to risk dissolving the class. I had apparently become an obstacle to their Utopia whereas I thought of myself as its agent. It all boiled down to the inevitable—if overworked and underpaid students in miserable mass education do not have to attend class, they won't, and I the teacher won't slowly wither but will rapidly dissolve like sugar in a steaming cup of tea.

Tea Time in Utopia: A Permanent Break in the Routine?

How to be democratic and still require attendance? How, indeed. Compulsion masquerading as freedom is the hegemonic status quo I hope to question, not copy. But, how can I practice my vocation as a critical teacher and educational change-agent if the class disappears?

Perhaps my fear that most of my students won't come to class unless required is not a problem at other schools, colleges, universities, or programs where the readers of this book work or study. Perhaps it is easier, more rewarding, or more attractive for students to attend class at other places. Because my working-class students have other things they would rather do or need to do—things more pleasurable, profitable, productive, or pressing—my course is low on their agenda. Also, official control in their lives has been dismal and dispiriting, something to evade, manipulate, sabotage, or put up with. Perhaps the institutional experience at more elite schools and colleges offers immediate rewards and eventual payoffs which make it easier to tolerate authority. Of course, I hoped to be a democratic authority who made the course inspiring, but that was a down-the-road potential. Critical-democratic pedagogy can offer a cultural experience not available elsewhere, but it's hard to make this convincing in the first class or two.

Stuck, then, in what I've called the discomforts of democracy, I wasn't fast enough in the negotiation to come up with an answer to Angela, but at least I knew how to stall for time. So, I posed the issue back to the students: "Does anyone else think that attendance should not be required and that you should be able to get an A, B, or C without coming to class?" Hands shot up all around the room, including some in far Siberia.

Class Dismissed? Stalling for Time

Being in control may help my self-image and my professional image, but the truth is that it guarantees nothing about student learning. In fact, the comforts of teacherly control can work against the intellectual development of students. They need to exercise authority and creativity in taking critical stances in all of the rhetorical settings of their lives. In class, their authority and creativity will involve risks for me and them, if some alternative development is to emerge. Conflicted as I am, a white male product of a gendered and class-divided culture, I have to face my own limits.

At the limits, my immediate need was for a response to Angela's proposal for no attendance. And, I had to respond in a way that rescued the group process, which meant negotiating in good faith, not legislating by command, not simply saying no. I couldn't violate the negotiating relationship by peremptorily outlawing a student proposal, especially a popular one. If I had said flatly to Angela, "That's out of the question," then I would have shut down the negotiation and converted the power-sharing rhetoric to a one-man, one-way discourse. Therefore, I had to present a rationale that respected her position while justifying her stake in required attendance, even before it was clear to these students that this class would be worth attending. I didn't have that rationale worked out, so I stalled by asking for discussion, while worrying that the class would vanish, ending with a migration of students out of the basement, driven by a hunger for free time and the light of day.

On this point, one of the deep Siberians, Dave, put it like this, "The college has strict rules about attendance. I thought that I am supposed to act like an adult, so why do I get treated like a high school student. If I could keep up with the work, why should I have to worry about attendance?" For Dave, being an adult meant making your own schedule, not being supervised. His use of the phrase "keeping up with the work" reiterated a concept often claimed by students over the years as they argue against required attendance. They mean *"keeping up with work set unilaterally by the teacher but done at their own individual time in their own choice of space,"* not in the time slots required by classroom attendance. They take an individualist approach to getting educated, seeing the course as a detached relation between each student and the teacher's assignments. This perspective fits their need to adjust education into their crowded working lives. But, in addition, schooling has provided them with too few inspiring experiences to make class attendance attractive. Thus, as I mentioned before, Angela, Dave, and the others generally don't question the content of assignments so much as they question the time demands of homework and attending class. They express no countervision of an alternative subject matter.

Hoping to rescue the process I had in mind, I turned back to Angela and bought more time by asking her to explain why she thought no attendance should be required and why she thought she'd have no trouble getting an A even if she never came to class. The story she told, which I will detail below, was confirmed by other students and left me awed. Other classes had expressed criticisms of their education in school and college; other classes had produced written and video reinventions of educational life; other classes had resisted this or that project and even my leadership role (one all-male remedial writing group once barricaded the door before I got to class, pushing the chairs up against it, daring me to break through the tangle of aluminum, formica, and fiberglass, which I did with the help of a co-teacher and a running start down the corridor, much to their delight); but, when Angela spoke, she offered a rendition of schooling I had never heard with such clarity in twenty years of teaching at the College. Yet, she merely reported a common experience which I knew from my acquaintance with student life. So, why did this everyday reality have such an impact on me and the process? Perhaps it was because of the context of negotiation in which it had surfaced and in whose midst the story had gained authority to change one corner of reality due to the constitutional process underway there. In the context of power-sharing, Angela's proposal and story became what Foucault called a disruptive "genealogy." Let me explain.

Mass education essentially silences the students' stories about what it means to have schooling done to them (Fine 1987). These unarticulated stories involve the formation of Siberia and manifold other devices of student accommodation and resistance. Angela's story, surfacing from the ordinary experiences of education in an extraordinary negotiation process, appears to me as an *"insurrection of subjugated knowledges,"* which Foucault defined as

> historical contents that have been buried and disguised . . . a whole set
> of knowledges that have been disqualified as inadequate to their task or

insufficiently elaborated: naive knowledges, located low down on the hierarchy, beneath the required level of cognition or scientificity . . . which owes its force only to the harshness with which it is opposed by everything surrounding it. (1980, pp. 81–82)

Foucault theorized that subjugated knowledges take shape not only as popular wisdom voiced by the "disqualified" and the "unqualified" but also as scholarly erudition by dissident researchers who reveal knowledge hidden by official histories and hegemonic canons. According to Foucault, popular and scholarly discourses rebel against the status quo by recovering *"historical knowledge of struggles"* (p. 83). When subjugated knowledges in scholarly or popular form recover hidden histories of struggle, they sometimes become tactically useful in concrete projects against authority. At this point of tactical utility in challenging domination, erudite or popular knowledges (or a union of them) become what Foucault called "genealogies" or reconstructive counterclaims that put the status quo on the defensive. In this scheme, then, Angela's upcoming story is a subjugated popular knowledge which surfaced in a transforming context (power-sharing) to become a "genealogy" tactically useful for putting authority (me) on the defensive and for challenging a mechanism of control—required attendance.

Generating "Genealogy": Angela's Story as "Subjugated Knowledge"

Angela the cultural warrior, objecting to my proposed attendance policy—one absence allowed for an A grade, two for a B, and three for a C—began her story by repeating that she could get an A in any course without attending. How would she do this? My interpolation of her narrative goes like this:

Most courses in the College are traditional ones where the teacher lectures, requires a textbook, gives a midterm, a final, and/or assigns one or two essays or a research paper. Covering the material from week to week in lectures, this kind of teacher allows little or no time for discussion. The teacher is too busy covering the material until the last minute of class to take questions from students or to have discussion, Angela insisted, and this teacher often talks past the end of the hour, making her late for other classes and for work. While most of her classes don't have much, if any, dialogue, her English classes have been exceptions, she said, where teachers often set chairs in circles. For the most part, though, she described classes where the teachers require $60 textbooks and say "read these chapters." Some teachers require expensive texts and then hardly use them, she reported, and other students agreed. Angela and the students were especially bitter about these costly and barely used textbooks. (A young woman student in another class put it like this: "I'm 18 years old and live on my own, so I bust my butt to be able to come here . . . I don't even want to mention the $200 I spent on books because it turns my stomach how college textbook publishers rob college people who, for the most part, aren't naturally wealthy.") I then asked the Utopia class why they thought the teacher required them to buy textbooks they didn't use. They weren't sure. Some thought that the texts were required for those students who didn't get it in the lectures, to give them something to read as a backup. Others thought the texts were there to make the course look good. (Later on, after Angela finished her story, I offered my backloaded thoughts on required textbooks, mentioning that a department may require a text even if the teacher doesn't want to use it, to satisfy accrediting agencies who examine departmental syllabi to see course themes, required texts, etc. Or, the department may require a uniform text to control what teachers do in these classes or to give certain teachers (considered subordinate or less qualified) a ready-made syllabus, as a substitute for staff development, in an age when low-paid part-time instructors are so widely used and exploited.)

Given her experience in the College, Angela concluded that her presence in class was not really necessary. From her point of view, to get an A, all she has to do to is memorize the lectures, read the assigned books or chapters (if any), show up on the days tests are given, and hand in any papers on their due dates. Her physical presence in class is otherwise irrelevant. It's a bureaucratic formality, a ritual of control, not an intellectual necessity—in a word, a nuisance, a waste of time. She's only a pair of ears and a note-taking hand in class. As long as she gets the lecture notes from a friend, she's "been to class," because "class" in this curriculum constitutes the teacher's spoken words. The teacher's lectures and material from the readings will reappear on the midterm or final as questions; and, the teacher's values are important to know for tests and essays. But, does she need to be there physically to get these choice items? No!, she insisted. She doesn't need to attend to get the notes because she has other means. Her story then became a tale of student collaboration to outwit authority:

Imagine three students in a traditional course working together to reduce their need to attend class. On any given day, one of the three will be obliged to come to class to take notes. (I like to think of the single attending student as "the designated listener" for that day.) This attending student is the ears of her or his partners who are absent that day. That student is obliged to be in class, to stay awake, and to take careful notes. Later that night, the two others in this clever student troika will call up the listener to have him or her read the class notes over the phone. Or, the listener could xerox her or his class notes and give them to the other two the next day. If they rotated the listening/attending function, they would greatly reduce the need for any one of them to be there. "And what would they be missing?" Angela asked rhetorically. Her story goes that if they read the required text (if in fact it is actually used), get the lecture notes, show up for tests, and hand in the papers, they have "done" the course. In sum, they really have to attend very little, not exactly never. Angela promised in my Utopia class to do all of the readings and to hand in all of papers when due, which would qualify her for an A because she planned to do that work well. When she finished her story, I noticed her tall neighbor Doug nodding in agreement.

Angela thus had a counterpolicy against the machinery of control, namely, no required attendance, work on your own at your own time in your own place, collaborate with other students to get by. She could better use her attendance and commuting time for other things, like earning money, getting job experience, and doing homework for other courses. Not coming to class would save her needed hours and cash. She'd have lower commuting costs (tolls, gas, repairs, parking tickets) and more time for schoolwork, jobwork, and private life. The opportunity for more free hours, lowered costs of living, and getting an A without coming much to class loomed as a genuine Utopia for her and others. Her proposal, expressed by a front-row scholasticon, not by a deep Siberian, showed how much the working students in that class had in common, whether front-seaters like Doug and Angela or rear-wallers like Dave above.

What could I say in return? I was morally disarmed first by my commitment to negotiate the curriculum, which meant I had to seriously consider student proposals, and second by my sympathy for their experience as working students who pay too much for low-quality education, who work too hard for too small a paycheck on the job, and for whom too few civilized services are provided in this wealthy society, like childcare and reliable mass transit. Still, I couldn't bring myself to risk losing the class to no required attendance. As I stated above, I needed to have them with me in the room to build a "democratic public sphere" (see Giroux 1988) as an alternative to the undemocratic ones we have been inhabiting in school and elsewhere. In this alternative sphere, students and teachers could meet to develop their arts of civic deliberation. But, could such a sphere become democratic if it was required? The contradictions were painful for me. I wasn't willing to let go of my critical intentions and yet I couldn't deny the justice of Angela's anti-authoritarian claims.

Everyone Has Good Intentions: Critical and Democratic Goals Clash

In reply, I began by saying that Angela was right about the education being done to her. Attendance in traditional classes was largely a formality rather than an educational need, a requirement that increased official control. How could coming to class become inspiring and meaningful, I asked, something compelling rather than compelled?

I went on to say that I believed that Angela and others could get A's in some courses with minimal attendance on their part. But, I planned to make this class different, unlike others where attendance seems pointless. I will not push words across the room at them. I will not lecture them into boredom. This will not be another episode of teacher-talk if I can help it. I believe in negotiating the curriculum, so that we build a mutual discussion here. I have a lot to say but only in dialogue, after I hear what they think about any subject. Because discussion would be the heart of our class, I thought attendance mattered here even if it was a formality in many other classes. I said that something is lost when human beings give up the few opportunities they have to meet for deep learning, because most of life is too busy to allow people to study together what's happening to them. Our class would be set aside from the rest of the week as a special time for this. Like them, I don't want to be bored in this room for the next three months. I care about learning and promised to do everything I could to make things different here than in other courses.

End of my speech, a spontaneous utterance provoked by the surprises of power-sharing. Perhaps my remarks convinced some of them to expect a break in the routine in this course. Perhaps my words were just a teacher's imposing announcement of what he wants, which cautions students to get along by going along. Rhetorically, I tried to communicate what I referred to earlier as my *ethos* (a face of moral values) as well as my *pathos* (an emotional core). Ethically and affectively, I did what I could to rescue my chestnuts from the fire. Would they believe my commitment to offer an alternative worth attending? I was unsure as I looked around at student silence and saw stolid faces in the Siberian edges. So, I intuited that I had to take a more dramatic step, to make some major concession other than relinquishing attendance to prove that this class would be a break with the official control of their prior schooling.

Utopian Concession: "Protest Rights"

At that instant, I took an intuitive risk to deal with student skepticism. Impromptu, I announced that in this class students would have "protest rights." Now, at the moment I said those words aloud, "protest rights," I didn't know what I was talking about. I had no idea what I meant by "protest rights" in the context of this curriculum. Having to invent the process *in process* and under pressure, I uttered "protest rights" without knowing what the function or consequences would be. Although I had been inviting students to negotiate and talk up, I had never said those words "protest rights" in any class before. I had been tacitly authorizing their rights to protest the process; now I found myself being explicit.

In the heat of negotiations, from the experiential warehouse of rhetoric, politics, and pedagogy accumulating in my brain, the phrase "protest rights" popped out. I said it and looked out to the baffled students. Not surprisingly, Angela wanted to know what "protest rights" meant, so I was pulled forward to explain these words. With thirty-five students staring at me in expectation, I invented a definition:

"Protest rights," I hypothesized on the spot, "means that each student has the right at any time to protest what we are doing. This means that students should notice how you are feeling in class, especially when you are unhappy or uneasy, bored, angry, confused, or lost in any way, and then *do something about it* instead of only swallowing it in silence or stewing about it in anger or acting it out in a negative manner. You should raise a hand and protest, saying, 'I'm bored,' or 'I'm angry,' or 'I'm confused,' or 'I disagree' or 'I don't like what we're doing.' We can then stop and figure out if we should do things differently. I'll invite the protesting student to explain her or his objection, find out if anyone else feels the same way, and then ask for suggestions and alternatives for us to do our work. We'll debate alternatives and vote on what to do next. With 'protest rights,' " I concluded, "students don't have to sit through a class that drives you nuts or leaves you confused or frustrated or angry or insulted or just plain dulled out."

Such an explanation, flying out of my mouth, amazed me. I wondered what I was doing. Could such a thing possibly work? What if the students took this seriously and protested a lot? How would I live with this? Just imagine, in any class hour, students are authorized to notice their feelings and to stop the process, explaining their bewilderment or boredom or anger, and thinking out loud about their preferred alternatives to what we are doing. I couldn't imagine how this would work day to day. But there it was, out of my mouth and into the basement room, a concession to student authority and skepticism propelled by my queasiness about required attendance. I was searching for a comeback to Angela's story and proposal, and this was apparently the first thing I could think of, an invitation to ongoing and permanent student intervention in the learning process.

I did not have to wait long to see the consequences of my proposal. Clever Angela used her protest rights immediately. She protested the lateness item on the contracts, where I had proposed one lateness allowed for each grade level. She wanted to know what time is "late." I responded that anyone not in class by five minutes after the hour is late. She rejected this as too little and proposed fifteen minutes. I asked her to explain. Angela reported that sometimes it's hard to find parking places, sometimes the bus is late, sometimes traffic is impossible, sometimes they have to run to the cafeteria to get in a rushed lunch between classes, and sometimes other teachers in classes before ours go on talking even though their time is up, making students late for the next hour. I posed the issue to the other students. Did anyone else agree with Angela? Of course they did. So, in a compromise, we agreed to ten minutes after the hour as "late."

But, Angela was not yet satisfied. She then protested the dismissal time for our class. I had not even mentioned dismissal in the contracts but she was thinking ahead, about two steps ahead of me. She asked what time our class would end. I said ten minutes before the hour. She objected to this. I asked why. She claimed legalistically that we had a double class hour, two hours long, so I'm required by College policy to give them a ten-minute break between hours or else I must let class out ten minutes early, at 3:40 instead of 3:50. She explained that each class hour is supposed to offer fifty minutes of instruction, and fifty times two equals 100 minutes for a double-hour class. If I let the class out at ten to the hour, I'd be keeping them 110 minutes, ten longer than I'm allowed. She wanted her ten minutes back. Did others in class agree with her position, I asked? You can guess for yourself their response.

Did I need a lawyer to get through this negotiation?

I was not comfortable with the turn of events, but there I was, knee-deep in their protest rights, which I had authorized. Would the deep Siberians soon move in to feed on my toes?

What some students in class did explain, at least, to soften me up, was that they have jobs, families, and other courses to get to after our class, and the sooner they get out, the better. Yet, the cultural conflict was unmistakable—I wanted to add minutes to the class and they wanted to subtract them. I lamented (to myself), "What about the critical learning process? What about its needed minutes?" I was lamenting the time lost for critical pedagogy while they were celebrating some freedom won from control. I like long classes for the time to question, listen, pose problems, write, meet in peer and project groups, and think out loud. They like to get out early and get to the other things in their busy lives. I saw prized minutes lost for learning. They saw prized minutes gained for living. Would this be what democratic empowerment looks like when students assume authority?

Now, I had lost five minutes at the beginning of class with the new lateness policy and I had lost ten minutes at the end with the new dismissal policy. But, do you see how I write about it? I write that "I" lost those minutes, as if "I" alone own them or "I" alone have a stake in what those minutes can do. Maybe *I* should phrase the pronoun and question differently: Did *we* lose this learning time because the students' working-class lives restrict the money and free hours needed for intellectual study? Did *we* lose those minutes because of the students' uninspiring experiences of underfunded mass education? Did *we* lose those minutes because only a pixilated professor on salary would want to spend extra minutes philosophizing in a steamy basement chamber? I thought of stories told by friends whose kids attended certain elite private schools where the children refused to come out at the end of the day at dismissal time, preferring to stay inside with their teachers, friends, games, books, and projects. The parents had to go in and get them to come home. Those pampered students did not need or want to leave class as soon as possible. Then I recalled the beautiful campus at Ann Arbor when I arrived as a 17-year-old freshman after an all-night train ride from the treeless South Bronx and how in the next four years at Michigan I preferred going to school to "vacation" time back home. I also thought of a humorous poster I saw in a bookstore, which declared that "Poetry Demands Unemployment." Art and intellectual life require a certain amount of free time and amenities which are in short supply for most people, like those enrolled in the basement Utopia of my budget-distressed College.

In the negotiations over lateness and dismissal, the students had gained a little more control at the cost of a little less learning time in class. Did I gain anything? Perhaps I was learning how to negotiate with them and how to tolerate anxiety in sharing power. I had named something called "protest rights," and now had to live with the birth of this democratic reality in the cinderblock chamber. Perhaps I was building a communicating relationship that might support some critical study of Utopia, I comforted myself silently, wondering what would come next.

Well, to grab the bull by the horns, after agreeing to dismissal at 3:40, I asked Angela to serve as time-keeper for the semester. When 3:35 rolled around, I asked her to wave a hand and let me know that we end in five minutes. When 3:40 came, she should announce that class is over (and she did).

But this was still not the end of the crucial "time" issue, which is so centered in control of the body, something physically expressed when students routinely start packing up to leave near the end of class, moving their torsos, arms, and legs to gather books and to put on coats, ready to bolt from their chairs, nonverbally signaling that class is over—an assertive rustling and squirming which I call the sound of students dismissing the teacher. That sound was approaching like an irresistible freight train as the class minutes dwindled down on our contract negotiations. Still without a final decision on required attendance, some students then took a fall-back position by proposing more allowed absences than my contracts specified. They wanted three free absences and one free lateness for all grade levels. They also proposed that any student could erase an absence if he or she did a makeup assignment after the three free ones were used. They then bargained to have one late assignment okayed for A and B levels, not just for the C contract. (See the Appendix to this chapter for a copy of the final version of the contract.)

They were embracing the process with lust. But before I congratulate myself on their democratic enthusiasm, I should repeat that their embrace of negotiation continued to shape the contract to suit their prior alienation from schooling and their everyday needs like getting to jobs on time after class. I, the professor, could feel differently about classtime because I had a privileged position in the process as the salaried teacher who is paid to be there, who makes a career of this, and who is treated better by the institution than they are. Still, I wasn't happy with the students' ongoing drive for less of a course. I felt the need to finish the attendance debate and contract negotiations by inviting students into fuller participation in the learning process, not merely winning more free time away from it. So, I followed another intuition, hoping that it would not only reconcile us after the contentious negotiations over attendance, lateness, and dismissal times, but that it would also encourage students to think about *making* the class, not just *evading* it.

Arts of the *Contract* Zone: Staying After Class Is a Choice, Not a Punishment

After my intuitive announcement of "protest rights," I found myself sensing the need for something more that would seal the negotiations. I had held on to required attendance, for which I was still feeling uncomfortable. I felt the need for a sweetener in the contract that would draw students into the critical process after they had used the democratic forum to reduce the course's demands on their time. My thoughts were drawn to inviting continuous student intervention in the syllabus, so that they and I would not simply slip back into passivity on one side and authority on the other. Thus, on the spot, I intuited and proposed that we form a committee that would be permanently in session over the term, for evaluating the class process and my teaching, to meet immediately after each class ended. I named this committee "the After-Class Group." I had never named or proposed something like this in any class. Once again, under the pressure of negotiation, I said out loud words I had never used before, "the After-Class Group." What did I mean by it? I didn't know. The students were looking at me for an explanation. I was searching my own mind for an explanation.

Speaking off the top of my head yet again, I found myself saying that the "After-Class Group" would be a voluntary committee of students who would stay after class with me to review the session we just had so as to decide what was working, what was not, what to change, and what to do in the upcoming class.

Well, I think that statement landed on its feet, but what was the creature that landed? The students were still staring at me. I wondered to myself, Why would students want to stay *after* class when they had just strenuously negotiated for less time *in* class? What could I possibly have in mind? Was my brain being addled by all of the contradictions? Besides, "staying after class" had always been the legendary punishment of prior schooldays, not a good association at all.

Nevertheless, following an intuition I only partially understood, I pushed ahead, saying that any student who volunteered to meet after each class to evaluate and plan the course could substitute the "ACG" for one of the two projects required in the A and B contracts.

Now, that might create some incentive, I thought—the AC group would be a credited class project to take the place of one other activity students would undertake on improving New York and the College, based on their own initial proposals to change the City and their education.

For a second time, following my impulsive utterance of "protest rights," I did not know what I was getting into. I had never organized an "After-Class Group"; the students had never taken part in such an activity. In all my prior years of teaching, and in the weeks of planning leading up to this class, the idea of an "After-Class Group" was as invisible to me as was the idea of "protest rights." (I remember one dear deceased colleague saying at a department meeting that he spent most of his time planning classes he never actually taught and teaching classes he never actually planned.) And there I was again, offering something I had never planned for, practiced, witnessed, read about, talked over, or imagined. My teacher's radar was pointing me in certain intuitive directions, which I pursued, hoping I made sense to the students.

They listened to my proposal for the AC group and appeared bewildered. I reiterated that we would meet after each class and talk over what went well and what needed fixing. This way, *even though attendance is required*, if any class session is awful or confusing or just plain boring, I and the AC students can face it and fix it right away, by coming up with ideas for changing it before the next class begins. I added, with a note of hopefulness, that if we do our work well in the AC group, we won't have two bad classes in a row. Then, maybe attending class will feel better. You might even look forward to it. In addition, I would also ask regular class members to evaluate the class from time to time and to make suggestions for changing what we do. But the ACG would be permanently in session, a bulldog against boredom, watching out for the quality of this learning experience, determined to prevent two bad classes in a row (which might answer the problem of education being boring but would not really get at the problem of too little time in everyday life for working students to embrace intellectual study).

I was apparently inviting students to join a formal group authorized to monitor the process class by class. Oversight of the class would no longer be solely a teacher's function and no longer merely punitive or administrative; it would be collaborative and corrective. Students were authorized to look at their own learning experience, to evaluate it, and to recreate it. This amounted to more than individual protest rights where students could object spontaneously, one by one, whenever. The AC group was to be a formal structure invested with an ongoing responsibility to review and revise the syllabus and learning process. I posed it as an option that required student volunteers to bring it into existence. No one was required to belong to it, and no one had to decide that day to join, I said. I asked students to make up their minds by next week if any of them wanted to choose the AC group as one of their contractual projects. If so, the volunteers should write their choice of the AC group on their signed contracts.

I waited and waited for students to question me on the proposed ACG, but no one had anything to say, which worried me. I didn't like this silence; it was ominous; perhaps I had been incomprehensible, going too far in pushing experimental pedagogy to this group. With this uncertain situation hanging in the balance, the intense contract negotiations came to an end.

A week later, to my surprise, nine students signed up for the After-Class Group: Stephanie, 20, the sophisticated college-transfer student who wanted a more literary approach to Utopia; Sammy, 19, a no-nonsense business major working twenty-five hours a week in sales, allied with Stephanie in criticizing the civic orientation of the course, even though he had been recommended to the course by a friend and wrote sincerely that New York City must find homes and food for all of the people on the street; Jeremy, also 19, the lone radical student who had also recently transferred to the College and hardly spoke in class but provided well-researched background for our discussions of the budget crisis; Colette, a 19-year-old sociology major working twelve hours a week as a salesperson, who came to the Utopia class because "I heard it was a very interesting course from someone who took the course already"; Maureen, the 20-year-old dietary clerk I mentioned earlier, a fan of "Murphy Brown" on TV, one of only two ACG students to sign up for a B-level contract (all of the others contracted for As), who took the Utopia course to fulfill a requirement and had complained about the overcrowded classes; Lisa, a 19-year-old international studies major also working in sales, who opposed any class time devoted to a discussion of the Gulf War because "I think we are hearing enough about it from the news," yet after the class discussion, chose to write a report on the War as one of her term projects; Jack, 19, a bank teller for eighteen hours a week who later would say that he wanted to become an English major because of the Utopia course and his experience in the ACG; Laurie, a 20-year-old liberal arts major, shy in class but very active in the small-group setting of the ACG, the other one to sign up for a B-level contract like Maureen above, both not high-achieving front-row students, but rather mid-Siberians; and Tommy, 20, a tall, thin, sweet Italian-American guy, an English major who wrote on the sign-in sheet on the first day that "students should have a bigger voice because we often aren't heard." Later on, one of the women paraprofessionals in class, Karen, 26, a deep Siberian who signed up for a B contract, decided to sit in on the ACG for no credit, just to be part of the experience. Of the original nine volunteers, I would say that six took active roles in regular class discussion, which puts their participation ahead of the deep Siberians. Thus, the ACG volunteers were a self-selected group from the more scholastic and younger side of the students in the room, which posed a problem for us—how to involve more people in class. Notice that Angela and her supporter Doug did not volunteer for the After-Class Group, despite their dogged participation in the contract negotiations. Both signed up for A contracts and were too busy after class to stay, which is one limit of the ACG, that it is most accessible to those students with the time to remain when the regular session ends. However, as time went on and the ACG developed into a small legend, Doug came to a few meetings, though he took full advantage of the three permitted absences while Angela missed only one class, even though she had led the charge against attendance.

The appearance of nine volunteers for the ACG overwhelmed me. I had hoped for four or five, not knowing who among the students would find such a project attractive, and also not knowing what an optimum number for such a group would be. (As it turned out, after several subsequent years of experimenting, I found that five to eight students is the best range.)

The ACG became an experience that changed my teaching life, just when I thought that most of my own teacher-development was behind me, after twenty years of learning on the job. And I think this After-Class Group changed the Utopia course and affected most of the AC students who took part in this experiment within an experiment (which I will report in the coming chapters), despite none of us being prepared for it when I uttered the words aloud and they risked joining something untested and unfamiliar. These nine and I crossed a border from the known to the unknown, taking a few more steps into the unpredictable and constantly evolving terrain of critical pedagogy, finding there some promise as well as some discomforts in a fledgling basement democracy.

APPENDIX

The Final Contract in the Utopia Course

Printed below is the final version of the Utopia contract negotiated over several sessions with the students. To summarize the above discussion of the results: The students bargained for more absences and a more lenient lateness policy. They insisted on maintaining the legal minimum of absences specified in College policy, similar to their legalistic demand for ten minutes less class time through dismissal at 3:40 instead of 3:50. I retained the discussion leadership clause for A-level students and the quality provision for written work at each grade level. The students also debated and accepted the use of plus and minus grading (A-, B+, etc., instead of just A or B). The college had implemented plus and minus final grading without consulting students, so I chose to present it to them as an option they could accept or reject. They also bargained for one late assignment without penalty. Here is how the contract shaped up after the negotiations:

Revised Contract—English 359/Utopias

Requirements for an 'A' Grade:
- 3 free absences allowed; grade reduction after 3 absences or do a makeup assignment for each absence after 3.
- 1 free lateness to class (2:10 is late), and after that 2 latenesses count as an absence.
- No leaving class early except for emergency.
- A-quality writing on all written work.
- A-level minimum number of words (1,000) on all written work.
- One late assignment okay without penalty.
- Home assignments can be rewritten for a higher grade if handed in on time and if redone one week after you get them back.
- Lead class discussion, respond to other students, keep the dialogue focused on the issue, participate every class hour.
- Do 2 project groups or 1 project and ACG; write final project reports and evaluation, and make class presentations.
- Write on all 3 assigned books.
- Plus and minus grading will be used on assignments and on final grade.

Requirements for a 'B' Grade:
- 3 free absences; grade reduction after 3 absences or do a makeup assignment for each absence after the 3 free ones.
- 1 free lateness to class (2:10 is late) and after that 2 latenesses count as an absence.

- No leaving class early except for emergency.
- B-quality writing on all written work.
- B-level minimum number of words (750) on all written work.
- Write on all three assigned books.
- 1 assignment can be handed in late.
- Home assignments can be rewritten for a higher grade if handed in on time and if redone one week after you get them back.
- Participate in every class discussion.
- Write 2 project reports (or 1 project and ACG) and make 1 class presentation.
- Plus and minus grading will be used on assignments and final grade.

Requirements for a 'C' Grade:

- 3 free absences.
- More than 3 absences require a makeup for each or a grade reduction will follow.
- 1 free lateness to class (2:10 is late) and after that 2 latenesses count as an absence.
- No leaving class early except for emergency.
- C-quality writing on all written work.
- C-level minimum words (500) on all written work.
- Write on all 3 assigned books.
- 1 assignment can be handed in late.
- Home assignments can be rewritten for a higher grade if handed in on time and redone one week after you get them back.
- Participate sometimes in group discussion.
- Write one project report.

FIVE

The "After-Class Group" Constructs the Unknown

Inventing the Unknown: Surprises in a Negotiated "Utopia"

I was surprised to find myself inviting students to join an unknown entity like the "After-Class Group." I was surprised again when nine of them signed up as ACG members in the second week. Then, some non-ACG students surprised me when they later decided to sit in on this experiment. Finally, I was surprised at how critical this group became of the course *and of me,* which disturbed and exhilarated me at the same time. In an experimental process, I should expect to be surprised and disturbed. "Power-sharing" can be thought of as a synonym for "surprise" because it is an unfamiliar, nonstandardized, counterhegemonic, localized pedagogy co-invented by the teacher and a diverse student group. Democratic culture, according to Mike Rose, "is, by definition, vibrant and dynamic, discomforting and unpredictable. It gives rise to apprehension; freedom is not always calming" (1990, p. 238). If I voluntarily distribute some of my professorial male authority to students who did not ask for it and have no experience using it, I have to expect surprises—some comic, some inspiring, some bewildering, some frustrating.

Cogovernance offers democratic power relations in contrast with the unilateral authority now dominating school and society. Such alternative relations were initiated by me as the teacher but were not legislated unilaterally by my decisions alone. A cogoverning teacher has special responsibilities to launch and maintain the process but not sole authority in it or over it. Some functions of authority are distributed to the group rather than monopolized at the front by the teacher. The AC students in particular watched over and adjusted the process with me, enacting an intense version of the general "protest rights" available to all students in class.

In this experiment, the ACG emerged as a formal structure for student authority without becoming bureaucratic—that is, not routine, rule-bound, or mechanical. Rather, the ACG felt like a homemade, handmade, hands-on invention.

Handmade Power Distributes Some Control: The ACG and Student "Protest Rights"

In the ensuing weeks, as soon as Angela had adjourned class at 3:40 according to our contractual agreement, nine student volunteers stayed for an AC meeting that usually lasted from twenty to forty minutes. The AC sessions had no time limits but rather ended when we felt finished or when people had to leave for jobs, for other classes, for family life, or to do homework. As the non-AC students left the room at dismissal time, nine volunteers drifted into a small circle of chairs, waiting for the postclass critique to begin.

In the first AC circle, I explicitly asked the nine students to be very honest. I advised them to say whatever they wanted about the class, the readings, the writings, and my teaching (of course hoping they would speak mostly praise). This is the only way the ACG could do its job, by facing reality honestly, I said (as if I knew from experience about something I had never experienced). I added that I am not the kind of teacher who gets insulted and holds grudges (at least I can hide it with the best of them). What I needed from the ACG, I explained, was direct feedback about what was working and not working. Their opinions and criticisms would make a difference in the course, I insisted (not knowing what I was getting into with this pledge, because I would have to prove myself by constantly adjusting the pedagogy to their suggestions). Following my remarks to the first ACG, no big bang from the nine students created this postclass universe. Instead, the AC group took in my advice without comment, as is often the case when I make speeches about anything to students at my College, who read a meta-narrative warning in such windy addresses—namely, that this is an area of high teacher investment, so be careful here and give the gorilla what he wants. And they did. For whatever reasons, I did not have to worry that this group would pull its punches. They threw caution to the wind. In the coming months, these students ate my liver twice a week while I lay chained to the rock of experimental democracy. To my amazement, they let me hear more than I was comfortable knowing. Perhaps they felt free to be critical because we had been through intense contract negotiations where we disagreed without me or them becoming insulted or insulting, not retreating into unilateral authority or condescension on my part, and not retreating into Siberian defensiveness on theirs. Perhaps they had been storing up grievances in a system that schooled and ruled them without asking their opinions, in preparation for a long life in a big country with a small democracy.

This remains memorable to me—the AC group became blunt and unintimidated. I had never received such probing and sustained criticism of my teaching as those nine students gave me week after week. After paying a thousand dollars in discomfort for the contract negotiations, I discovered that the deal included a bonus—fourteen more weeks of head-to-head in the ACG. I think of this episode as one example of what Paulo Freire (1970) meant when he urged the reconciliation of teacher and students as the first problem of education. It's fair to say that this reconciliation led the AC students to take *my* education as seriously as I took theirs. They challenged my lesson plans, my classroom management, and my various presentations. I tried to smile through all they said until my cheeks ached and my ears were aflame. Intuition told me that I had no choice but to restrain my defensiveness if I wanted this ACG to reinvent power relations. I had to learn how to sit in close quarters with students who were dissecting a class I just led, but I sensed that questioning authority in-process at the immediate site of power relations (as Foucault urged) is exactly what a critical-democratic process should produce. In the early years, I had moved to Siberia and taught from the rear of the classroom, invading student space and making them uncomfortable; now, they were returning the favor, invading (by invitation) my space of authority.

As I mentioned above, I was obliged not only to listen to their criticisms (which I will detail below) but also to respond thoughtfully and to use their ideas in the regular class. I had to demonstrate that their critical feedback was altering the course, to legitimize power-sharing, protest rights, and the ACG. They had to see from class to class that the syllabus and learning process adjusted to their interventions; if the course's new power relations did not change the curriculum, then the constitutional assembly was a fake, and so was I. This not only pressured me to react to AC criticisms and to enact its consensus, but I had to do this in a short time, with only a few days between classes. My time for adjustment ended with the start of the next class, because without fail the nine would be back again after the next double-hour session, ready to judge what happened. The ACG thus kept me honest as a critical-democratic teacher. I found myself *immediately and continually accountable to students,* which is the practical meaning of teacher-student reconciliation and of democratic authority. Immediately accountable, class after class, I felt pushed to the limits of my teaching skills and my democratic commitments.

But, there is a dialogic rainbow at the end of this democratic downpour: the demands of power-sharing are a *three*-way street. Let me explain what I mean by this. When a power-sharing teacher accepts discipline from the students by being immediately and continually accountable to them, she or he disconfirms the one-way authority students learn to expect in the traditional classroom (which models the undemocratic power relations of all social institutions). By disconfirming unilateral authority, by accepting student discipline, a power-sharing teacher then becomes *democratically* (not *institutionally*) authorized to make higher demands on the students because students have been authorized to make higher demands on the teacher. The discipline becomes reciprocal; the students then become accountable to me not merely because I am the institutional grade-giver, as before, but because I am in a reciprocally accountable relationship with them (as Piaget [1979] advised). With the contracts publicly setting the terms for grading, and with the ACG criticisms affecting my practice, the students had more authority and less reason to sabotage the class and their own intellectual development (see Willis 1981). Such a power-sharing process can take off when a *critical mass* of students (*not* necessarily a *majority*) accepts and uses its new position of reciprocal accountability. A mutual process is then negotiated step-by-step, gradually and partially emerging from the Siberian restraints of the old regime, like the way Michelangelo's half-finished statues struggle to emerge from the marble blocks encasing them. Lastly, if teacher-student discipline becomes reciprocal, then, a *third* potential emerges which can alter *student-to-student* relations, that is, students begin assuming the authority to make higher demands *on each other,* not expecting that only the teacher will evaluate and educate them but that they can do these things for and with their peers (the *three-way street*).

Thus, the more authority exercised by student-constituents in the process, the more legitimate is the teacher-authority in the eyes of many, but not all. The more legitimate the teacher, the more she or he can ask for and comment on, the more promising become the conditions for critical learning. By sharing authority and consulting/ accepting student judgment/discipline, I gained a new legitimacy to evaluate students and to teach to their limits of democratic participation and critical thought. Perhaps this sounds like a battle royal with everyone pushing everyone. I'd have to say that it was very busy, intense, and often difficult as well as conflicted, but it was also, from my view, convivial and enchanting.

Congenial and conflicted, the basement Utopia became a trial by fire for me at a time in my career when I thought the big fires were behind me. In twenty years of classroom research and writing, I had never reflected so hard in-progress on my teaching and had never consulted so intensely with the students during a course. Until the basement class, I had simply not imagined an agency like the ACG to authorize students. Instead, before this course, I had been asking students to negotiate contracts, to vote often during class hours on various options for reading and writing, and to write anonymous evaluations and suggestions in-progress. In my own development as a critical teacher, I crossed a certain threshold of democratic practice with the formulation of the After-Class Group that semester in B-34.

Along with its difficulties, I would have to describe the AC group as a teacher's friend, if I can use that expression. Can I explain the weight lifted from me when nine students accepted some responsibility for continually codeveloping the class? No longer alone in dealing with the Siberian Syndrome, I became part of a constituent structure which oversaw the curriculum, and a deep winter of discontent moved one day closer to spring.

The Changing Climate: How the AC Group Worked

When the AC group convened each time, I would begin by asking the students what worked and what didn't work in the class that just ended, what they liked and didn't like, and why. Each student had a chance to make a statement, and then we had general discussion. I took notes as they spoke, asked questions to draw out their remarks and suggestions, encouraged student-to-student crosstalk, and backloaded my responses. From the notes I took at each session of the ACG, I can report some of the specific interventions which came out of these meetings.

In our first AC, students told me that the Utopian concepts I had introduced on Day One were not well understood by them and others. To deal with this, they advised me to begin the next class by writing on the board fuller definitions of the four ideas I had introduced up to that point—futurism, questioning the status quo, social engineering, and decision making—and then ask the class for questions and follow up with more examples.

I received some other advice at the first AC meeting. The AC students asked me not to repeat what I said in class for latecomers because that bores the students who come on time. They did not want me to accommodate the late people at the expense of those who were in their seats by 2:00 P.M. Now this was a curious item. Here was an unaccommodating attitude toward student lateness expressed by some students themselves, a critical position that did not emerge during the contract negotiations. Perhaps the ACG freed up some students to voice higher expectations from their peers who tend to be late. Perhaps student solidarity restricted this position from being verbalized during the contract session, insofar as those who campaigned for more absences and latenesses appeared so confidently and popularly on the offensive. In any case, this peculiar item demonstrated that students don't always agree with each other. Besides this advice on not repeating material for late people, the AC urged me to raise the profile in class of the student who volunteered to be a rewrite counselor available for revising papers. I was asked to meet with her to make sure that she knew what she was doing. Their attention to such details surprised me for this early moment in the AC process.

Using AC feedback, in the next class I did not repeat material for latecomers (though I should have deliberated on this item with the whole class before implementing AC policies, which I began doing shortly thereafter as my own practice evolved). I also reannounced the availability of the rewrite tutor (Tina, the older woman student who was a paraprofessional in the public schools) and asked her to see me privately to discuss her tutoring work. I then reintroduced the Utopian concepts by writing them on the board with definitions and examples. I contextualized them again in terms of our negotiation process (questioning the status quo of unilateral teacher authority, socially re-engineering the decision-making process in the curriculum, experimenting with shared power to develop a future-oriented alternative education). Lastly, I distributed stories of Utopian communities for students to read so that they could then write a paper at home on which of the concepts were at work in each case, which we discussed in the following week's class.

After that class session, the AC group convened for its regular review. Regarding the reintroduction of the Utopian concepts, my notes show them saying that our discussion on "questioning the status quo" went well but the part on "social engineering" got off the subject. They wanted me to bring it back into focus by making summary remarks on social engineering at the end of the next class. Consider what it means for the AC students to commission and authorize this upcoming classroom lecture by me on "social engineering." They were identifying their learning needs through critical reflection on the previous class and then calling on my academic expertise to serve their self-conscious learning. I would not be routinely lecturing them in a front-loaded, teacher-centered, "banking" manner from my unilateral control of the syllabus. Instead, they were re-engineering my academic role in the process by giving me advice on what needed to be said. I was called into the position of lecturer by students reflecting on their disciplinary needs. This development in the ACG left me a little speechless from their careful attention to their learning process.

In addition to focusing on the need for me to speak more in class about "social engineering," the AC students also made another major proposal. At that second meeting, they suggested that before we write papers on any book we should have a class dialogue on the text. Instead of students bringing in already-drafted papers on the day a book was due in class for discussion, they wanted to have a discussion first as part of a their "prewriting process" (though they didn't use that term from composition studies [see Ede 1995]). A previous Utopia group had made a different suggestion in this regard: They wanted to bring rough drafts of papers to class and go over them in peer-writing groups before handing in the paper and before having whole-class discussion of a book. In this course, the AC group preferred a book discussion before writing their papers on the text. I presented this suggestion to the whole class the next time we met, and the students approved it, which is the writing method we followed.

Regarding the choice of alternative writing processes—talk first and then write a rough draft or write a first draft and then talk it over—my practice had been to ask for a paper or a draft on the same day a book is due for discussion because experience told me that if a writing assignment is due in class, the students will more likely have read the book for that day. But, the AC students had a different perspective. They wanted to use class discussion to help them clarify their ideas for writing on the book. The students in the previous Utopia class saw peer-group discussion as a tool to help them revise drafts of papers they had already written. Which writing process is best? They are both workable. Class discussion, like conversation generally, can be a "heuristic" or "invention strategy" to discover meaning (see Britton et al.

1975; Lauer 1984; Lindeman 1995). What matters is that the AC students were reflecting on the writing process most comfortable to them and taking the initiative to structure the class around their preferences. In this and other instances, the AC students could see that their role was authentic and effective; their proposals influenced how we studied books and wrote about them.

Their further interventions in the writing process evolved as the term went on. For example, when studying the difficult and unpopular text *Walden II*, the ACG and I agreed on an elaborated form of their preferred writing process—talk first/draft paper second—in an effort to cope with their resistance to this book. The elaborated model took a longer route into the text so as to generate interesting ideas from which to write about a novel that interested few of them. The extended process resembled the "component theme method" which I use in other classes and originally wrote about in *Critical Teaching and Everyday Life*. Essentially, this involves dividing texts and topics into component parts for peer-group writing and discussion, with each student group examining and presenting one component. In the Utopia class, the study method for *Walden II* went like this: Break the class into discussion groups, ask for and suggest topics or questions about the book, let each group choose the one it wants to talk about and write on, have each group meet by itself for thirty minutes to discuss its particular theme, then have group reports for thirty to forty-five minutes to the class as a whole, and end with a half-hour of individual writing in class so that students can compose a rough draft of their papers on the book, to be revised at home and handed in a week later.

For the *Walden II* discussion, I listed nine thematic sections of the book and asked students to divide themselves into nine groups of three or four, each of which chose one theme to talk about and report on. I decided spontaneously to add "free writing" (best described in Elbow's *Writing with Power*) to the method by first asking each student to write for ten minutes on the theme chosen by her or his group, then read their writings to each other in the group as a way to kick off their internal discussions. My intuitive addition of free writing here represents the maintenance of some pedagogical autonomy on my part, in the role of a teacher who knows some worthwhile learning methods, especially through written composing. Finally, in this exercise, I reconvened the whole class so that each group could successively lead discussion on its theme. Through this method, I didn't lecture on the book but backloaded my comments into a dialogue based in each group's presentation.

My AC notes following that class on 28 March indicate that students disagreed on the success of that writing/study method. The big issue was that we only made it through two of the nine thematic groups in the study of *Walden II*. The AC students debated whether this was satisfactory progress or was too slow. Their various statements conflicted (as recorded in my notes): " 'we didn't cover all the groups'; 'should we have covered them all?'; 'the flow of class should not be interfered with'; 'covering the book in-depth is more important than covering more material quickly'; 'material is never "covered" or "finished," but rather should "spark our interest" to think about other issues'." In this instance, from their various opinions, no consensus was reached, but they were addressing matters you would expect to find in teachers' journals. Still, I picked up from the group that I should move the class dialogue faster.

As the study of *Walden II* went on, hostility to the book grew, even as students were able to write about it and even as I was able to pick up the pace of class discussion. Students in class and after class protested it as boring, irrelevant, and pedantic. To make matters worse, just then, a heat wave struck New York in April. Our basement chamber became a furnace. My notes on student statements at the 9 April AC meeting read like this: " 'Meet outdoors? Why not?'; 'Too hot to hold class? Yes'; 'Now I understand *Walden II*, by going through the groups'; 'good use of time, wasn't slow or boring'." But, other AC students then said that " 'People hate the book, hard to read, clumsy'; 'says things in too many words, too drawn out, not hard or difficult, mind drifts away'; 'is there an updated version of *Walden II*? Rewrite it for the 1990s?'" They wanted me to "personalize" the narrative to "bring it close to their individuality," as one AC student, Jack the 19-year-old bank teller, put it. They preferred studying an academic text in a way that spoke to their subjective contexts, which the component writing/discussion groups had apparently not yet done for them.

The relation of texts to personal and social contexts is an important issue which Freire has often raised through his idea of "reading the world and reading the word" at the same time (Freire and Macedo 1987). The students still wanted to know how a fifty-year-old book related to their lived experience. Because I am the teacher who chose this book, they happily dumped this problem in my lap, which I had no choice but to accept because I did choose *Walden II*, after all, and I think it is does relate to my life and theirs. Still, their protests forced me to question my choices. My lifelong book learning creates some imposing cultural differences between me and the students. I got to

Walden II through a different social development than they did. As a former "scholarship boy" (Hoggart 1992 [1957]), I saw books as a ladder out of the working class of the South Bronx (a story of climbing up by internalizing elite cultural capital, told by Linda Brodkey, Mike Rose, and Richard Rodriguez, among others). I did well in courses and seminars in college and graduate school, many of them plain dull. I read carefully, even if a text or teacher was uninspiring. In college, I learned how to write 'A' papers on books and topics that were of marginal interest to me. For my students at Staten Island, academic life is not the same kind of promising ladder to upward mobility. Few, if any, will become academics, writers, researchers, or publishing scholars; few will get jobs that dramatically change their incomes or lifestyles, as my job changed mine; few of my students read much outside of school and even fewer read critical material; few read things in school that inspire them, so books often feel like pointless obstacles to their careers rather than as ladders to them. In their first years of college, they would benefit most from an interdisciplinary, field-based curriculum focused on ethnographic reporting and on critical projects about knowledge, society, and experience—which is opposite to the bookish curriculum they now get. So, the stiff erudition in *Walden II* sounded to them like more of the teacher-talk that addresses them in an academic discourse about remote issues.

As they protested boredom with Skinner's book week after week, at least they were not just grousing in deep Siberia or stewing in silence. The negotiation process had brought their experience out in the open where we could face the conflicts instead of denying them. Thanks to persistent student protests over Skinner's book, I began questioning my own professorial position and began to wonder if Skinner's narrative was too boring indeed. Painted into a corner of doubt, I accepted responsibility to connect the text with their personal and social contexts.

Connecting Text and Context: Philosophizing Experience and Experientializing Philosophy, or Extraordinarily Re-experiencing the Ordinary

To accommodate the students' request for relating Skinner's Utopia to their lives, I proposed to the AC group two exercises we could do in class: (1) What is your idea of "the good life"? and (2) What "code of conduct" would you be willing to live with in a Utopian community? Students would write their answers to the two questions and then examine

Walden II to extract its definition of the good life and its code of conduct, to compare with their own. The AC group liked these two plans. But, as it turned out in class, I was able to implement only one of the exercises, "the good life," because of too little class time (from my point of view, an institutional scheduling problem) or because of my failure to move quickly enough through the peer groups (from the point of view of AC students who later criticized me for poor time management).

I began with "the good life" because I intuited it as an attractive theme for writing. First, I frontloaded the students' discourse on this theme by asking each of them to write her or his image of the good life. In addition, to put this theme into a real social context, I brought in a feature article from the *New York Times* reporting the poignant story of a white high-school baseball coach in a largely Hispanic neighborhood of upper Manhattan, whose dreams of the good life changed from selfish glory to community service, which I will describe below.

With their first drafts on the good life written, I asked students to read their texts aloud in unison as a way to exercise again their self-editing skills (the "voicing" technique for literacy development I mentioned before and wrote about in *Critical Teaching and Everyday Life*). After they voiced their texts a little slower and a little louder than in normal conversation (slowing down to give their less-developed reading eyes a chance to compete as a language instrument with their highly developed, automatically corrective voices), I invited them to make any changes, additions, deletions, or corrections they wanted. Then, I asked them to exchange papers with a partner, read each other's texts, and discuss similarities and differences they found in their definitions. After some peer dialogue proceeded on these self-defined texts, I next asked each of them to consult a section of Skinner's novel where the Walden II theory of "the good life" is articulated. After that, I asked them to write a comparison of their individual versions of the good life with that of the Utopian community. Lastly, I asked them to return to their partners and discuss their comparisons, how each of them saw his or her version of the good life in relation to Walden II. When they had completed reading and discussing each other's papers in two's, I then convened a whole-class discussion about this issue. Here are some students' versions of the good life and their comparisons to Walden II.

Carmen

"The good life would be becoming a teacher to help educate others. Having money so I can donate to charities or medical research. I would also like a house in the suburbs and maybe a summer house. My dream car is a green Jaguar. Also, I would hope to have a healthy and happy family. This is most important to me." (NOTE: This young woman student then wrote: "I think my life is selfish compared to Walden Two. I am thinking only of myself and my family." The suburban home, summer house, and *green* Jaguar made an impression on her, vis-à-vis her material desires. She criticized her "selfishness" despite the sentences in her text about helping educate others and about making charitable donations to medical research. Is she too hard on herself? Did the Utopia class encourage or oblige such moral self-reflection on private goals and material desires? She had some *social* goals and images for herself as a teacher and as a supporter of philanthropy. Then, why did she indict herself as selfish? In a consumerist society, teaching and charity as social goals can't compete with the lure of *green* Jaguars, suburban homes, summer houses, and a happy family life. When she surveyed her own discourse, I think she knew which side had the greater subjective pull on her feelings.)

Kathy

"The good life to me would be to complete my education in a decent school and go into a field of work of my preference. To be happy with my friends and family. To not have to experience the stress, tension, and problems I am so often confronted with. To be able to form one happy, loving, long-lasting relationship with a special man, and to one day form a family. To experience peace of mind that our world might someday be a happier, healthier and more secure place to live in." (NOTE: This young woman hopes to finish her degree "in a decent school," so I suppose she is not happy with the quality of our College. Like Carmen above, she also combines private and social dreams in her discourse. She wrote about Skinner's Utopia: "They have time for sports, hobbies, crafts, etc. They have time for relaxation and rest—I don't have time for any of these things . . . I have written down family and relationships where they didn't mention family at all." Again like Carmen, Kathy's discourse is weighted affectively in favor of personal items in private life. Social goals appear in her final sentence and are not accompanied by discussion of how she might act to promote health and security in the world. These social goals are also more abstract than Carmen's previous mention of donations to medical research. In such texts, where private and material desires are vividly foregrounded, the students' social goals often become an imageless, colorless discourse. There is nothing comparable to a green Jaguar in their imagination of civic values. Instead, there is a blind quality and cool register to social goals which is in striking contrast to the vibrant imagery and warm feeling attending consumerism and private hope. Kathy's social/ personal imbalance generates concrete images of private life—go to college, find a good job, marry a "special man," have kids, set up a happy home—but no concrete images in the final socially oriented sentence. Her private dreams may be romantically adolescent, but they fit a society that defines people as consumers first, privileging buying and getting. The contrast between vivid narratives of private hope and meager stories of social concern is common in everyday discourse; to address this imbalance, a critical pedagogy needs to offer some vivid images of transformation, which unfortunately *Walden II* had failed to do up to that point, I have to admit. The next novel, *Ecotopia*, did better in this regard, which I'll describe below. Besides Utopian literature that sometimes offers lively images of alternative societies, media stories of real campaigns underway in society are other resources for elevating the profile of civic change.)

Pauline

"The good life for me would consist of teaching around the corner from where I live. Making a substantial amount of money so I can afford to feed myself, my dog, get a car that works, a house of my own. I would not have to follow a certain standard in teaching in my classroom. I would have six children and one para in my classroom. Classes would start at ten and end by three. Find a cure for my allergies. Living near school (college). Not having to waste time commuting places. Have more free time to work on my art. Have money to keep taking college courses that I find interesting or helpful instead of worrying about a degree." (NOTE: This text on the good life wove personal problems into a social context. It shows some sense of the social construction of the self, I would say. For Pauline, a 25-year-old white psychology major who worked forty hours a week as a paraprofessional in school, her needs are wrapped up in a hectic schedule of living in Brooklyn, teaching in New Jersey, and attending college on Staten Island. Commuting, being "on the road," was not a romantic American experience for her, a working-class woman, not a hippie traveler. Pauline needed relief from the hard time she had getting to class and to work. Walking to work and to college are luxuries available to those students who can afford residential campuses or life in a college town. Her next concrete image of liberation, after walking to work and college, concerned her job as a teacher; she wanted small classes, a paraprofessional to assist her, and no restrictive, required syllabi from outside authorities (freedom from following "a certain standard in my classroom"). This was an interesting conjunction of personal and social goals because she had a critique of unequal funding and top-down authority in mass education from the point of view of a teacher who is controlled in the school system. A class size of only six sounds luxuriously small, quite "Utopian," but one of the students in class, Stephanie, had transferred from an elite private college where professors taught eight students in a course (not thirty-five like in my College). Apparently, this feature of the good life already exists for those few who can afford it. Her dream of the good life ends with her need for money, a tool of freedom. Another female student put it this (unedited) way, "Without money you cannot get the things you want in life." A third began her text like this, "I would want a lot of money," and went on to write that "I would want a castle for a house. A yacht to live on in the summer. I would want a in-ground pool, and hot tub. I would want an expense car, like a Lambergi or Forerri. One red and one black." A young male student from deep Siberia, Bobby, the fellow who worked in a pizzeria thirty-two hours a week, wrote, "The good life for me means having a good job, making good money. I would like to have a comfortable place to live with one garage and two cars." Some don't ask for "tons of money," as Stephen the chef put it, just enough to be secure in comfort. Pauline the paraprofessional represented money as freedom from hunger for her and her dog, and freedom from fear that her car would break down on the road (disabled cars in New York can mean the loss of pay from missing work, the loss of education from missing class, the loss of time to shop, clean, cook, study, and relax, and the loss of peace of mind because breakdowns can be chilling experiences, especially for stranded women). Moreover, money means her own place to live in—a house, freedom from family supervision and from the family noise that makes studying and creating art difficult for working students. Lastly, money to her meant the class privilege enjoyed by wealthy collegians, *studying what you like rather than studying what you think will get you a job;* you might call it freedom from the class structure restricting your choices in the curriculum and the economy. Finally, about the good life in *Walden II,* Pauline picked out the values of "good health, minimum amount of unpleasant labor, a chance to exercise talents and abilities, relaxation and rest, general tolerance and affection, thinking as a whole group, choose work freely, honesty," as the issues in the Utopia which spoke to her immediate needs.)

Tommy (an ACG member)

"For me, the good life means being free to make my own choices. This means working for myself instead of having a boss telling me what to do all the time." (NOTE: This young student expressed a lively social consciousness in his other written work. In his short text here, he focused on freedom in choosing work, similar to Pauline, but he contextualized the issue as freedom from a boss telling him what to do, a common desire of working people. Thinking more generally and socially, Tommy compared his good life to that in Skinner's community in terms of achieving "the greatest good." According to him, what was fortunately absent in the Utopian community and unfortunately present in our society, was the idea of "wealth" as the basis of the good life.)

Tina (the adult woman paraprofessional in the schools and the self-selected "rewrite" tutor in class)

"A society that functions as a whole. Considerate toward others. Cooperating with others, less conflict with others. All individuals doing their share. Leading a comfortable life without always struggling. Helping others, trusting others, honesty. Doing what we enjoy doing. Living in a cleaner and safer environment. Not trying to get ahead at the expense of others. A system based on honesty and not greed. Equality for all individuals. Life without jealousy and resentment for others." (NOTE: Unlike Pauline above, who was also a paraprofessional, Tina is less focused on private needs and more oriented toward social goals, perhaps because she was older than Pauline and more settled into her own family life. This woman wrote with a maturity and sophistication ahead of the other students. In general, at my College, older women students tend to be more focused, academic, socially concerned, collaborative, and open-minded than are younger females or males of any age. Yet, while numerous socially minded older women are now in college, only some assume a critical role in the classroom; many simply stay quiet, out of tiredness from a long day on the job or raising kids or doing housework and homework, or out of a sense of unfamiliarity or inadequacy with public speaking, or out of a fear of sexual vulnerability in drawing public attention to themselves in the presence of strange men, or out of a gendered identity discouraging women from being assertive in public. This low profile is also common to the liberal minority of students who are impatient with, contemptuous of, or overwhelmed by the aggressive conservativism of the majority. Sometimes the liberal minority is quiet simply because it is self-absorbed with getting out of college and into a career with the least trouble. Keeping a low profile in discussion, Tina chose not to read her text during the good life debate in class. She also said very little in that class about other students' ideas. Her text was very different from the self-centered, consumerist stories which predominated the other students' writings, but she chose not to reveal her difference. I read her paper after class and realized what had been lost to the discussion; it was too late to integrate it when it would have created some valuable student-to-student debate. Later on, Tina wrote a fine report on the Gulf War, which I will present in another chapter. But, her critical posture toward the status quo had no impact on the group process because she rarely spoke in class and did not challenge the statements made by more traditional students. For a critical teacher, it's a great asset to have some students take responsibility for questioning the status quo. But Tina did not accept this responsibility even though I directly invited her into the conversation and wrote praise on her papers. In a critical process, the less the students undertake questioning the status quo, the more the task falls to the teacher, who can easily begin talking too much.)

Tina's text on the good life expressed a civic-minded discourse more common in evening classes, where the students are older than those in the day session. More mature, more fully employed in careers (not just part-time jobs), and more likely to be raising families, evening students still seat themselves in the Siberian Syndrome on the first day. But, the night-time Siberian corners contain older students who more easily emerge into the class discussion than do the deep Siberians of the day. For comparison, here are some texts on the good life from an older evening Utopia class.

Janine (in her 40s, a white woman)
"The good life means that everyone would have adequate food, clothing and shelter. All children in the society would have equal access to education. As you had mentioned, every child's education would be equally invested in. A 20 hour work week would definitely be a move toward the good life. Being exposed more to cultural wants could only be an improvement. A clean and safe environment should be provided even if everyone in society has to work to create this. Cities especially need more parks and greenery. Wealth should be distributed equally. Everyone should be able to afford luxuries here and there."

Rose (35, an African-American woman)

"A good life is living in an environment free from pollution. People making their own choices. Nothing like racism should exist. People should live in peace and harmony. Sharing interests best to all. People should be allowed the same opportunities. People free to live anywhere. Equal job opportunity. Wealth should be shared evenly. Wants and needs are satisfied. There should be plenty for all."

Bernard (in his late 30s, a white man)

"A clean, pristine environment. No crowds. Plenty of open space to roam and wander among natural beauty. No competition among people, everyone has their own sense of self-esteem and is content. All of society is taken care, there are no impoverished people. Man has compassion for his fellow man. People put the needs of those less fortunate in front of their own needs. People put the welfare of society in front of their own welfare, there is no personal greed, Everyone has a sense of belonging, the feeling of family permeates all relationships. Less work for all, no need to suffer to try and get ahead."

These older students more frequently expressed civic goals than did the younger ones in the day session. As working adults, they not only valued more free time but also social peace on the job and in public life. However, I received a statement from one evening student, a white man who was about 35 years old, which echoed the material dreams predominant in the younger students in the basement day class: "The Good Life—a wide open road, the wind blowing through my hair, driving 130mph in my yellow porsche Cabriolet with a beautiful girl at my side, a set of golf clubs in the back seat and enough money in my account to choose when I want to work or how long I have to work for! Owning a business or business' that don't require me to be around often. A ski house, a summer house, a penthouse apt. in the city, a very big sail boat, privacy, a very big house with a pool, golf course." The luminous details of his affluent wonderland reminded me of the TV show "Lifestyles of the Rich and Famous." Yet, a decisive number of older students did not reference the good life to consumerism, perhaps because work and family life in a downsizing economy have made them realistic about what the system has to offer them and their children.

Still, to complicate these varieties of consciousness, the day students in the Utopia basement—younger, more volatile, and more materialistic—were more defiant than were the older students at night. More hostile to authority, the younger ones were also more authority-dependent, looking *to be told* what things mean and what to do, as well as looking for ways to manipulate, outwit, or undermine authority. Some of these students negotiated the curriculum more militantly than did the evening students, bargaining hard for more control and less work. Compared with the older students at night, I would say that the younger students questioned my authority more vigorously while also requiring more supervision. Perhaps the defiant assertiveness of some of the younger students had to do with their late adolescence, their need to assert autonomy and their lack of confidence and familiarity in doing so. Perhaps the maturity of the evening class allowed them to more easily understand or trust the conceptual framework of shared authority. Developmental differences such as these make it necessary to deploy a situated pedagogy rather than a standardized syllabus. One size does not fit all.

Sizing Up a Situated Utopia: Walden II versus Mainstream America

The other Utopian novel we studied, Ernest Callenbach's *Ecotopia*, posed strikingly different conduct rules than did B. F. Skinner's community. While Walden II favored modesty and frowned on people standing out from the crowd, Ecotopia encouraged eccentric personalities, allowed wild individuality in dress and speech, promoted nontraditional communal families, and enjoyed open sexuality (in a pre-AIDS age). Students read Walden II's way of life as too strict and unemotional, too many rules and too few family relations. They preferred the more contemporary story in *Ecotopia*, especially its passionate sexuality, strong personal relationships, large family groups, individualism, and environmental cities filled with parks and served by nonpolluting electric mini-trains. When one student called Ecotopian tree worship extreme, another replied, "Do we worship money the way they worship trees?"

Still, despite their preference for Ecotopia, the younger students in the day did find that some of Walden II's goals actually intersected with their own, like short workdays, free time, good health, work you like doing, many social relationships, and material security. They liked Walden II's chances to pursue arts and sports without paying fees. But, they did not accept the absence of nuclear families or the limits on "personal freedom," which means to them doing what you want to do when you want to do it and getting what you want when you want it without feeling responsible to a community or to a group process. Maureen, a member of the AC group, put it like this: "I don't want to have to wish for things; if I want something I want to be able to go out and get it." Most essential, though, to all students, was having their own distinct families. They objected to the communal childrearing of Skinner's Utopia. Not living in a private home with their own parents and siblings would make them feel like orphans, not like communally nurtured offspring. This reminds me of Hoggart's observation that "The more we look at working-class life, the more we try to reach the core of working-class attitudes, the more surely does it appear that the core is a sense of the personal, the concrete, the local. It is embodied in the idea of, first, the family, and second, the neighborhood" (The Uses of Literacy, 1992, p. 32). My students' most intense emotions appear rooted in their current family life, in their home communities, and in their sentimental dreams of future family-building, providing powerful grounds for the conservative appeals of the 1990s to "family values," which Stephanie Coontz (1995) has criticized as ignoring the diverse nature of American family life now and in the past.

Family happiness and neighborhood fit into the students' privatized notions of the good life. The students' distant public lives are largely impersonal and unrewarding, as they go from work to school in a succession of institutional experiences. Family life is emotional and noninstitutional, even if it can be exhausting, restrictive, and even abusive. If not for the emotional anchor of the family and the local identity of the neighborhood, what would be the center of life?, they wonder. Also, family life offers help when you get in trouble and includes recreational consumerism (from Sunday dinners to June weddings to Christmas gifts to outfitting the house for the new baby's arrival). Some emotional fulfillment and sense of control come together in the home, unlike the lack of control and unfulfillment typical of public life at school, at work, on the road, in court, at the doctor's office, etc.

Older students have learned how hard it is to live up to the myth of the happy family and the prosperous household. Their experiences at home and on the job make it easier for them to see that the good life is not merely a private achievement to be won or lost by each family on its own. Family life needs civic supports beyond home and neighborhood to make it work (see Coontz's argument that social programs have always affected the successes and failures of family life in the United States). Yet, despite a more civic notion of the good life, the older group in these conservative times has not been closer than the younger one in taking action to change society. In fact, as the term wore on, the younger students in the windowless basement became more impatient to act. Despite their privatized visions of consumer happiness and sentimental family life, some asked more and more each week, What can we do? How do we act on these ideas? They didn't want simply to know what was wrong; a good number wanted to know what to do about it, at which point it became appropriate for me to raise the profile of social campaigns, citizen activism, etc.

Civic Dreams: Questioning Private Visions of the Good Life

To propose civic values and a sense of the social construction of the self, I then introduced the baseball coach's story referred to earlier (Rimer 1991). The white baseball coach, 37, managing a high-school team of Hispanics in Manhattan, had once been a teenage pitching prospect from Brooklyn. Scouted by the New York Mets, he wrecked his knee at 17 in a schoolyard basketball game and had to give up his great dream of major league stardom. Twenty years after his shattered knee ended pitching his way to fame, he told the *Times:* "Sometimes when I'm coaching third base, I think to myself, 'I can't believe I'm here.' I never thought I could help anybody with anything. I was never the kid who wanted to be a fireman or a doctor. What did I care about anybody else? I was going to be a baseball player and get all the glory. Now, I just want to do the job. Let the kids get the glory" (p. B1). To me, this touching report was a mythic story of *felix culpa*, the "fortunate fall" motif I encountered years ago in the epic paradise poems of John Milton and in a favorite eighteenth-century novel of mine, Oliver Goldsmith's *Vicar of Wakefield*. It took a dramatic reversal of pride and fortune before the coach found his way to civic redemption in the unlikely heaven of a Latino high school in a rundown neighborhood. As a kid, he had a self-centered goal of striking it rich with a golden arm. As a man, he had fallen and risen, and now wanted others to have the glory. Lucky for him that he fell from graceless pride only to discover civic grace in the end. Arrogance deflated, he passed through the eye of the needle and stood on a shabby infield diamond in the shadow of heaven's gate, a happy man.

My high-status literary discourse is occasionally appropriate in a book like this but not in the rhetorical setting of the Utopia basement, where it would risk subordinating and silencing the working-class students with its high-culture allusions. So, I did not deliver a frontloaded belletristic lecture on how I read this baseball story vis-à-vis Milton, Goldsmith, and *felix culpa*. Instead, I asked the students to read the article in class, write their understandings of the coach's experience, and discuss it in groups, especially comparing the coach's teenage hopes of great fame and personal glory with his new purpose of serving the needs of the young Hispanic players. Then, I asked them to compare his changing vision of "the good life" to their own and to that in the community of *Walden II.*

When I asked the students to read aloud their responses to the news story, I heard how the coach's teenage loss affected them, how they empathized with the knee injury ending his brilliant career before it began. They were also moved by the coach's self-amazement at his civic satisfaction from helping others. To draw out the social meanings of his changes, I asked a variety of questions: "Why did civic purpose come late to him? Why did dreams of personal glory and conquest come ahead of civic feelings? Is this only a boy's story or boy's dream of individual success? What do girls dream about in our society? What values do boys and girls grow up with in Walden II?" In discussing these questions, there gradually emerged in a number of students a sober recognition of the competitiveness we absorb and act out in a society like ours. To make the social construction of the self concrete, I asked students to consider how the coach might have grown up if he was born into a cooperative, noncommercial society of minimal consumption like Walden II. Would he have wanted to be a star pitcher at 17? Some students replied that had he grown up in Walden II as a pitching phenom, he would have had civic goals taught and modeled to him as a child, so that by the time he became a teenager he would already be concerned with the community benefitting from his talent, not only as an adult fallen from promise after an unfortunate accident. The discussion then centered on how Walden II was organized to develop the civic interests of children especially. In this way, the largely invisible "system" became a little more visible; the competitive, individualist ethos of society emerged as an influence on a person's thoughts, values, dreams, and actions, especially in comparison with the cooperative ethos in which the youth of Walden II (and Ecotopia) come of age.

Remember that I argued earlier that my students don't see their "real selves" as dominated by the "system," whereas I view the self as socially constructed on unequal terms in a culture dominated by an elite hegemony. The coach's story changed some of the students' denial of the system being implicated in their development. The baseball article connected the text to personal and social contexts; that is, it was a subjective window for them, a relevant way to view their own individualism in light of dominant values in society. For some students in the class, this discussion raised civic questions, making the learning process into what I earlier mentioned as a "zone of proximal development," as Lev Vygotsky (1962) described it, that is, a space where the growth possible from teacher-student interaction is greater than the growth students can enact on their own.

With their own texts on the good life thus compared with the poignant baseball story and with the good life in Skinner's Utopian novel, interest in the book finally began to pick up. In the AC group, I heard at last some praise competing with the protests, as my notes on student remarks from the 16 April meeting report: " 'Good Life exercise interesting'; 'Walden II related well to our lives'; 'everyone got to use their imagination to dream about our good life'." But one student, Jack, still insisted that "Walden II is torturous: Who would publish a book like that? Ecotopia is fantastic next to it. Walden II is too technical." Sammy, the unforgiving, no-nonsense business major, then focused on the class process and reminded me that "we didn't get to the conduct code." Some of them kept my nose to the grindstone with high expectations from my performance as the teacher, which is disturbing but good, because students should expect a lot from their teachers as a sign of their own intellectual seriousness and as a balance to the teacher expecting a lot from them. Once again, Sammy made clear, my "time management" was not working well enough; I fell short of introducing the second exercise on the code. But, that day in the AC group, Jack, the bank teller, said after we discussed our study of Skinner's book, that "I couldn't tell another teacher if I was bored. A lot of teachers don't care if you're bored. They just keep talking anyhow . . . Teachers suck here for most part. They only care about covering the topic, getting in the quota of material to go on to next topic. They only want discussion to see if things they say are understood."

Through negotiation, AC students were assuming some authority and asserting some protest rights, including the right to say "I'm bored" in front of the teacher without fear of reprisal. They expected me to listen to their criticisms and to act on them to make the class better, which I accepted while trying to include them in imagining solutions, not only in announcing problems and not only in pointing out my mistakes. And, while some moved decisively into power-sharing roles, they were emerging only slowly as social analysts and critical thinkers. I wanted the critical learning to catch up to the pace of the democratic process. Could I make that happen after we debated "the good life" in a windowless room hilariously unfit for life and learning?

APPENDIX

"Conduct Codes"

The basement Utopia class never got to the "conduct code exercise." Here is how the older evening class developed a conduct code for a Utopian community: First each student wrote down one or two rules of conduct he or she would be willing to live with and thought important for the community. Then, I collected and collated their individual suggestions, combined repeated ideas, and re-presented a list of their ideas. We discussed their composite agenda and voted on which items to keep. Following that, I asked the students to form small groups to read *Walden II* so as to extract a conduct code from it. Each peer group met, read the text, and came up with a report to the whole class from which we compiled a Skinnerian conduct code to compare with the one devised by the class itself. We now had two texts of conduct codes—the student version and Skinner's version. The two texts, side by side, became the occasion for more class discussion on Utopian thought, and looked like this:

CONDUCT CODES FOR A NEW COMMUNITY

A. FROM THE CLASS:

1. No violence; no sanctions based on force; all arguments will be solved nonviolently and will be mediated by a committee.

2. Equality for all; people share work and wealth equally.

3. Respect for each other; treat others as you want to be treated; no one can gain anything at the expense of anyone else.

4. Money brings no prestige.

5. No products allowed if they cause health problems.

6. Everything should be agreed upon; everyone must agree with the rules of the community.

7. Everyone should be supportive.

8. Put the good of the community above your personal wants and ambitions; social advancement must come before personal advancement.

9. The needs of the least fortunate come first.

10. There should be no superior members.

11. Reading time should be set aside each day so people become aware of what is going on in the world.

B. FROM *Walden II:*

1. Don't talk to outsiders about the affairs of the community. (Planners are exempt.)

2. Explain your work to any member who is interested. (The "Apprenticeship Rule")

3. Don't gossip about the personal relations of members.

4. Don't wait to be introduced before speaking with a stranger.

5. When you are bored, say so out loud.

6. Do not argue about the Code of Conduct or about a work rule with other members. Speak to the Planners and Managers, who have the last say on rules.

7. Dress and act modestly. Do not stand out from other members and draw

attention to yourself. Do not compete with other members for anything. Personal fame and victories are to be avoided.

8. Treat all children as your own. Do not lavish special favors or attention on your own children. Give free affection to all children, and to adults also.

9. Do not say thank you to other members. Avoid personal expressions of gratitude.

10. Don't condemn someone for poor work. He or she will be transferred to another job.

11. You must contribute 1,200 work credits a year.

For *Ecotopia*, the night group began by extracting from this novel a conduct code that it could compare with its own and to the one from Skinner's Utopia. They worked again in peer groups during class to analyze *Ecotopia* for its code and then reported and discussed the items in relation to *Walden II* and to their own self-constructed rules. Here is the code they derived from Callenbach's novel, which I wrote down as notes from their reports and read back to the class for editing and discussion:

ECOTOPIA CONDUCT CODE

1. Don't allow cars.

2. Express feelings openly—positive as well as negative emotions but violence is not acceptable unless authorized (the "War Games").

3. All laws must be obeyed.

4. Recycle used material.

5. Sex is free for all—if it feels good, no one will get hurt, do it.

6. No thoughts of overthrowing government; cannot shake the foundations of Ecotopia.

7. Consume less.

8. Worship the land—don't damage environment—give back what you take.

9. Eat natural food.

10. Do not steal.

11. Free dress code.

12. No harm to others.

13. Referee other people's arguments to prevent violence.

14. Be aware and involved in government functions and in environmental issues.

15. Be physically fit.

16. Do not overwork yourself—twenty hours a week maximum.

17. Enjoy whatever you are doing.

18. Biodegradable materials must be used.

19. No violent sports.

20. Women in high political positions.

21. Respect everyone's ideas—give equal opportunity to women—their ideas are taken seriously.

22. Boys should be taught to treat women equally.

23. Women are as free as men to express their sexuality.

When I next asked them to compare Ecotopian life with the good life as defined in *Walden II*, they came up with the following similarities, despite the great differences in the two imaginary societies:

- good health and easy access to health care
- absolute minimum of unpleasant labor
- freedom to choose the kind of work you do
- a chance to exercise talents and abilities, through sports, arts, crafts
- intimate and satisfying personal contacts
- freedom from attitudes of domination and criticism, and from serious conflict
- relaxation and rest
- having your needs met

Such a critical study of Utopia offers students a chance to conceptualize and judge alternative models of social life. By exploring diverse forms of society, students are encouraged to see the current system as historical and changeable, to imagine options to the status quo (which Brookfield [1987a] identified as essential for critical thinking).

SIX

Power Is Knowledge: "Positive Resistance" and "Ultra-Expectations"

Students Pushing Back: Resistance and Rising Expectations

After an eight-year study of nearly a thousand schools, John Goodlad wrote, "We will only begin to get evidence of the potential power of pedagogy when we dare to risk and support markedly deviant classroom procedures" (1984, p. 249). Agreeing with Goodlad's conclusion, another lion of school reform, Ted Sizer, wrote after touring the nation's high schools that "It is astonishing that so few critics challenge the system . . . The people are better than the structure. Therefore, the structure must be at fault" (1984, p. 209). A power-sharing critical pedagogy is a process for restructuring authority, teaching, and learning. This Utopian adventure produces some creative openings as well as some interesting problems. For example, in the last chapter, I reported how frequently students protested *Walden II*, challenging my choice of this famous book. I was called upon in class and in the AC group to defend and rethink Skinner's tome as part of the syllabus. This is one example of student "protest rights" in action. By protesting in-process, students keep the learning program on the table for scrutiny rather than leaving it routinely unquestioned in the hands of the teacher, who traditionally is not obliged to justify her or his choices to the class.

With knowledge and authority question-able, some students will take the lead in negotiating the agendas of the class and the teacher, whose unilateral power to dominate knowledge-making ends where power-sharing begins. This democratic disturbance of the teacher-centered classroom confirms a primary goal of shared authority: to restructure education into something done *by* and *with* students rather than *by* the teacher *for* and *over* them. For students especially, the experiential quality of this restructuring amounts to *extraordinarily re-experiencing the ordinary*, which I first described in *Critical Teaching and Everyday Life* (1987a). This re-experience of education recovers what Freire called "the attitude of being a curious and critical subject" that is denied "whenever the learner is made the mere passive recipient of the teacher's word" (1981, p. 30).

I also reported in the previous chapter that one student, Jack the bank teller, softened his criticism of *Walden II* by adding that he wouldn't be able to tell his other teachers to their faces that he was bored in class. I enjoyed this ironic compliment. At least he gave me some good news along with the bad, which is certainly better than receiving bad news alone. Jack, a tall, good-looking Italian-American guy with an olive complexion and short black hair that stood up oiled, displayed some of the authority he was gaining through the negotiations, enough to address a teacher directly on his dislikes, which he felt he couldn't do elsewhere. Certain levels of alienation and inequality were declining between me and a number of the Utopia students, so that they could extraordinarily speak their minds, without the ordinary fear of reprisal. The teacher's materials and interpretations were no longer "sacrosanct," to use the word of Sheila O'Brien, who reports negotiating the curriculum in her Idaho college class: "Student involvement begins with the syllabus itself. Before I hand out the syllabus, I emphasize its draft status . . . I ask them to suggest course materials, particularly materials relating to gender, race, and class. Students do make suggestions, I adjust time frames accordingly, and all of us benefit from the rich interdisciplinary and cultural diversity within the class itself" (1992, p. 2). O'Brien also asks students to choose essay topics for their exams, which are negotiated in a whole-class forum that sometimes votes for the teacher's suggested topics and sometimes not.

In experimenting with curricular negotiations, I have found that "conflict" does not disappear in our interactions, but that some "constructive conflict" and "positive resistance" emerge. These two positions differ from the students' residual alienation and defensive withdrawals into the ordinary Siberian Syndrome, where they wait to be told what to do and what things mean, ambivalently desiring and resenting their own authority-dependence. As a qualitative marker of the negotiating process, the degree to which students negotiate the syllabus is the degree of "positive resistance" emerging against the Siberian Syndrome, which I have been defining as a dependent posture of negative resistance, a defensive position of "getting by" in a non-negotiable setting.

When some positive conflict develops, students express what I call "reconstructive intentionality," that is, they begin framing purposes which reshape the process to meet their emerging intellectual interests. This is one way I see them being "released into language," to use Adrienne Rich's (1979) eloquent phrase from her essay on teaching Open Admissions at City College. This new discourse positions them as subjects and constituents of the process rather than as objects, clients, or spectators. A constituent process—synonymous with power-sharing— seeks to overcome the anti-intellectualism ordinarily generated by traditional classrooms, painstakingly recorded by Paul Willis (1981) among alienated working-class British schoolboys and by Herb Kohl (1994) in a wonderful narrative of "creative maladjustment" among some American students. Because students authorized as constituents can push into the process and change it, they have less reason to push away from it and sabotage it. When the numbers of students embracing negotiation form a critical mass, the process takes off.

However, as students push farther into power-sharing, other parallel problems may emerge, one of which can be the lack of a consensus through which to move ahead, requiring the teacher to consult her or his intuition for what to do, to move in several directions at once to satisfy conflicting tendencies, or to alternate directions first one way, then another. In addition, there is a peculiar problem I alluded to earlier—what I judge as student expectations being raised too high, which result in what I call their "ultra-expectations" and their "surplus criticism" of me and the process. From my point of view, not theirs, surplus criticism is an exuberant or militant position emerging from the students' new experience of shared authority. Power-sharing as a pedagogy of constructive conflict can dramatically raise some students' participation and expectations. As I argued in the last chapter, in terms of the metaphor of "the three-way street," the students' repositioning as authorities can encourage them to expect more from themselves, from uninvolved students, from me, the texts, the assignments, and the discussion. The good news is that higher expectations work against the depressant, anti-intellectual effects of the Siberian Syndrome. The bad news is that I, the students, and the process cannot continually deliver on rising expectations, for reasons simple and complex, such as the lack of class time, inadequate student experience in democratic arts, prior habituation to unilateral authority, demands of current jobs and private lives, institutional limits on me, such as required letter grading, my divided attention across three crowded courses each term, etc. Over the years, I have been learning the dangers of promising more than I can deliver. So, the exuberant release of some students' expectations is a problem that can and did trouble the ACG especially. Of course, I ask myself right now if I am merely searching for excuses to explain away my discomfort with not always meeting student expectations. By using the words "exuberant," "militant," and "surplus" I ennoble and ratio- nalize my own position vis-à-vis their alleged naivete in these matters. This won't do; it's too partial a view of the situation, too much like special pleading to justify my role and performance. I admit that my practice falls short in too many instances, like my habitual inability to do effective "time management" in classes that don't get to the end of our agreed-upon agenda for the day (criticized often by the Utopia ACG, as I have mentioned). But, I am willing to describe these failures and am not using the words "ultra-expectations" and "surplus criti- cism" in a merely defensive manner, though I do find the concepts and the conditions perplexing. Perhaps it is fortunate that I can at least limit my own "ultra-expectations" because that releases me into patience and humor, which are essential resources in a problem-posing process that evolves unpredictably.

Still, ultra-expectations in students often bewilder and amaze me. When some of them become passionately involved in power-sharing, they turn the tables, pushing the teacher and the process to change faster. Even as some deep Siberians continue resisting involvement by preferring a teacher-centered class, some transforming students assail me and the course because they want more change than they are get- ting. For example, some AC students criticized me for not producing 100 percent student participation in class discussions. I'm generally sat- isfied with 50 percent at a distressed commuter college like mine, given the prior and current educations of the students, the large classes and bureaucratic processing, and their overcrowded, underfinanced lives. But, some exuberant students wanted everyone involved, urging me to accomplish this, but not yet taking responsibility to make it happen with me, displaying the authority-dependent *residues* of traditional schooling (let the teacher do it, let the authority take charge), residues of authoritarian education which Giroux called "sediments" and Willis called "accretions," where education deposits layers of Siberian habits based on the teacher's unilateral processing of the students. Meanwhile, as one group of students desired complete participation, other nonparticipant males and females clung to Siberia, dragging their feet in the groups researching improvements at the College and in the City. This is a strange dialectic for a teacher, to face resistance for engineering too little and too much change at the same time. However, it's not uncommon in my experiments with critical pedagogy because of the diversity of the students. They are not a self-selected protransformation group with uniform lives or intellects. In democratic discourse, an uneven spectrum of thought and feeling should emerge and contend. Perhaps this also exemplifies the phenomenon of *combined and uneven development* where parts of a complex reality are moving in different directions at different velocities at the same time, with some students moving into participation and ultra-expectations, while some move into gradual engagement, even as others cling to Siberia with negative resistance and hostility to the process. Welcome to Utopia.

Combined and Uneven Development: Power Is a Learning Problem, Learning Is a Power Problem

Uneven student development had another peculiar relation to my teaching experience in the basement Utopia. One AC member, Stephanie, the transfer-student who left an exclusive liberal arts college that her family could no longer afford, came to class with an academic background far ahead of the others. This bright young woman with progressive values and dressed-down bohemian garb, a healthy complexion and good teeth, was apparently passing through my crumbling campus on the way to another life, as she spoke to me of her plans to leave soon for the West Coast. Stephanie seemed to be uncomfortably bouncing down the ladder of class privilege, from a manicured, upper-crust college to the basement chamber at Staten Island with thirty-five people packed into a fluorescent cinderblock room. From the first day, she appeared different to me, not dressed-up or done-up like most of the other women from a mainstream culture that obliges females to look neater and more stylish than the men. (Makeup, jewelry, perfume, and bright fabrics are a lot cheaper than good dental work.) At the elite campus Stephanie had left, the young women were apparently allowed to dress down with the same casual demure as the young men. In addition, she was comfortably academic, similar in this regard only to Jeremy, another transfer student with progressive ideas. She was active in the ACG but rather quiet in class, sitting toward the rear wall on the first days, near deep Siberia, not out of academic inadequacy but rather out of what seemed to me like cultural displacement, perhaps a cultural "discomfort with difference" as Sonia Nieto (1994b) has called it.

Discovering Stephanie's intelligence and progressive views, I hoped she would become an ally to raise critical questions that eluded other students. On Day One, she wrote a *counter-Siberian* statement on her sign-in sheet in regard to improving the College: "Smaller classes, more student interaction and personal attention from teachers. It's difficult to learn when students isolate themselves from the class. In small classes, isolation isn't really an option." It sounded as if she was recalling the small classes of her previous college where the formation of Siberia was unlikely. I know well the elite campus she left, one that oozes power and prestige, bathing its fortunate graduates in a honey of privilege that will sweeten their lives for decades to come. Still wearing that sugary scent in our basement, Stephanie wrote in a global, empowered voice about improving City life: "Better health care. My problems with New York City aren't really specifically with New York but with the way the country is run. We can't be a strong country unless each member of the country is strong. People are dying of AIDS and living on the streets but others don't seem to care." Stephanie had a wonderful civic imagination oriented to change-agency. Still, despite these sentiments, she took part erratically in class dialogue, perhaps because of her gender in a macho campus environment, perhaps because she was soon planning to leave this wretched place for the Coast, perhaps because of her small stature and delicate physique, perhaps because she related to education as an individualist exchange with the teacher where each student promotes her or his own development by a transfer of knowledge from the front of the room.

Quiet but impatient in class, Stephanie was assertive in the small setting of the ACG. For example, she was the chief proponent for a more scholarly and literary class, more reading of books and more analysis of textual meanings, less of a civic-oriented, student-centered discourse. She argued intelligently that students had a lifetime ahead of them for implementation and only a precious short time in class to delve into theory and literature. Stephanie already accepted civic-mindedness (an activist stance she took for granted and felt no apparent need to promote here in others). She was used to the professor having a high academic profile in class from which student high-achievers could absorb knowledge. Seeing her dismay in class, in the ACG, and in our office conversations, I invited her to a do a special study on Utopian literature directly with me, which she declined without explanation. The class, though, remained civic-oriented and student-centered because, unlike Stephanie, most AC students preferred it that way. But, Stephanie remained critical. After our final session on *Walden II* (about which some AC students said, "Really good today; we could all relate to it; brought out emotions, anger/curiosity; judging the quality of education is not that easy; is higher education necessary in society? are electives doing any good for you?"), Stephanie complained that "Sometimes the AC group is a second class; it should focus more on evaluation of the class itself." She felt that AC time was taken up discussing class material instead of evaluating class effectiveness. Her criticism surprised me because I thought the AC group resembled the small seminars she had liked on the elite campus she left.

She was right about the group becoming an informal second class to continue discussing subject matter, but a majority of students in the AC group constructed that function, as part of their own rising expectations I would say. They liked the intensity of small-group learning in the AC group, a luxury rarely available in nonelite education. Still, this didn't satisfy Stephanie and two others, so a conflict emerged in the group between some who only wanted to do course evaluation and a larger number who wanted an informal seminar on the course themes after the regular class was over. Because most AC students preferred maintaining the dual character of the AC, I went along with the "second-class" or "after-class seminar" function of the ACG, which a student majority had constructed with their authority and agency, not mine, but I felt constant pressure from Stephanie to focus on processing the process, not the content.

Communication Is Not Consensus: Other Conflicts in the AC Group

The conflict over making the AC group into a second class is one good example of how differences of opinion took shape there. As I mentioned above, at certain times I couldn't take away a consensus to help me plan the next class. For example, on 21 April, when the regular class was tackling *Walden II* theme by theme, peer group by peer group, one AC student complained that the "groups are taking too much time, limit them to a half hour each," while other students said that the class "went well; talking about new things; able to focus on ideas," and still another complained that "each group should have spoken to its theme for a few minutes more to give more feedback to other groups in class— each group should make a statement on its discussion of the book, then have the group's secretary write it on the board." This last student wanted the whole-class dialogue for that day to begin with a series of statements from each of the eight or so peer groups before we went on to discuss them serially in depth one by one. Still another student that day said "best class we ever had—wish all teachers would talk over the class with us." As I've indicated before, a persistent criticism was that peer discussion groups in class took too long and we were not getting through the groups fast enough and thoroughly enough, a problem that would certainly be solved if we had the elite luxury of eight to twelve students to a class. However, others in the AC group felt that we were going into depth on each topic and the pacing was correct. I could not decide between the two positions and accepted that sometimes we would not agree on what should be done. Faced with contradictory advice, I decided to follow my own intuition. But, I was edgy about this in class, unhappy with this pressure to move faster because it meant listening less to each group report, going less deeply into student perceptions and reflections. This conflicted with my ethnographic interest in student thought and speech and with my role as problem-poser/questioner. Their needs as students were conflicting here with my needs as a teacher-researcher, it seems—but, really, whose process is this anyway? Our interests are simply not identical in this struggle over controlling class time. Perhaps my explanation is once again a rationalization, beautifying my failure to move well through discussion groups by gilding it with the apparent importance of my "research," an academic god-word.

Even if I sometimes conflicted with the ACG or couldn't find consensus from it, I did notice that the students were seriously debating the learning process and coming up with alternatives. Their growing self-regulation of the ACG was an exciting moment (humorously, I have called it "the withering away of the teacher"). My leading/organizing role in the ACG declined as students undertook some self-management. In this situation, I become repositioned in the process as a special participant, not exactly equal to the students and not exactly separate from them either. Affectively, in power-sharing, I experience a changing role which feels like *moving with* instead of pushing, a lightness of *being part of* instead of the weightiness of *being solely in charge of*.

Shared authority is thus a transformative "apparatus of power," as Foucault might have called it, a means to overcome unilateral authority by democratizing power relations and a means to critically study subject matter. I'd like now to go further into reporting the critical study of the subject of "Utopia" itself. On its own, cogovernance challenges the socialization of students into an unequal, undemocratic status quo ("normalization" in Foucault's terminology). Shared authority helps create the conditions for a critical study of knowledge, power, and society. To see how a critical study of the status quo grew out of a power-sharing arrangement, I'll report on the study of the second novel, *Ecotopia*, and then go on to the project groups researching the City and the College.

A Utopia With War Games, But No War

In approaching *Ecotopia* (1974) by Ernest Callenbach, I followed the democratic/dialogic method of frontloading student discourse. I first asked students to write down the themes and questions they wanted to start with in discussing this intriguing fable of a Pacific Northwest secession that led to a new society there in the 1990s. After they wrote for some minutes, the students reported their ideas so I could list them on the board. I then asked them to reflect on the items so as to classify themes, after which five items emerged as their self-perceived categories: urban mass transit, family life, male/female relations, environmentalism, and the "War Games" (an approved ritual where groups of young men dress like savages, fashion crude weapons, and challenge each other to stylized combat, cheered on by female supporters, until a casualty ends the game with an attendant victory celebration, triumphant sexuality, and reconciliation between the warring sides). I then asked students to divide themselves voluntarily into groups, one for each theme. The groups met in class, did free writing for ten minutes on their chosen theme, read their texts, held discussion, and then reported serially to the class, with each group posing a question to begin the larger dialogue.

As groups reported and posed questions, I re-presented their material to the class, took notes, and posed my own backloaded questions and comments. Here are my class notes and reflections on the five group presentations:

Urban Mass Transit. The question this group posed to the class challenged the status quo: "How come our system has regressed instead of progressed when we have the technology to reach a transportation system equivalent to or better than that of Ecotopia?" They began with their impatience vis-à-vis New York's poor mass transit to the outer four boroughs (Manhattan being overserved and overdeveloped). The reporting group said Ecotopia's transit system enabled the development of small cities instead of large ones, helping to "spread out the population with electric trains." Students were impressed with Ecotopia's ban on private cars (which remained only in the autonomous minority area called Soul City) and its construction of inter-urban commuter rail; they attributed this aggressive transit policy to Ecotopia's "environmental concern," which they generally approved. However, some students in class had a different perspective, insisting that Ecotopians were "nature nuts," in their words, who went too far. Others in class said, "We're used to our politics," which means to them that people here are too set in their ways to change, so "it's not possible to achieve Ecotopia here in twenty years" as was done there. "How long will it take to do what they did?" one student asked, liking what he read yet doubtful about reaching it here. The committee's other questions for class discussion were, "Ecotopia includes three West Coast states with a population of fifteen million people—how did they get mass agreement to give up their cars? Were there incentives or punishments?" They also had a technical question which was sensible: "Do electric cars produce acid waste from batteries?" On the whole, the class had trouble believing that people in our society would give up private cars, given their dismal experience of mass transit in New York and the various needs and pleasures which cars represent; they can't imagine doing without cars in remote Staten Island, with no subway and few buses, thus requiring automobiles to make life possible. This was a difficult discussion because the majority feeling was in favor of the mass transit/ anticar policies of Ecotopia but felt powerless to make a difference in our area. When I raised my profile, I backloaded comments on developing earth-friendly mass transit here, which would be safe, clean, convenient, quiet, and on time, like the BART in San Francisco or the Metro in Paris, referring to systems in the here and now which were superior to New York's. I mentioned the powerful highway lobby in the United States which promotes truck and automobile use over mass transit. For example, I said, New York City used to have electric trolleys that were nonpolluting until Mayor LaGuardia in the late 1930s agreed to their replacement by diesel buses made by General Motors. Then, because political groups campaigning for mass transit are invisible to students, I mentioned Ralph Nader's Public Interest Research Group and suggested student government as a place to set up a transit committee to lobby for student needs.

Family Life. This group reported that Ecotopians live in large diverse communal families, with some members blood-related, some work-related, and others being friends. Some families are three-generational, while others have either no kids or no grandparents or have only adults of the same age group. The Ecotopians prefer extended nonbiological families instead of the single-parent households and two-parent nuclear families common in our society. The advantages of the Ecotopian choices, according to the students, were "childcare, split bills, male/female equality in the home, friends gained, love from more people"; the disadvantages, to them, were "lose privacy, real relationships lost, nuclear family lost." According to them, "real relationships" involve a traditional nuclear family, not the communal families of Ecotopia. This group was doubtful about Ecotopian alternatives. It asked for discussion around the questions "Why did these people change from an American life to living in an Ecotopian life? What didn't they like about the family life while living in America compared to living in Ecotopia?" For the students, a warm, traditional family life is something they cherish or crave, so this is a point of contention when it comes to family experiments in Utopia. I think their predominant youth also played a role because many have yet to form their own families and have romantic hopes for that in the near future, unlike older students who have spent ten or more years in married life and know the hard work of maintaining a household. The students did like the reliable childcare Ecotopian families could provide for themselves, the gender equality that raised the status of females in the family, the easier time of making ends meet because of multiple incomes in communal households, and the conviviality of a large household. Still, they clung to traditional family life. My backloaded comments focused on what Ecotopians hope to gain from their communal families, in terms of providing stable family life for adults and children of divorces, for single parents who are abandoned to their own resources in our society, for retired folks who Ecotopians will not dump into old-age homes, and for unmarried, childless adults who share family life without having to bear their own kids. But, my comments stirred little interest, I would say, because of their young age, their romantic family ideas, and their fond dependence on their own nuclear families for help and emotional support in a commercial/competitive society.

Male/Female Relationships. This group reported that in Ecotopia the partners in a romantic relationship were "not so individually oriented"; partners "discuss things together" and are "psychologically open"; they "don't hide feelings"; students thought that these relations were "not much different" from those in our own society, which I had trouble believing. I did wonder if my age was an obstacle here: Was I too far from them in years to know about their dating experiences? But, then, at their age (nineteen to twenty-two mostly), how much experience could they have had with relationships? Probably less than me. They were shy in talking openly about dating, boyfriends/girlfriends, and spouses, which is understandable because of their desire for privacy. None hinted at any interest in homosexual or lesbian partnerships, an extremely risky admission in this locale, and a theme ignored in *Ecotopia*. My hunch is that they were not revealing difficulties in their existing relationships, but this is too private an area for me to question. Rather, I should have used thematic materials from other classes where gender relations were posed as a social problem not as a personal quandary to hide from public view (see *Empowering Education*, especially the Introduction). I could have done this with articles about date rape, or about parental restrictions on the social lives of their daughters in families where the sons get more freedom, or about wife battering, or about homophobia, etc., to raise the profile of sexual violence and gender inequality in society, underreported in the media. Before that Utopia class, I had been accumulating a racial violence/inequality file to use when this theme emerged in class, and then I began to keep a gender inequality/sexual violence file as well, a few years before photos of the painfully battered face of Nicole Brown Simpson appeared on TV. Still, in regard to this theme, other opportunities emerged in the Utopia class. For instance, one member of the reporting student group asked why women in Ecotopia are in sole charge of birth control, "Shouldn't men also have to share the responsibility?" Some students agreed with her point, but there was a shyness again on the part of most of these younger day-session students to talk openly about sexual matters. So, I referred them back to sections of the text itself for answers on the Ecotopian attitude of leaving reproductive decisions solely in the hands of the women. In Ecotopia, childbearing is completely voluntary—women decide when and if to have children, how many, and how to manage the child's early years, with men taking larger roles later on if the couple stays together. Turning to the text helped reduce the personal privacy of this issue, so more discussion could take place. In general, class opinion (in a group about two-thirds female) favored the equality of the sexes in Ecotopia and wanted to declare this equality already operative in our society, which was wishful thinking. To characterize some of the gender inequity remaining in our society, I was able to provide data on salary differences between men and women at similar levels of education.

Environmentalism. This committee was very interested in Ecotopia's biodegradable technology, which avoids metallic building materials because of their environmental costs, preferring natural and biodegradable products such as wood and a special "living plastic" which can be molecularly unlocked for decomposition in contact with soil. To make urban areas into earth-friendly and health-supporting greenbelts, the cities have trees everywhere, greatly reduced pollution thanks to no automobiles, and nontoxic food, land, and water because no pesticides and herbicides are used in gardening or farming. This student committee concluded that the Ecotopians "live a cleaner, healthier life; nature benefits them in the end," which is much different from our society, they pointed out. Then, they asked the class, "How can we get our government to make an environmental policy?" and "Would our society be willing to use woods and living plastic to build our homes instead of the materials we use nowadays?" The first question indicates their interest in taking action, even though ongoing environmental campaigns are largely invisible to them, which requires teacher-provided information in the syllabus about what groups are already active in the field. This is also an appropriate place for what I call a backloaded "dialogic lecture." With the students' question as a springboard, I made some extended comments about environmental initiatives taken in and out of government, including New York City's emerging, embattled, and popular recycling program. My remarks focused on the federal weakening of air-quality standards to accommodate recalcitrant auto makers, the generally weak enforcement of environmental regulations when it came to industrial safety and pollution, and the paltry investment in a recycling industry that, up to now, has not been able to absorb the tons of materials accumulating from recycling programs. Then, a student who opposed such active government supervision of industry, Sammy the 19-year-old business major and ACG member, protested the official Ecotopian "blacklist" of polluting companies and unhealthy products as unfair to business. He wrote that "Producers are blamed for production methods and packaging and nothing is blamed on the consumer who created the demand for the product. How can they get away with advertising that soda producers are responsible for cavities? The consumer is responsible for his own oral hygiene." Now, this was an interesting antiregulation position against my own support for strict government oversight of industry. Sammy was a proponent of laissez-faire economics, a "let-the-buyer-beware" policy. I posed back to the class the problem of consumer demand, asking, "Does industry produce what people want or does industry teach us what to want by advertisements and media images?" A good discussion ensued, during which I referred back to the text, bringing in Ecotopia's policy against using TV as an advertising medium.

The War Games. This ritual intrigued the class, including the deep Siberians, who were drawn in, I believe, because of its closeness to violence and sports, two themes with a high profile in everyday life. The reporting group said that the War Games constitute an "anthropological experiment" in Ecotopia that allowed young men in communal households or in work organizations to form warrior tribes to fight each other with spears after drinking an intoxicating home-brew from a steaming cauldron. In savage dress and makeup, they went off to "war" chanting, accompanied by female supporters. Throughout Ecotopia, some men were killed and wounded each year in this bizarre macho game, which ends only after a casualty is suffered on one side. After a war game, the victors console the losers and make up with them; the losers' female companions lament their casualty in strenuous outcries of public grief while some winners celebrate by having sex with female partisans nearby. The wounded man is carried off as a Christ-figure who made personal sacrifices for the sake of purging male violence in the community. The experiment is meant to create a ritual that Ecotopians hope will limit male aggression while safely and socially satisfying the male need for heroic posturing, bonding, risk-taking, and macho physicality. The game is supposed to be a civic quarantine for male violence, not a brutal, commercial spectator sport like hockey or the infamous Super Bowl. The theory being tested in Ecotopia is that the War Games will release male aggression while protecting society from it. But, the students wondered if this would lessen violence in everyday life. They were intrigued and appalled by this practice and its essentialist theory of violent masculine nature (though they don't use such conceptual language). They acknowledged that Ecotopia had such Games so as "to relieve anxieties, gain less violence, for less crime," yet wondered if it was a "senseless" idea, leading to "more violence and crime" because "violence leads to violence"—"a friend gets hurt, you feel vengeance and start a vendetta," one said, so "killing cannot lead to a better society." They had difficulty seeing beyond the violence in their own communities, where public insults or assaults lead to retaliation, not reconciliation. The grudges played out in their families and neighborhoods make a strong impression of the long-term risks of male-to-male violence (which has different rules than wife-beating or attacking men of a different color). Their imaginations were Utopian in ways different from Ecotopia's War Games, that is, they were proposing a pacifist society without war or violence in any form, not a society with a violence-containing ritual targeted at men specifically. All in all, the War Games provoked a disturbing discussion in which it was hard for male or female students to face male violence in the direct and conceptual way Ecotopians did, to theorize it as a social problem which requires some dramatic intervention via experiments like the War Games. The basement group resisted my suggestion that the amount of rape, battering, gay-bashing, child abuse, gang violence, racial attacks, street harassment, and stalking in our society make the question of male violence urgent. The Ecotopian manner of gendering male violence was either too far ahead of their thinking or too close to their experience for them to face, and I felt frustrated by the wall I ran into here.

Climbing Walls with Global Issues

Ecotopia and *Walden II* offered comprehensive visions of Utopian change detailed at the levels of society, community, family, and everyday life. I also asked students to read *50 Simple Things You Can Do to Save the Earth* (1990), a practical handbook filled with environmental suggestions aimed at consumer purchases and domestic behaviors, like reducing the amount of water with each toilet flush, not shaving or brushing teeth while the faucet is running, using cheap cleaning agents like vinegar to replace toxic cleansers, etc. The students liked most of these suggestions, which related to their everyday lives. In addition to discussing the fifty items in class, I asked students to take an activist posture toward knowledge by testing the book's proposal to "spread the word." Specifically, I asked them to read their favorite proposals from the book with any two people outside of class and hand in written reports on their conversations. Such extramural discussion of class material can offer students experience as informal teachers and low-risk change-agents. They create in their everyday lives critical discussions ordinarily absent, taking the questioning process out into the community.

Some students in class criticized me for spending too much time on *50 Things*. Perhaps they were right. I hung on to the book to hear about their experiences in their outside dialogues and to push analysis of the difference between individual consumer action in private life versus civic action in society against industrial pollution, the biggest environmental threat. The book *50 Things* did not take on the systemic industrial level, so I introduced it, lengthening the time spent on the book and provoking protests from a number of students, which led me to go on to the two Utopian novels, followed by project groups organized from the first-day's writing on what they would change in the College and the City. As I mentioned, a third project group emerged because some students chose to study the Persian Gulf War. When the project groups began their reporting, I asked AC students to become in-class evaluators of the reports.

For College improvement, students formed groups on the registration process, insufficient class offerings, parking, oral tests for teachers (whose English, some students said, is not understandable), the costliness of books, and improving teaching. For the City, the students' topics of choice were homelessness, crime, welfare, drugs, racism, pollution, and improving the schools. I asked students to volunteer for the groups each wanted, keeping in mind the contract we had negotiated, where an 'A' required two project groups, plus written and oral reports; a 'B' two written reports but only one oral report; and a 'C' one written project. Researching, writing about, and reporting on the Gulf War also counted as one project. To accomplish this, each group met once in class and once outside to plan its work. In addition, I reiterated the basic Utopian concepts—futurism, questioning the status quo, social engineering, decision making, and systemic thinking—with the request that students think about these concepts when designing their solutions. Further, I offered a five-part heuristic for organizing and presenting their research:

1. *Description:* What is the problem? What does it look like and feel like? Who is being affected by it and how?

2. *Diagnosis:* How did it get like this? What caused it? What are its roots? Who set it up like this? Who benefits? Who loses?

3. *Solution:* What are some answers? Propose and explain three possible solutions to the problem you are analyzing.

4. *Implementation:* How would you go about implementing each of the three solutions? What do you need to get started?

5. *Evaluation:* How would you evaluate the success or failure of each solution? One year from now, what would you want to see changed? Five years from now?

This five-step heuristic or invention strategy is an extended version of a three-part visual paradigm I first developed in the 1970s and wrote about in *Critical Teaching and Everyday Life.* The earlier method was essentially the first three steps of the above model, which I originally named "the Problem Method" because, in a Deweyan sense, it defined critical thinking as naming, defining, and solving experiential problems. The expanded model above is a more activist research paradigm, what I could call a Freirean extension on a Deweyan base, because it draws specific attention to intervention in society.

As I have used them, three-step or five-step paradigms are not abstract cognitive exercises in thinking *skills*. "Critical thinking" in this pedagogy doesn't mean "micrological analytical skills," as Richard Paul (1993) called philosophy-based thinking methods such as induction, deduction, fallacy detection, etc. In a Deweyan-Freirean model, critical reflection is more social than the "thinking skills" practiced as logical operations. I define critical thinking as a holistic, historically situated, politically aware intervention in society to solve a felt need or problem, to get something done in a context of reflective action (see Dewey's model of thought in *How We Think* and Freire's discussion of dialogic inquiry in *A Pedagogy for Liberation*). Further, as Stephen Brookfield (1987a; 1995) has argued, this form of critical reflection is not an academic exercise dissociated from the many venues of everyday life; rather, it involves questioning the cultural assumptions underlying our thoughts, feelings, and actions in all of the sites of daily living, from home to work to education to politics to media, as well as questioning the values and practices of the institutions and society around us. According to Brookfield, critical thinking means imagining and acting on alternatives to the culture we are part of. This fits Freire's (1970) definition of critical consciousness as subjective intervention into history, as consciousness of, for, and against something, as "intentionality" vis-à-vis social experience, a reaching out to rethink reality and to act purposefully in it.

Rethinking Reality: Sturdy Problems, Shaky Solutions

I also took the initiative in distributing responsibility for evaluation, as I mentioned just above, by asking the ACG to do written assessments of the oral project reports, which I then relayed to the groups. In addition, I gave each group my own written evaluation and a group grade. Each project group member also handed in an individually written report for an individual grade. One AC member, Jack, told me that "student peer evaluation of project groups is harder than they thought." They had to listen carefully to their peers in a structured way, then evaluate them, and finally give a grade. They did not ask for this responsibility. It was unfamiliar and risky (vis-à-vis making other students angry at you for judging them), and the results were uneven. Grading made the student-to-student assessment especially awkward— I will say more on that below.

To see a profile of student thinking in these projects, here are excerpts from the report on "Not Enough Classes" handed in by one of the Hispanic women in the class, Elena, a 19-year-old secondary education major who worked thirty-five hours a week as a cashier. I judged it about average for the students in that class in terms of the writing and thinking:

"The government wastes its spendings when they could be put to better use. For example, government officials hire employees for high salaries when they don't even work all the time. If the government made just a few minor cutbacks in one year's time more courses would be open to students. The money could be used to pay teacher's salaries so the classes can be available. This would also allow for smaller classes because more sections of the classes can be opened.

"We can close or cut back on certain courses that aren't in demand and open more sections in the classes that are in greater demand. Students should have the opportunity to decide which classes can be cut. This will be effective one year from now because there will be more courses open that we need and less electives. If students are given a choice which classes are more necessary, then more money can be invested in those specific subjects. More sections of these mandatory classes can then be available to students. This solution can also help students finish school earlier. If they don't need to take electives this can make more room in their schedules to fit the more mandatory classes. As a result, students can earn their degrees in less time by avoiding the unnecessary courses.

"CSI's new campus will be effective because maintenance will be lower. It will be replacing both the Sunnyside and St. George campuses. With only one campus open there will be no shuttle bus expenses to worry about. This means with all classes given at one campus, students will only have to commute to and from one campus. Since the Willowbrook campus has already been paid for the building of it is not any extra expenses. With one large campus there will be room for many classrooms and maybe fewer students in each class.

"If the government cuts back on spending and if students decide which classes can be cut, the government can use this extra money for much more needed courses. CSI's new campus will also be an effective solution in the continuing problem of not enough classes."

She began with a predictable focus on government waste, a theme much echoed in the media, which do not focus on corporate waste or corruption with the same zeal directed at the public sector (Cohen and Solomon 1995). Money saved by cutting government waste would be one way to solve the educational budget crisis, Elena proposed, and another solution is to expand the number of required course sections by letting students decide which electives to cut, ending the liberal arts distribution requirements which force students to take electives in various disciplines. In effect, she proposed abolishing liberal arts education, favoring instead basic requirements (like Freshman Comp) and career education (those required for a major).

Elena's frustration at having to take "required electives" at a time when fewer and fewer courses were available led to a solution which I often hear voiced by working students who find liberal arts courses to be "talky" obstacles to graduating with a degree and with training that really count for a job. This frequent hostility to the liberal arts is akin to their impatience with teacher-talk and "theory," which Paul Willis saw as derived from "the class function of knowledge" in an unequal society. That is, for working-class students in school or on the job, Willis wrote, there is a

> massive feeling . . . that practice is more important than theory . . . Practical ability always comes first and is a *condition* of other kinds of knowledge. Whereas in middle-class culture knowledge and qualifications are seen as a way of shifting upwards the whole mode of practical alternatives open to an individual, in working class eyes theory is riveted to particular productive practices. If it cannot earn its keep there, it is to be rejected. (1981, p. 56)

Willis's analysis applies to my working-class students' skepticism about the value of liberal arts for their future careers and incomes. To many of those underprivileged in education and the labor market, liberal arts seem like luxuriously abstract indulgences far removed from the real world of finding good jobs and earning a decent living. Liberal arts are genteel theorizing to many working students. To them, if theory does not concretely relate to experience and practice, it is useless. As Willis put it, these working students feel that "theory is only useful insofar as it really does help to do things, to accomplish practical tasks and change nature. Theory is asked to be in a close dialectic with the material world" (p. 57). The premier form of theorizing—academic discourse—is a high-status marker which facilitates upward mobility for some. This high-status idiom—which tends toward *theorizing theory* rather than *theorizing practice*—is cultural capital for those seeking upward mobility via education. Those students with high aspirations, like Stephanie the elite college transfer, are interested in liberal arts theorizing more than in civic practice, while most of the others with lesser economic options see it as delaying their progress toward a degree and employment. In rejecting liberal arts, working-class students are *not* being anti-intellectual or *atheoretical,* but rather are expressing the terms of their lives, which orient them to prefer theorizing about practice rather than theorizing about theory.

Elena's critique of liberal arts was positioned inside of a larger group report, which my class notes recorded as follows:

> *Description:* Classes are too large—13,000 students now on a campus built for 5,000; not enough sections of courses; students from expensive private colleges now "flocking into" CSI because it is cheaper; students are shut out of classes they need—wait till they're offered again—students required to stay extra time and delay graduation; students and teachers feel cheated—quiet people fade into the background; smaller classes would give students more time to get educated; students get lost in large classes—Budget crisis has reduced sections to least ever!
>
> *Diagnosis:* Budget cuts—Gov. Cuomo's cuts—part-time teachers cut to keep ones with tenure—most cuts in adjuncts are in Computer Science, Business, and English, so these lose classes; students from private colleges coming here; 10 to 13 thousand on campus; maintenance costs and shuttle bus lead to extra expenses on two campuses; classes are now larger—even with tuition hike classes will still be overcrowded; budget cuts are the root of the problem.
>
> *Solutions:* (1) Budget cuts—Gov. Cuomo and the State are giving money to other fields but education should be a priority ahead of other fields; (2) Raise taxes on the rich—charge them more to pay for schooling; (3) Stop government waste—White House has 30 staff photographers [NOTE: Just imagine how such an obscure detail like this on White House photographers reached everyday life through the media and lodged itself in the students' worldview.]; (4) There are too many students in classes, so some required classes should not be required any more [NOTE: this is the solution emphasized by Elena in her individual report above.]; (5) We need a strong student government to protect our interests.

While this group's solution to cut required liberal arts electives was popular in the Utopia class, its report did not get to the implementation and evaluation phases, which was a common failure of the student projects. The first three phases of the inquiry appeared to exhaust their capacities. Phases four and five involve an activist imagination where students assume a stance of intervening in society. This activist posture is the weakest link in their thought and feeling, which I expected given my familiarity with the constituency and with the political climate on and off campus. Implementing a project for change is daunting at any time, more so in a conservative age, so I can understand why their reports ended where they did. But, in this instance, student silence does not oblige teacher silence, so I take their end-point as my starting-point to raise questions of social action.

Their proposal for raising taxes on the rich was a novelty, unlike the predictable call for ending government waste. One AC student wrote on her evaluation of this project group, "Tax the rich, great idea." However, this proposal to tax the rich was not indigenous to this group; it was imported, but not from me. The idea came into the group through the lone activist student in class, Jeremy, who did background research on this issue because he was involved in campaigns against budget cuts. Jeremy rarely spoke in class, out of shyness, I think, but he did voluntarily sit in on the "Not Enough Classes" group and made the following research available to it and to the class:

> Presently, New York State is facing a $6 billion budget deficit. The proposed Executive Budget intends to make up most of this deficit by cutting already-existing programs. These cuts will affect a broad range of social programs, which will mostly harm the state's poor . . . Of the $92 million being cut [from the City University], only $40 million will be covered by the tuition hike. The rest of the money will be made up for by a reduction in student aid, faculty, and courses offered . . . Economically, it makes a lot of sense to pay the $1,450 a year required for these students education, rather than, later paying $8,000 a year to put them on welfare, or $40,000 a year to lock them in jail. At this point in history, a requirement for a decently paying job is a college education. When people complain about how bad crime has gotten, or how we need more jails for the criminals the cause is going to be because those "criminals" had no other choice, and resorted to theft in order to support themselves. I'd like to know the percentage of people in jail [who] earned over $50,000 a year . . .

> A proposal regarding how New York State could raise more funds was made by State Senator Franz S. Leichter. This proposal stated that, if New York State were to impose a 3 percent income surcharge upon people making more than $200,000 a year, we will earn over $1 billion a year in revenue. This tax surcharge would only affect 2 percent of the state's tax payers. A billion dollars would cover the amount being cut from the CUNY budget by more than 10 times; and it wo[u]ld almost

cover the entire CUNY budget (which is $1.1 billion). According to a news release from Leichter's office of Nov. 28, 1990: "Leichter said that during New York's economic boom of the 1980s, the personal income tax rate paid by the wealthiest New Yorkers was cut nearly in half, from 13.5 percent in 1986 to 7.875 percent currently. At the same time, many low and moderate income New Yorkers saw their tax rate double from 2 percent to 4 percent . . . Unfortunately, it is extremely doubtful that legislators would even consider imposing a tax on the rich, since they are rich, and it will affect them and their friends . . .

Besides targeting the wealth of the super-rich to solve the apparent budget crisis, the remainder of Jeremy's paper proposed that the end of the Cold War meant there should be a peace dividend (which never materialized), with funds being transferred from the military into education, housing, health care, etc., "which will improve the quality of living." His political positions actually appealed to many students, who agreed that taxing the rich was a good idea, so there appears to be support among working students for class-conscious politics.

Next, the largest project group to report investigated registration at the College. Here are my notes taken in class during its presentation:

Description: too many signatures required; after getting a course schedule worked out, students find that the classes they want are closed; advisors aren't any help; too many people on too many long lines; old ladies in registrar don't care about you; counselors take more time; classes are still closing as you do it.

Diagnosis: the administration is all over the school and on two different campuses; advisors not in one place; process not consolidated; people who work here don't like their jobs; students need better help in advisement, especially freshmen; the school is too big, needs to be broken down into 1000 or 2000 students, into specialized schools like science or nursing, break up the big college; New York City is too big, population is too large, resources too taxed.

Solutions: divide school into smaller colleges, which would be easier to get to, each campus would have its own requirements, too many students are registering at one location and students become just numbers, students and teacher need to get to know each other better; the current distribution requirements are too rigid, students should be free to choose their own courses, take as many in science or other departments as they want, no distribution requirements; freshmen and sophomores should take only required courses, juniors and seniors should get first choice on courses and should be allowed to make up their own schedule, with both groups doing mail-in registration with an on-campus day set aside later on for students to make adjustments if courses are closed; there should be a special "help area" during registration to solve problems; seniors should help and advise other students and these peer advisers should get academic credit; staff should be trained in a "customer service program" because some people are nasty to students (One student said, "What we do not need is people who do not care, and have nasty attitudes. I think this is where the problem starts."); don't keep changing the college catalogue and its announcement of requirements; set up a computer data bank available to each advisor and to students at registration to find out what's still open.

This was an ambitious and interesting report, though I was offended by the "old ladies" reference in the "Description" concerning the women who work in the Registrar's Office. I wondered how to comment on it without sermonizing against sexism and ageism. I knew there were hostile relations between the clerical/janitorial working people at the College and the working students enrolled here. The institution put them into conflicted relationships, with both feeling harassed by the problems of the other in a distressed college. While some students use terms like "old ladies," some secretaries have unflattering ways of referring to students. Too many students needed too much help from too few secretaries; too many students were packed into a facility whose budget allowed for too few groundskeepers to clean the rooms; and too many students were competing with each other for too few courses. This situation reminded me of the robber baron Jay Gould, who boasted in the nineteenth century that he could hire one half of the working class to kill the other half.

Like the other project group, the "Registration" committee favored cutting required electives and letting the students choose which courses to take. Also like the other group, this one did not do steps 4 and 5, implementation and evaluation, once again the missing area of civic imagination. It ignored student government as a potential advocate in changing the registration process. Evaluating this group, one AC student gave a grade of B+ and wrote: "I like the idea of smaller campuses, but it is an unrealistic goal. The ideas on what classes should be required due to student interests are great ones. I also feel that they are achievable." About a student's remark on the nastiness of college staff, he added: "I don't think she understands the CSI employees. Registrar is not at fault for school rules & shortcomings. When students get turned away for these reasons & rightfully get angry, then these people also get upset. We must first look at the system we're working with, & then the people." He thought that there was actually "too much conversation" following this group report because it was "something that everyone can relate to . . . it hit home."

Following this report, the next one on "Improve Teaching" was made by an interesting triad of Stephanie, the transfer student and ACG member most critical of me; Pauline, the paraprofessional commuting from Brooklyn to New Jersey to Staten Island, the one most critical of the school system, who wanted smaller classes and more freedom in class, and whose paper on "the good life" I presented in the last chapter; and Karen, the 26-year-old paraprofessional working twenty-seven hours a week in the schools, who sat in unofficially in the ACG. With some inside knowledge of schooling, they produced a well-developed report. First, they criticized a lack of dedication in many teachers at the College, an attitude due, in their opinion, to overcrowded classes, low pay, the low status of the institution, and administrative overregulation, as well as from what they judged was an unhealthy mix of two-year degree students in the same classrooms as four-year baccalaureate majors. This group said that teachers can't work individually with students when classes are crowded, so they develop low expectations for the students, rather than challenging them. They also criticized students for their lack of interest in studying, blaming it on the low input students are allowed into the syllabus, on the difficulty of registering for classes they need, and on their feeling that teachers talk down to them. Many students don't value education in its own right, this group claimed, but think of the money they can earn afterwards from it (an interesting counterstatement in support of liberal arts education, not surprisingly from a group led by Stephanie). Overall, they judged that students were bored in their classes, not excited. They diagnosed the causes as inadequate public school preparation and funding and a lack of national standards for high school graduation, which lead to undereducated students becoming college students and future teachers ("Our English teachers make grammatical errors," they said in dismay.). This group asserted that government doesn't fund education adequately at any level, thus leaving college labs underequipped and campus activities impoverished.

From a global point of view, to solve the budget crisis, they wanted military spending cut, foreign trade tariffs raised, and extra taxes put on the rich to support education (echoing the class-conscious politics announced by the "Not Enough Classes" group). Higher teacher pay, more student evaluations of teachers, stricter and higher requirements for those entering the field of teaching were also parts of their agenda. Some of Stephanie's leading progressive values were apparent in their report, but it also included an elitist appraisal of the nonbaccalaureate students, who were characterized as remedial nonachievers degrading the performance of the serious BA/BS group, a portrait which led to some hot debate because they were denouncing some of the very students sitting in the Utopia class. Here was a student/student conflict. I backloaded my comments into their discussion, mentioning how two-year students admitted to four-year colleges tend to blend into the general student population, doing about as well as the allegedly superior baccalaureate group (see Karabel and Brint 1989; Dougherty 1991 and 1994). Demonizing and segmenting parts of a constituency into a category like "two-year students" has a divisive effect useful for bureaucratic control but not useful to student solidarity, which suffers when students are socially constructed into rival castes ignoring their common interests.

(Do) I Love NY?: Racism and Improving City Life

The last project I will report on is from the City group on "Racism." Just below is a brief text by one student from this group, which led to intense class discussion. It was written and read to the class by an Italian-American female in that group, Nikki, a 20-year-old psychology major who had criticized racism on her first-day sign-in sheet and whose all-woman group included two other Italian-Americans and one Hispanic:

> New York City Project—Racism
>
> One of the largest problems in New York City is Racism. Large media coverage of events such as the Howard Beach attack has brought cause for much alarm and hatred. I feel that alot of this coverage brought about racism that wasn't existing before. In order to attempt to solve the problem we must first understand why we have it.
>
> School Situation—In Boston, a study called "Locked In, Locked Out," came up with the findings that Blacks receive a "significantly different" education from that of their peers. Teachers seemed to have lowered expectations of them. This reduced their chances for academic success.
>
> Statistics show that 17 percent of Blacks aged 17–21 years old were dropouts in 1985. That number was down from 27 percent in 1975. Their graduation rate has increased to 71 percent from 61 percent.

The unemployment rate now is 12.2 percent for blacks, as compared with 4.6 percent for whites.

In the study, the major causes of dropouts were listed as low achievement, alienation, economic reasons, peer pressure, pregnancy and drug and alcohol abuse.

Racism in schools has risen by 50 percent. School related racial incidents have also increased. One reason for this seems to be related to the tougher competition these days for a job.

Groups like the Skin Heads and the Ku Klux Klan have both been targeting the young for recruitment. These groups have a strong desire to keep their "race pure." This is a clear example of dysfunctional ethnocentrism, which is another name for racism.

I feel that these youths are being targeted because teenagers tend to act aggressively. Therefore, teenage forces combined with racism can be deadly.

Students at the University of Florida have formed the "Coalition Against Bigotry." This seems to have helped student tensions at that school.

My solutions for this explosive problem all deal with education. We can educate people about racism.

(1) People must be shown the dangers of racism. Tell about the Civil Rights movement in the 1960's.

(2) Educate minorities—this will help them get jobs.

(3) Create clubs at school for the integration of races. The more races interact with each other, the more comfortable they will be.

(4) Reeducate parents—this is where children first learn to be prejudice.

In her statement, Nikki praised University of Florida students who formed a "Coalition Against Bigotry" and recommended such a project for our own campus, a proposal that I reiterated in my remarks as an invitation to student action. In her agenda of solutions, she also emphasized a familiar remedy, more education against racist attitudes. It is a good idea, I think, to include the Civil Rights Movement of the 1960s in school curricula, as she suggested, but this can easily quarantine such an event in a distant past rather than posing civil rights as an ongoing battle for "social justice," a theme which Sonia Nieto (1994b) focused on as most appropriate for multicultural education. Nikki's report also included a call to "educate minorities—this will help them get jobs," suggesting that their lack of education is responsible for their condition, which comes close to a "blaming the victim" attitude, because minorities have been denied equal access to education and to jobs even when they had sufficient credentials. Minorities with similar educational achievements as white employees are paid less as a group (Hacker 1992; Pincus 1995). Regarding this solution to racism, I wrote a note on her paper asking, "Are there enough good jobs for all who want them? Are minorities uneducated? Is that why they lack jobs?"

Further, I often hear whites at my college say that media coverage of racist incidents "brought about racism that wasn't existing before," in Nikki's own words. She asserted this even though her second paragraph cites a report documenting long-term racist conditions in a big-city school system like Boston's. She turns to statistics, history, and critiques of skinheads and the Ku Klux Klan, yet falls back on blaming the media and aggressive teenagers for the problems of racist violence in New York. She is apparently not yet integrating the knowledge she already possesses, which I addressed in my backloaded comments.

We came to the issue of racism after being drenched in a series of violent racist incidents in the City, which received intense media coverage. Her text suggests that such media reports on racist attacks caused "alarm," which then led to "hatred." In one way, I agree with her perception here, because sensational media coverage can create fear that intensifies racism, sexism, homophobia, xenophobia, etc., but blaming the media is only part of the story and too easy an answer, I would say. Some white students deny the racism already existing in themselves and their communities prior to any notorious incident. There is also a tendency among whites to use "racism" as a word to describe the behavior of many minority members, as if to say that blacks are as racist as are whites, so we are all guilty, a conclusion helped along by the high media profile given to alleged black tendencies toward crime, drugs, violence, illegitimacy, welfare dependence, etc. Media coverage is indeed often sensational in a tabloid town like New York, and in its negative depictions of African-Americans, the media help develop and confirm the racism of many whites. But, in specific coverage of racial incidents, the media are highlighting the racism already here, not creating it. White students seek some comfort and self-justification by blaming the media for provoking racism which their own white communities have simply not faced up to. To Nikki and the class during this discussion, I posed the problem of whether the media create racism through their coverage of single events or whether the media merely report only some of the racism that has always been here. To use writing as a method for bringing out knowledge and feelings about racism, I asked three questions to the students for anonymous composing: "Is racism a big problem now in New York City? Has it always been a problem or is it only recently an issue? Will it always be a problem or is there a way to solve it?"

Only three students wrote anonymously that it is not a problem, while the rest of the class agreed that racism is a big problem now and has been for a long time. Here are some excerpts from unsigned student papers on whether or not racism will always be a problem, and how to solve it:

1. "Yes. Because human nature has been molded so that we will always discriminate."
2. "It was probably always a problem but now the media has sensational-ized it. How do we stop it? I don't know."
3. "As long as there is capitalism and class differentiation, there will be racism."
4. "People will always be taught to hate."
5. "Start teaching children at young ages color means nothing everyone is the same."
6. "When the black people were slaves to the whites, the whites made the black race look like they were subhuman to justify their acts and it stayed with the black race. How can we change some people's views of black people?"
7. "It will always be a problem no matter what."
8. "I feel that people need to be educated."
9. "I believe that the tension has gotten so bad and that people are so hung up on their 'race' that it would be difficult to try to forget what color we are and to remember we are all humans."

With these statements frontloading their perceptions, I subsequently commented on racism and the media. I also provided background read-ings from my racism file, which I mentioned above, a xeroxed packet of news clippings on racist incidents in New York and elsewhere over the years, about long-term racist discrimination in housing, hiring, the military, the FBI, education, the media, sports, advertising, etc., includ-ing statistical tables comparing educational and income levels among the races. No one has a simple solution to a problem like racism, so the best I could do was supply in-depth material via the packet, encour-age the formation of a Coalition Against Racism like the one in Florida, and mention to the Utopia class that next semester I would be teaching an experimental course on race relations where we could continue the discussion (which I did offer the following term).

End of the Dialogue

On the whole, doing two project groups was too ambitious. I was criti-cized in the AC group for this. The students thought there was only sufficient time for one. They preferred "improving the College" be-cause it was close at hand and immediately related theory/research to practice/needs. New York City's problems, from racism to home-lessness to crime, seemed to them like an overwhelming distant swamp where research only took them deeper into vexing, menacing issues.

As for the improvement groups themselves, I would say that they were uneven. I had mixed feelings about the quality of their reports. Some were well-researched, provocative, and clearly presented; others not. Some groups did not look deeply at issues they themselves selected, like racism and rape. In addition, oral reports require skillful verbal delivery which few students have been allowed to practice. It's very possible for reporting students to bore each other even more than teacher-talk bores them. It takes experience, authority, an engaging style, and well-informed background to make a good oral report. But, if these talents are not yet possessed by most of the students, they have to develop somewhere; so our class was as good a place as any for stu-dents to develop as oral communicators. While their nonacademic speech is very complex, the students do not develop in school as aca-demic rhetors.[1] They have not had a dialogic curriculum where diverse, contending voices think out loud and discover meaning. Students rarely experience each other as sources of formal knowledge in an academic setting, so they lack habits of listening carefully to each other and of thinking together in class, where the words that count and the grade-giving power that matters have routinely belonged only to the teacher.

To encourage their habits of academic analysis, I have to discipline my own voice so that it creates a "zone of proximal development" (Vygotsky 1962), that is, a zone of discourse where my questions draw out their analytic abilities. For a dialogic process to evoke critical stu-dent discourse, I have to speak first in questions, and then integrate my backloaded comments into the profile of their expressions rather than expecting them to respond to my frontloaded lectures. To accom-plish this, I pose problems that provoke students into more discourse. In the AC group, after the first few project reports, the students told me that the probing questions I asked after each group report were

1. See Hoggart 1992 [1957], Willis 1981, Heath 1983, Ohmann 1987, Rose 1990, and Fox 1990a for analyses of working-class discourse.

good, that they helped relate the problems to everyone and inspired a lot of people to participate. I was very glad to hear this.

Like me, though, students in the AC group were often not happy with the lack of depth in some group reports, as my notes from ACG sessions indicate: "anecdotes were too important in the group reports; people should talk to class about solutions instead of complaints." This student in particular felt that mere complaining predominated when students reported on the College, while solutions were less developed. Certainly, it is easier to criticize something than to imagine and act for its transformation. Talk is cheap, it is often said, and grousing is the cheapest talk of all. On the other hand, this lesser engagement of alternatives by students is also the problem of an isolated critical classroom in a traditional institution where students have few if any chances to negotiate, to think critically about the status quo, and to practice change-agency. Then again, the high profile of complaints and the low profile of transformative solutions in student reports speak to the distance of classroom inquiry from the areas under scrutiny; the more concrete and at-hand the social project, the more involved and transformative students are likely to be in reconceiving it, because they would be doing theory in an immediate context, their favored praxis. Lastly, there is also the problem of students' undeveloped civic imaginations due to their lack of activist experience. Except for Jeremy, and perhaps Stephanie, none had taken part in protest culture. Those two alone had arrived with some sophisticated critical stances toward society. Jerome Bruner (1986) urged "stance" as the key posture for students and teachers in constructing education as a cultural forum for the negotiation of meanings. But, to take a stance, a person has to feel authorized by, committed to, and well-informed in the discourse and activity underway, because critical thinking and action are domain-specific, that is, supported by the familiarity a person has with a specific context. If students had more experience in changing public arenas of their lives, they would speak and write with more assurance and commitment about alternatives to the status quo. But, if they had more desire to make change, they would also seek to gain more of such experience. This chicken-and-egg dialectic is where power-sharing plants its feet, to create the desire and imagination of change while also creating the experience and skills for it. The critical-democratic class, then, is a context for change that develops the desire and imagination needed to make change.

Still, even partial social critique can be provocative. One AC member said in his evaluation of the group projects that the reports "went by so fast, people were really into it, people were outraged by it." The students chose problems they cared about, even if they couldn't imagine how to implement solutions. Though incomplete, these class reports stimulated discussions in the AC group about organizing students to solve the various problems studied. It would be a big step forward in a conservative time and place for a learning process to lead students to action outside of class. Recognizing the need for and the difficulty in taking civic action, Jack the bank teller said that at a commuter college like ours there is too little time for working students to organize themselves for social change. Their lives are too busy and fragmented, he opined, and they are not on campus long enough to work together. Once again, we came back to the issues of institutional control of time and the discipline of the body, emphasized by Foucault—call it the overorganized day—a theme which had fueled the long negotiation over required attendance in the first week of class. The ACG students wondered how to get around the time problem in lives already stretched thin. So do I.

Yet, the issue of change-agency refused to die. After several rounds of reports, Angela stunned the class and stopped the dialogue by announcing that "We must change the whole system, not small parts. The project groups are a waste of time. The whole system is the problem." She had heard enough. She wanted action. Her verdict provoked yet another student-to-student discussion on how to act on the problems they had researched. I added that civic action is a good idea, but that it should be well-informed action, which meant that research was important. A good number of students agreed with both of us, that we needed to gain more knowledge and then use knowledge to change things, not just complain or talk in a classroom.

But Angela insisted that we had to act and change the whole system, after which Lisa from the ACG once more voiced her frustration that she couldn't do something about the social problems we were examining class after class. I put the question to them directly one last time, "How could they organize to solve some of these problems?" They thought it over but remained uncertain. I directed them to groups already afield, like the tenacious New York Public Interest Group on campus and to CUNY-wide groups acting against budget cuts, which Jeremy also spoke about from his own involvement. They did not have to invent the wheel. They could join existing organizations. Some of them had reached the river's edge—the choice of whether or not to take part in organized action for change—and were stopped there, toes in the dark water. And I had the split feeling of being in two places at once—on the stuck side of the river with them as well as on the other bank where my nomadic and activist life had taken me. It appeared that the process was developing desires in a number of students to use knowledge outside of class to make change, which is significant, but further development in this political choice was still ahead of them.

At the water's edge, the compelling issue stared us in the face: How to act socially from the knowledge gained in class? How to bring knowledge and activism together? This concern had a long run in the theater of the basement Utopia. Power-sharing practice was developing in me and in some of them, along with some critical theory and civic desires, as we continued our subterranean encounter with disturbing knowledge and discomforting democracy.

SEVEN

Can Siberia Become a Critical Territory?

Cultural Production in a Critical-Democratic Zone

As the April heat wave in New York dragged on that semester, the basement hole became a busy mining operation producing a lot of ore as well as soil, dust, rock, and muck. Some students resented and protested the quantity of work, perhaps feeling that I had them laboring in an overheated salt mine. My sweat was just as salty as theirs, but I could put up with it better because, after all, I was earning a salary underground, unlike them, and because I had a long-term personal/political/professional stake in this experiment which none of them shared. For sure, some students preferred the predemocratic days of undisturbed Siberia, which power-sharing had disrupted if not dissolved. At least, now, residual Siberia had to contend with provisional Utopia, as the self-regulating project groups reported nonstop from the front of the room, where the student rhetors sat and the teacher didn't. With even deep Siberians included in the reporting, the student groups ran the sessions themselves, a pleasure for me to watch as I perspired in the steamy back of the room, remembering how a previous remedial class had insisted that I chair their project groups (see the Introduction to *Empowering Education*). This time, students took charge and ran their own sittings.

Each group's report on improving the College or the City was followed by discussions in class and in the ACG. Furthermore, individual students in each group handed in written reports. At the same time,

AC students were writing in-class evaluations of each group for me and for the reporting students, while I similarly produced written evaluations of the groups. Papers, reports, evaluations, and comments were flying in all directions, from students to students, from students to me, from me to students. The two-hour sessions were not long enough to process all of this material. I wearied at the pace and marveled at the activity-level in a process whose engines seemed to be running all at once in every direction. I digested as much as I could, but there was too much on the table. With so much activity during and between classes, the hot and dingy room below ground became a center of ferocious cultural production, but I still have to come to grips with the big question: *What exactly was being produced?*

A productive, congenial classroom is far preferable to an unproductive, chilly one, but it takes more than productivity, collaboration, and circle-seating to make a learning process critical or empowering. Being busy and collaborative is not the same as being critical of the status quo (see Sapon-Shevin and Schniedewind 1991). The borders of critical culture appear when a discourse questions existing knowledge and unequal power relations, when it imagines democratic alternatives departing from authoritarian business-as-usual, when it connects subjectivity to history while relating personal contexts to social contexts and academic texts, when it situates the theme of "social justice" at the center of the knowledge-making enterprise (as Sonia Nieto [1994b] has suggested). These borders were on my mind as I listened to, read, and responded to the students' reports. Were we crossing them?

Producing critical thought in an anticritical culture is about as challenging as producing democratic relations in an unequal school system. For example, consider the quotidian nightmare of commuter colleges: parking. Earlier, I reported that the student group examining this *bete noir* of everyday life proposed solving the parking mess by cutting down trees to expand the already huge parking lot into a wooded greenbelt bordering the College. A few years later, after we had moved into the larger new campus with its even bigger parking lots, other classes would favor the same solution to the unresolved parking problem: cut down trees and pave over lawns to make more space for cars. As it happened on the new campus, frustrated commuter students didn't wait for the College administration to implement this plan—they simply began parking their cars on the grass and wherever. The administration responded to this "grassroots" undiscipline by ticketing, booting, and towing the offending cars. Students who had to retrieve cars or pay fines became only more disgusted. Too disgusted to wait for adequate legal parking, for adequate mass transit, or for adequate numbers of classes to be available at registration, some began dropping out, and enrollment declined. Essentially, parking was expelling working students from college. Parking, along with impossible registration and higher tuition, were three institutional obstacles to mass higher education structured into student life by mass higher education itself. The problem of "getting into college" no longer involved only good high school grades, high SAT scores, and deciphering admissions applications. Mere acceptance into this allegedly "open admissions" public college did not guarantee actual access to the campus and its classes. "Getting in" became increasingly physical and fiscal as well as academic. The legal ability to "get in" did not equal the actual power to "get in" to classes or the campus, thanks to the disempowering features of parking, registration, and ever-rising tuition.

Unable to afford the class-based luxury of attending a residential college, like Stephanie's former campus, some students concluded that it was not worth the struggle to pay for and stay in a college like this. In such a bizarre situation—legal "open admissions" contradicted by de facto barriers to access (resembling the restricted access to "legal abortion" in the 1990s)—I am tempted to say that every course actually begins in the parking lot and in the checkbook, or more dramatically, that intellectual work is dominated by the parking lot and the student's checking account. The way students "get in" influences what happens in the classroom. In the case of my troubled budget College, parking problems, registration issues, and tuition are disabling experiences that dissociate students from intellectual life. For this reason, no pedagogy is autonomous of society because every pedagogy—not just my critical-democratic one—is dependent on the larger social conditions enveloping every learning process.

Parking is thus one condition of everyday life that delivers many students to class angry, resentful, distracted, and exhausted. No wonder, then, that their imaginations dream first of building even bigger parking lots where ("expendable" and "useless") trees now stand. This is understandable and should not be interpreted as thoughtless anti-environmentalism or as yahoo autophilia (car-love) on the part of working-class students. Rather, their weak relationship to environmentalism reflects their everyday struggle to meet their needs in society. If they had the power to design a campus for themselves, the students would not construct one with such commuting, registration, and parking problems; the administration with input from faculty (who have their own nearby and gated parking lots) approved such a campus in collaboration with state agencies and professional architects. Woods, trees, grass (romantically idealized as *the environment* as if traffic jams and inner cities are not environmental) don't have a chance in this conflict between unorganized students and a powerful oligarchy.

Well, of course, it was easy enough for me to become the sentimental defender of pretty nature in these discussions regarding parking in the Utopia class. My own privileged access to a faculty lot and to a salary that pays for a good late-model car, make my environmentalism a class luxury that my students can't afford in a society like ours, at a time and place like this, in an unorganized working-class constituency like theirs. How could they put trees and grass ahead of their own struggle merely to "get in," to reach campus, park, and come to class on time? Green vistas and critical theory soothe me as I cruise into my professorial parking space, but philosophy and grass are no substitutes in student life for easy access to parking by whatever means necessary (like cutting down trees).

Perhaps I should admit right here how uncomfortable I am to find myself still thinking and writing about parking at this late date (1996) and at such a late point in this book. When I first drove my red Volkswagen beetle onto campus in 1971, my new eyes saw gray, squat concrete buildings dwarfed by the vast parking lot, which stood on a rise overlooking the diminutive academic quadrangle where classes were held. Back then, I intuited this parking lot as an interference to critical thought (see *Critical Teaching and Everyday Life*) because it occupied so much social and physical space. I feel embarrassed to be consumed and bedeviled by parking twenty-five years later and almost three-fourths of the way through this book. I would rather simply take credit for my Smokey-the-Bear defense of pretty nature and pat myself on the back for being an angelically Green Promethean. But that's not the way it is, whether I like it or not. The nagging truth is that I have a superior class position that allows me to love trees and still park my car in comfort. The different class position of my students gives them a different relationship to trees and cars at the College and in society. Environmentalism is not a moral issue but rather a class one here.

More than three decades after having left the working class of the South Bronx and more than two decades after first meeting these working students on Staten Island, I am still obsessed with the icons of everyday life—the parking lot, the fuming car, the bad teeth, the mottled complexion, the ubiquitous candy bar, the furtive cigarette, the dripping soda can, the greasy hamburger, the white styrofoam cup redolent of acidic coffee, the sleepy eyes in evening sessions, and the fiberglass classroom chair. In this iconography of student life, *the parking lot* stands above them all as an awesome fixture, an epitomizing shrine of unacknowledged class conflict. The brilliant Frenchman so favored now, Foucault, whose awesome intellect inspired me when I heard him speak years ago, might call this parking lot a discipline device for institutional control of behavior. If Foucault returned to life, he would find embodied here his theory of how dominant authority achieves hegemony by circulating through the everyday actions of individuals at local sites of experience, in the way hundreds of student drivers constantly circulate the campus in search of parking, an activity that restricts their relationship to trees and to intellectual work while professors and administrators conveniently park and stroll to classes or offices.

In the Utopia class, I raised some global issues involved in this parking problem, but I failed to relate environmentalism to social class in terms that would be meaningful to the students. My attention was too exclusively environmental and didn't sufficiently integrate ecology with class. On environmental grounds, I questioned the commonsense solution of cutting down trees to build more parking lots to make room for cars. Would a bigger parking lot meet environmental needs like lowered air pollution, less noise pollution, and reduced consumerism, all goals of the *Ecotopian* society, which the students liked? And, would a bigger parking lot actually solve the problem? I pointed out that urban traffic tends to expand with each new highway, bridge, tunnel, parking lot, or garage, leaving New York and Los Angeles tied for the worst traffic in the nation (L.A. has the worst air). Pro-car policies produce more cars; pro-Earth policies produce more mass transit and fewer cars, which reduce pollution and control costs while easing commuting.

Despite my critical words on this issue, students stood by what Paulo Freire might call their *limit logic*—thought constructed within the limits of their existing social positions (class, race, gender, etc.). In their lives, building bigger parking lots is the logical answer for a place with too many cars, too few spots, so many trees, and so much acreage. They turned away from activist or visionary logic, if I may use that phrase, which would point toward such things like pushing government to provide adequate mass transit (what Freire called "limit-acts" or action against the limits). I proposed more mass transit as a solution, along with ideas for decentralizing our one large campus into several smaller ones closer to their homes. But, they rejected these options, not because they are anti-environmental or because I was inarticulate in presenting my case but, rather, because my perspective violated their logic, in this case their desire for short-term relief, not long-term transformation, an urgent desire which turns them toward what is possible in the near-term. Their immediate need for more parking fit into a whole dominant "way of life" (Raymond Williams' [1977] definition of culture and hegemony): save money, buy a flivver, find cheap insurance, fill the tank with low-test, jump into traffic, take shortcuts to campus, circulate until you get a spot, park on the grass if you have to, and run to class hoping you're on time and that the car is still there when you get back, not towed, ticketed, booted, or broken into. All of which means that I didn't get very far in my basement arguments against cars and parking lots.

I like to think that you win some and you lose some, which is a comforting frame of mind through which to consider the next project group, "Communication Between Teachers and Students." The reporting students here took hold of a real problem but got tangled up in the analysis of it. For example, in defining the problem of classroom communication, the students conflated the *pronunciation* difficulties of foreign instructors with the rapid-fire, one-way *teacher-talk* of native professors and adjuncts. Students reported that both native and foreign teachers apparently used the teacher-talk or lecture model, but they didn't separate the "banking" pedagogy problem from the linguistic accent one. Still, this group's report was well received by the class and the AC evaluators, who were apparently fed up with the struggle to learn from hard-to-follow foreign and native teachers alike. The level of resentment among students was surprisingly high here. A later student's remarks characterized the feeling in the Utopia class: "I'm currently taking a Geology class which isn't one of my better subjects. The lab instructor can barely speak English. I think he's from Russia and I'm sure he's an intelligent man, but I can't understand what he's saying. All I'm saying is that I find Geology difficult, and I would appreciate an instructor who could speak comprehensible English." For this problem, the reporting group proposed several solutions: ongoing speech and communication courses for all teachers; oral testing prior to and during a teacher's employment; and the effective use of student evaluations of a teacher's performance. These proposals seemed sensible to me. In the context of current academic policy, they represent a constructive alternative to the present low regard for teacher-training, for teacher-student communication, and for student opinion. In the discussion following their report, I backloaded some comments, including a distinction between foreign teachers and native full-time/adjunct faculty who lecture students into silence. Then, I questioned why foreign teachers are being hired just now (nonstop budget cuts at an impoverished public college like mine result in hiring the cheapest academic labor available).

In the presentation that followed, "Homelessness in New York," the reporting students were sincerely outraged at the disgrace of people sleeping on the street, picking through garbage for their food, begging for money on subways. But, they too did not ask systemically why homelessness became a major problem in New York and other cities since the procorporate/prorich tax policies of the Reagan-Bush era (see Barlett and Steele 1992; Greider 1993; Cassidy 1995). Not questioning the conservative politics of the time, they assumed the efficacy of traditional answers in their proposed solutions: open more temporary shelters (which are actually expensive to run and pose security problems) and promote more personal charity from individuals (which tends to rise and fall with the state of the economy). Desperately seeking solutions, this group even suggested that City residents draw maps for the homeless to help them find their way to the nearest shelters. Desperate necessity was certainly the mother of peculiar invention here, for what was necessary in this exercise was imagining the unimagined and, up to that moment in the homeless tragedy of New York, no one had yet distributed shelter maps to those seeking beds for the night. For my interventions in this discussion, I provided readings on homelessness which presented it as a social product of corporate-government policy to defund the public sector and social services like public housing, the federal budgets of which declined precipitously in the Reagan years. In addition, homelessness dramatically increased during the prolonged period of high unemployment, declining real wages, and soaring executive pay which characterized the decades from the 1970s to the 1990s.

In yet another group report, two women in the "City Crime" project focused on rape but couldn't agree on what "date rape" was or if it actually happens. One focused her critique on the judicial and media treatment of the rape victim, who, she said, was victimized a second time by insensitive courts, aggressive defense lawyers, and voracious news organizations. The other young woman denied that sex on a date could be characterized as rape, preferring instead to define rape as a violent attack without a social context, even though rape is often committed by males known to the female victims, which I mentioned in class. These women proposed remedies such as stiffer sentences for rapists as well as some strong advice to women: avoid walking alone in dark places, learn how defend yourself when attacked, and be sure to report the assault to the police. This advice was sensible but did not go to the root of the problem. So, in my backloaded comments, I asked how Ecotopia or Walden II would handle rape, reminding the class about the War Games ritual of Ecotopia. Could War Games reduce the male violence known as rape? The students still had difficulty conceptualizing how War Games would lessen male violence against women. So, to become concrete and closer to home, I then asked if schools should have K-12 programs in rape prevention which would focus on nonviolence training for boys while giving self-defense training to girls. This proposal appealed to more students but not all. Given the pervasive sexual violence against women and girls, I am sure that some female students in class have been harassed, assaulted, or raped—but were understandably unwilling to disclose such an experience—and I am sure that some men in class have committed these acts or have sisters or girlfriends who are victims of them (see Stein, Marshall, and Tropp 1993; Katz 1995). Sometimes I think that this theme is best taken up in all-female and all-male settings (as done in the Antioch College harassment program; see Gross 1993), but in 1995 in two mixed classes, some younger and older women were able to speak openly and effectively about the sexual harassment they have experienced, unlike the shy underground group in the Utopia class.

Lastly, the "Pollution in the City" committee stood strongly behind vigorous recycling of consumer materials and industrial waste. Local oil spills and illegal toxic dumping were apparently out of control, as reported in articles I had asked them to read and in other articles which they had provided. One young white woman, Melanie, a 22-year-old English major who worked forty hours a week in a hardware store, asked, "Why doesn't anyone swim in the waters off of Staten Island? When my grandfather was my age, he swam and fished in the waters of the Kill Van Kull." She recommended that the news media broadcast each night the proposals of the book *50 Simple Things You Can Do to Save the Earth,* but went beyond the consumer/individualist remedies in that book to offer the following appeal "to create a better system," in her (unedited) words, which begins immediately with the idea of praxis (putting theory into practice through reflective action):

> People can have all the knowledge they can possibly get their hands on, but if they do not use it, nothing will change. If people are not committed to making the world safer and cleaner, than it will not become so. Things can only change if we want them to, and if we do something about it. Laws need to be changed so that they serve the interest of the American public, and the best interests of the planet. New and more

stringent regulations of factory pollution, stiffer fines for companies that dump toxic waste illegally. Enforce fines for littering and such. All these things will help stop the spread of pollution.

Melanie was one student who attempted a systemic critique focused on civic action.

Overall, though, uneven analysis was common in the project groups. Some took the projects more seriously than others; some were more militant about the issues than others; some more than others acknowledged that a system was behind particular problems; and some were more comfortable in public speaking or in writing than others. Every class is a diverse gathering of students, an assembly of people with varied abilities and agendas. I had invited students to exercise civic imagination against and outside of the status quo. At moments, some students did that, like when Angela burst out that the project groups were a waste of time because the whole society had to be changed, not just pieces of it; or when Melanie, as above, understood the need for praxis in using knowledge to make change. These declarations offered a few sublime moments of critical perception that other students could ponder or deny, embrace or ignore.

Time to Measure the Sublime: Students Are Always Thinking, Sometimes Critically

As the project groups reported, and the hot spring cooked our brains nicely in the windowless basement, I asked the ACG: "Is Utopian thinking going on in the reports we are hearing? Are students thinking in ways that are futuristic, questioning the status quo, engineering non-traditional solutions, and proposing new means for decision making? Is systemic thinking happening in class?" Sensing my doubt, Jack the bank teller said, "We haven't yet had a full semester of this, so there's not enough time to do this in depth. The students are trying to come up with solutions, but the teacher has a better way of thinking—when the teacher looks at something you look at it well-thought out." I asked his advice about how to draw out more systemic thinking, but he simply encouraged me to continue my backloaded comments and questions, which he said were helpful. I had to make do with this endorsement because the ACG students were still not ready to share with me the job of evoking deeper thought in class.

Shortly after Jack's comment in the ACG, I made a mistake in class which changed the focus of AC discussion. Impatient to draw more critical thought out of the project groups, I took over a reporting session prematurely and effectively substituted my thinking for theirs. On a particularly warm day, I hastily intervened in one group's presentation because I was too eager to model systemic thinking. I pre-empted the "Books Too Expensive" committee by suggesting that one alternative to overpriced commercial textbooks was to replace them with materials written and published by students and teachers themselves, as part of the College's academic program. Through credit-bearing courses in a writing-across-the-curriculum, literacy-in-context format, I proposed setting up textbook publishing classes that would write materials and revise them each year according to feedback from students and teachers using them. This would include printing and selling inexpensive, collaboratively authored works at the College, thereby creating some desktop publishing jobs for students on campus as well as providing the benefit of less costly, noncommercial, locally designed books. I emphasized the Utopian cooperativeness, activism, and efficiency of this alternative, but the students in class had never imagined such a thing and could not see themselves as authors, editors, and publishers. This proposal of mine not only stopped the group report that had been underway but it also stopped class dialogue, period, because students could not speak to a big new idea requiring time for digestion, namely, reinventing their relationship to authorship and textbooks. Too late, I realized that I had intervened too soon. Also, I intuited that to produce my textbook alternative across-the-disciplines I would have to lead a class in writing educational materials to develop cadres of students and teachers who could pioneer the project with me.

But, more to the point of the Utopia process, the AC students criticized me for breaking in early with such a lot of commentary. According to them, I cut in too soon, spoke too long, and started the class conversation on the committee report before the committee had finished. I tried to defend myself by saying that it was a very hot day and students seemed sleepy, so I intervened to raise the attention level. I also explained that I wanted to highlight certain parts of the students' report which were not developed or presented well. But the AC students were unsympathetic to my explanations. They said that my comments cut down the remaining time available for the "Improving Teaching" group, the next one scheduled to report. The AC group was especially miffed because they thought this group on improving teaching was one of the better attempts to engage in Utopian thinking. I was advised by the AC group only to intervene briefly to focus attention on an issue, not to cut off the committee or to call for whole-class discussion until later on, and to limit the whole-class discussion before it pre-empted the time needed for the next group. In correcting me, the ACG was exercising its new authority to discipline the old authority, thereby defending a dialogic process against antidialogic teacher-talk. I felt some satisfaction here in seeing the responsible way the ACG related to that class session. I also felt some defensive awkwardness, which I did my best to control, just as the special Gulf War group began its long-awaited presentations.

What They Learned about the War

"When I think of the United States," wrote Doug, Angela's tall supporter against required attendance and a member of the Gulf War research group, "I can't help but feel warm-hearted." He went on to write that

> The United States, since it's very beginning, has stood for freedom and justice, and although we have had major contradictions to this theme (such as 200 years of slavery) it is usually our country that is looked upon as a guiding light. Indeed, our country is a growing one that has never stagnated in its quest to becoming a better one. However, recent events seem to have set our program back a few steps. What I am talking about specifically is our involvement and policies in the Gulf War Crisis.
>
> At first I was pro-war like the vast majority of my fellow citizens. I watched the news on TV and read some newspaper articles and drew certain conclusions which were not entirely accurate. As I started doing some research for this assignment I began to uncover some facts that were never found on the front pages of newspapers or on prime time television. It now seems that much of the news we received was carefully screened by our government. In other words, our propaganda machine was virtually 100 percent successful.

Tall, smart, and handsome Doug (who received one rejection after another that term from the medical schools he applied to until one finally accepted him) voluntarily chose to research the war after a class discussion on it in the early weeks of the term. I mentioned in chapter 1 that the first-day sign-in sheet included a question asking students if they wanted any time devoted to the Gulf War then underway. Doug and a strong majority voted 29–6 in favor of discussing it. I would not have used class time for this issue unless they had authorized it, and I did not make a speech to the class on how to view the war. Once the students voted in favor of a war discussion, I compiled a media packet as background, because few students had read much about it even though many had already developed strong pro-war positions. Only later, after we had read and discussed this packet, did I backload commentary, discussing the war in the context of Utopia/Dystopia. I cited how Utopias seek to reduce violent conflict through egalitarian economics, cooperative social life, and civic means of negotiating differences, whereas Dystopias tend to be police-states run by manipulative elites who secure power through violence, war, media control, secret intelligence operations, and scapegoats, by scaring, dividing, misinforming, and distracting the populace.

But, before I backloaded comments on Utopia/Dystopia, and before handing out the reading packet, I took an anonymous opinion poll in class, using the following form, to profile the starting point of student perceptions:

PLEASE DO NOT PUT YOUR NAME ON THIS PAGE
ARE YOU
IN FAVOR OF THE WAR ⎯⎯⎯⎯⎯⎯⎯⎯⎯⎯⎯⎯⎯⎯⎯⎯⎯⎯
OPPOSED TO THE WAR ⎯⎯⎯⎯⎯⎯⎯⎯⎯⎯⎯⎯⎯⎯⎯⎯⎯⎯
UNCERTAIN ⎯⎯⎯⎯⎯⎯⎯⎯⎯⎯⎯⎯⎯⎯⎯⎯⎯⎯⎯⎯⎯⎯⎯⎯
UNINVOLVED ⎯⎯⎯⎯⎯⎯⎯⎯⎯⎯⎯⎯⎯⎯⎯⎯⎯⎯⎯⎯⎯⎯⎯
PLEASE EXPLAIN WHY YOU FEEL LIKE THIS:

As it turned out, only five students opposed the war, while seven wrote that they were uncertain, and the rest supported it. Here are some anonymous and unedited explanations offered by the twenty-odd students in favor of the war:

- "I feel that Hussein must be stop in order for the world to be at peace (He is nuts)"
- "Hussein must be stopped. He thinks he can do whatever he wants and could soon develop nuclear weapons. He must be stopped before he tries to conquer the world."
- "Hitler did the same thing!"
- "He is another Hitler and must be stopped."
- "I feel Kuwait is strategically important to not only the world's supply of oil, but also to the balance of power in the Mid-East. Israel must be protected from future aggressors & Saddam Hussein is just that, an aggressor. I firmly believe if he was shown no resistance after invading Kuwait, he would've moved into Saudi Arabia. Hitler did the same thing!"

• "I don't think war is a good thing, but it is what we have to do when dealing with insane leaders trying to ruin our country and the world."

• "I feel that Kuwait was violated by an aggressor nation . . . I also feel that the United States has the responsibility as a world power or super power to help smaller weaker nations fight for their rights to freedom and independence. It's what democracy is all about!"

• "I am in favor because I think as citizens of the United States we should back our country. I am more in supporting the troops than the war itself. I only feel that President Bush should have tried to avoid the war for a little longer. Maybe there would have been peace instead of war."

• "I am in favor of the war but I do not follow the news too closely. I'm really not as involved as I would like. I don't really read the papers and only catch a quick report on the 11:00 news."

• "I feel this way because our soldiers are out there fighting for us, as soon as it is over we should be very proud of them. I hope for their sake and for many families the war is over fast."

• "I think President Bush made the right decision at the right time. I think fighting the war is important and I hope there will soon be peace."

• "I am not a warmonger but I feel that the U.N. is an important organization in the world and countries have to learn to not ignore its resolutions, even if it means war."

In these statements, what is striking is the repetition of Saddam Hussein as an "insane Hitler" with the power to threaten and destroy the world. Apparently, the White House "spin" equating Hussein to Hitler had been successfully conveyed by the establishment media, scaring Americans with a psycho-demon soon to possess nuclear weapons and able to conquer the world. In addition, some pro-war students were supportive of the war because the men and women overseas came from their own families and neighborhoods. Those with this sentiment did not know of a dissident organization of families whose relatives were serving in the Gulf, led by Professor Alex Molnar from Milwaukee, whose Marine son was over there. This group and other antiwar formations were effectively quarantined from the American public.

The few students who opposed the war wrote comments like these:

• "If we continue to attempt to resolve conflicts through agressive means, eventually we'll lose. There will always be a bigger bully. We spend more money trying to destroy life and property in other countries than we do protecting the lives of our own citizens. We should develop our domestic life rather than destroy foreign worlds. Iraq's invasion of Kuwait is no worse than our invasions of Panama, Grenada, Nicaragua, etc."

• "The President knew all along he was going to war but he wasn't honest with Americans."

• "I feel we could have gotten Iraq to accept the U.N. resolutions without the use of military force. In time sanctions would have force Iraq's compliance with these resolutions. I feel we have other motivations in this war besides Iraq's compliance with U.N. resolutions."

Outnumbered by the large pro-war group, the anti-war critics were quiet when discussion began. Their fear of speaking might have been eased if I could have changed the rhetorical setting from one that silenced and marginalized dissent to one that legitimized it. If I could have opened the discourse to a broader spectrum of opinion than allowed in the corporate media (see *EXTRA!* magazine, 1991), then I would not have had to solely carry the rhetorical load in questioning the war. This democratic undertaking, to legitimize dissent and contention rather than hegemony and conformity, does have its risks. In another class that same term, with the rhetorical load of questioning the war mostly on me, I was rebuked by a group of night students who berated me for challenging White House policy. In that class, I was all-but-silenced, but I did have one ally in the person of Keith Hefner, a brilliant director of youth journalism for inner-city high-school students in New York, who had taken my course to study dialogic pedagogy and was overrun with me in the war debate. At least Keith and I had each other, which did make it a little less painful for me to run into the pro-war wall. Having a student *group* lead the questioning of the war in the Utopia class made a world of difference.

In the Utopia room, there was an aroused and officially authorized student majority in favor of the war and a silenced handful opposed, but there were also some Utopia students who declared themselves "Uncertain," with doubts like these:

• "If all the news reports are true about Hussein & Iraq then I'm in favor of the war, but at this point I don't know what to believe."

• "I don't really know all of the facts, therefore, I can't really decide. From what I do know, I'm not opposed to the war."

• "I feel uncertain and uninvolved because I'm not that well informed about it. It's really not all clear to me why there's a war and from what I've read and heard, due to the press and government official we are not told everything that there is to know about what's going on."

• "I am very frightened by this war . . . I understand there are specific reasons for being there, however we have a right to question those 'reasons.' . . . Whatever may happen in this war, people should keep in mind the Vietnam nightmare. 40% of the people living in the streets in NYC are Vietnam veterans—Let's not forget the veterans of tomorrow."

In general, those uncertain about the war knew about as much as those in favor of it, mostly from the gross images provided by the Bush Administration and CNN. So, I handed out two news stories for them to read from two newspapers which had editorially supported the war: a column by Knut Royce from Long Island *Newsday*, tracing what Royce called a "trail of distortion" in the White House's claims against Hussein (that he had gassed the Kurds in his country, that he would soon have a nuclear bomb, that he planned to invade Saudi Arabia, etc.); and another report by James LeMoyne of the *New York Times*, recently back from Kuwait, describing how the press was censored there and how the Pentagon managed the news to guarantee favorable public opinion at home. I asked the students to study them outside of class and to bring in written responses to read to each other in discussion groups. For class discussion, I then xeroxed two student comments on each article, so that the dialogue on this sensitive issue would be built from their frontloaded expressions. Here are excerpts from the student papers I xeroxed for the whole class to read and discuss:

A. Royce
1. "Royce's article offers concrete evidence that the Bush Admin. has a policy of misinforming the American public about occurrences in the Gulf . . . It is obvious that this is a war Bush wants to fight whether or not it is truly warranted . . . We have to learn by ourselves to discern truth from propoganda . . . I don't know whether or not Royce knows the ultimate truth . . . but his article makes me angry. It makes me question even more readily the things I hear and read. That's what I should do."
2. "This article reveals how our govt. has attempted to make us believe that everything they have done was right and everything Hussein has done was wrong. It shows us some interesting facts such as the possibility of a nuclear device and the fact that maybe Iraq was provoked into war. These are things we never hear on the news or by our govt. . . . I believe we are right in attacking Iraq but do believe we have hid some facts about Hussein and what he has done. However, I see nothing wrong with this.

Everyone does this, show their side of the story . . . Hussein is sick and we should not worry about proving him justified and moral, just support our military and get this psycho out of office."

B. Lemoyne
1. "This article was written by a reporter who was in the Gulf from Sept. to Dec. He tell us how the Pentagon limits the reporting on the battlefield. Officers and reporters who talk negatively about the war are cut off . . . Events are staged for cameras and coverage is swayed in favor of the Pentagon . . . I agree with what is said by Lemoyne. However, I disagree with the Pentagon. I think the press should be allowed to report whatever they wish without conditions. The Pentagon is taking away rights of the press and the troops by swaying coverage in favor of themselves . . . I think that by having such strict rules placed on the press, troops are forced to ask themselves just what kind of leaders they are risking their lives for because everyone deserves the right to speak."
2. "Reporters covering the war claim that restrictions imposed by military authorities obstruct informed and objective reporting. Pentagon officials deny access to reporters if critical views are expressed . . . I have mixed feelings on the censoring of the reporting. Logically, I can see why officials want positive coverage to support the war but on the other hand, I also believe that the American people should have a right to see what is actually going on in the Persian Gulf."

I asked students to read these four statements, which took different positions, to write their own responses and read them to each other in groups of four, and then to choose one text or a synthesis to read aloud for whole-class dialogue. As it turned out, the Royce and Lemoyne articles provoked some uncomfortable doubt among the pro-war group concerning the logic and truth of the war. Doubt can become a door to transformation, and in this instance, doubt did transform the political climate in class, creating an opening for the anti-war minority to speak about press censorship, government lying, and Hussein being a Hitler. This was a modest step forward in raising the profile of dissent in one small public sphere. The rhetorical setting opened for contending points of view during a heavily managed and censored moment of public life. This rhetorical opening pleased me, so I kept the discussion going, but this angered some AC members who criticized me later for taking too long with this topic. Following AC protests against further war talk, in the next class I instead offered students a chance to research it as one of their term projects. Six students took on this topic, for which I provided materials and for which they found their own in the library. Eventually, they reported to the whole class as more-informed peers.

In their reports, the Gulf War group primarily presented background about the conflict's history and about Pentagon-media censorship. Their reports were largely sobering but easier to listen to now that the war was over with apparently "small" costs (about 300 Americans dead, some $50 billion spent, perhaps 100,000 to 200,000 Iraqis killed, while some 20,000 U.S. Gulf veterans eventually came down with a strange "Gulf Syndrome" illness later on). Here are a few (unedited) excerpts from the final reports of the Gulf War group as they were read to the class:

DENISE: "Virtually all the major news organizations agreed that the flow of information to the public was blocked, impeded or diminished . . . resulting in their inability to tell the public the full story . . . It is my opinion that economic sanctions could have been effective if given the chance . . . Press censorship is expected in Communist countries, not in America. I was under the impression we live in a democracy."

DOUG: "Instead of spending billions of dollars on a war in the Gulf we should have put the money into research and development. We could have explored better ways of using sun and wind energy; experimenting with alternate fuel vehicles or more efficient gasoline ones. The real war should be waged on our own inefficiency and wasteful ways of life. We should leave the oil in the Gulf alone and work on ways to becoming a self-sustaining country . . . U.S. policy makers should look within our own borders for problems to solve. We need to do something about our ailing economy, failing school system, loss of competitiveness and failing social system."

LISA: "I believe that most Americans have been brainwashed rather than well informed. Many have come to believe that supporting the troops is synonymous with supporting the war. Many war protestors have been actually intimidated about speaking out, for fear of being labeled unpatriotic. America is awash in war glorification . . . I think our problem lies in our passivity and acceptance of the status quo as it exists . . . Power as it exists in this country is holed up in a vacuum, with a very privileged few having enormous control and influence . . . We have potential power in our sheer numbers alone. Politicians simply don't ignore voters, although they may ignore a minority, which has been war protestors."

One student in this group, Dave, had been a deep Siberian all semester. He comfortably supported the war, apparently unintimidated by and uninfluenced by my opinions or the critical readings. Dave was a likeable 20-year-old electrical technology major who worked twenty hours a week as a stockboy. Friendly and mellow, he had written on the first-day sign-in sheet that he wanted the death penalty restored in New York, as this was his suggestion for improving life in the City. Although a Siberian who clung to the corner, Dave wrote on the first day that he took the Utopia class because a friend who had it before recommended it, which made him "very interested in the topics . . . and the books," not because it was merely a requirement. He never missed a class and rarely spoke in any of them; he went straight for the Siberian corner, but signed up for an A contract and handed everything in on time. His complex character is a caution about seeing the Siberian Syndrome one-dimensionally as simple exile, passivity, and withdrawal, because Dave was affable (not hostile), self-possessed (not dependent), and workmanlike (not careless), who resisted my efforts to question the status quo like a rock resists raindrops.

Here is an excerpt from the report Dave read in class:

> I believe that two good things came from this war, one being that Kuwait was liberated and its government restored, but we really don't know how good that is. Number two being that strong pride was reborn in our country. Faith in our military was restored and people came together to support our country and its leaders in a time of serious crisis. I feel that this was the most important outcome of the war, the way it brought our people together.

His differences from the others in his group allowed the debate to begin from opposing student positions, into which I backloaded comments about the antidemocratic government of the Emir of Kuwait which was restored to power without instituting democracy (for example, women were still not allowed to vote or drive cars in "liberated" Kuwait). All in all, the war research group provided a student-led, in-depth second forum on this issue at a time when it was extremely difficult for opposition to be heard in any media or public forums.

War Ends, Peace Is Yet to Start: Evaluating the Utopia Process

The war was over and so was the Utopia class, or nearly so. The Gulf War report and debate concluded as the basement Utopia reached its final session, with only an end-term evaluation of the class by the students left to accomplish. I placed responsibility for designing the final course evaluation in the hands of the AC group. The AC students worked on it over several meetings before coming up with their self-designed form, which I will present in full in the next chapter. But, here are the first two questions asked by the ACG on its form:

1. Has this class opened you up to new ideas and changed your way of thinking? How?
2. Do you feel motivated to take action in student or civic government or in other classes to change things?

They put "change" high on the list. They focused immediately on "action." I couldn't predict if most students would report being changed or would announce desires to take action, but I knew that the ACG students had learned to ask a few good questions.

APPENDIX

In later semesters, I asked ACG students to act as "interpolators" who would take minutes of the meetings. The students rotated that job, with the result that the minutes were uneven, some being more detailed than others. For a flavor of ACG dialogue, I reproduce below an excerpt from an ACG meeting (11/22/94) after an "Introduction to Journalism" class. Earlier, during class that day, I had posed these questions to students: "Why do major newspapers have 'business' sections but not 'working day' or 'labor news' sections?"; "How would you research the claim made by authors Jeff Cohen and Norman Solomon in *Adventures in Medialand* that the news media have a procorporate tilt?"; and "If newspapers have a procorporate tilt, what would a newspaper *without* such a tilt look like?"

Here is the student interpolation of that day's ACG discussion, in which you can see the dual functions of the ACG, as a small-group "second class" to pursue issues in a seminarlike setting and as a means to evaluate the process itself:

GREG: How would a paper with no procorporate tilt look? This was a great question. I think there is no answer.

KIT: I don't think it can be done.

STAN: Me, neither, the people at the top always dictate what goes on, it's all about money.

IRA: What if we exposed all tilts, all points of view, in the news media?

KIT: Yeah, but someone always has to own the paper. Whatever they say goes.

ALICE: Even unions have tilt. Business has to be run by someone. It's the big guy who gets their way not the little guy.

TED: You can't get away from tilt. We live in a capitalist system. Money runs everything . . . It's an elitist country, it always has been run that way.

IRA: How about our [analysis] of the business section? Any criticisms about that part of today's class?

ALICE: I think maybe you could've asked the question a little differently. Instead, maybe you could've asked "If there was a working day section [in the newspaper], what would you put into it?"

IRA: Yeah, last semester we did projects illustrating what people thought a "working day" [section] would consist of . . . Do you think we should go deeper into this?

ALICE: I don't know, there's only one more class to go.

IRA: In the last class I wanted to do that broadcasting exercise with the anchor, feed, and commentator. A thirty-second film clip with a voiceover, taking information from the [recent November] elections. What do you think?

ALICE: I think it sounds like a good exercise.

KIT: Is this a group thing?

IRA: It will start out individually and then move into a group exercise.

KIT: What does the anchor do?

IRA: He or she writes a small text like a direct lead. You'll have to choose from data and organize it into a newsreport.

KIT: This sounds good.

DENISE: I don't know, it sounds complicated.

STAN: It sounds like it can turn into a mess.

IRA: Well, it's the last class . . .

[NOTE: After more discussion, the AC students convinced me not to do this broadcast exercise, favoring instead a discourse analysis of a videotaped segment of TV news.]

EIGHT

Siberian Harvest: Measuring the Yield of Power-Sharing

Shared Authority Distributes the Teaching Function

"I didn't know how to share responsibility with my students," wrote Nancie Atwell in a widely read essay, "and I wasn't too sure I wanted to. I liked the vantage of my big desk; I liked setting topic and pace and establishing criteria. I liked being in charge. If responsibility for thinking and planning shifted to my students, what would *I* do?" (1985, p. 36).

Atwell took a risk and shared authority "to help students discover and act on their options." The results she recorded from her eighth-grade English classes rewarded her break with tradition, but it isn't easy for teachers to let go of unilateral authority, the only form of power relations most of us have witnessed and practiced. Even though an old saw of education says that the best way to learn something is to teach it, many teachers hesitate to authorize students to share the teaching function. Yet, the notion that teaching enables the teacher to learn the most is hard to deny because teaching requires constant exercise of our questioning and communicating habits. Intuitive and analytic, a good teacher sets an example for informed reflection and for using language critically and creatively. If these homely truths are uncontroversial, then the benefits of power-sharing for students should be apparent. By sharing authority and assuming teacherly roles, students take greater responsibility for their educations, which can translate into a more intense relationship between them and the learning process.

By opening the process to student authority, power-sharing repositions students from being cultural exiles to becoming cultural constituents, from being unconsulted curriculum-receivers to becoming collaborative curriculum-makers. In this way, a negotiated syllabus
challenges the Siberian Syndrome, creating the option for students to
be leaders and stakeholders in the process, which means they can occupy the enabling center of their educations, not the disabling margins.
Of course, not all students will buy into the process, for reasons I've
been defining throughout this book. Not all classes will develop a critical
mass of participants to pull the negotiations forward. Not all teachers
will be able to share the authority needed to open the process. Those
who accept the invitation into cogovernance will often find it difficult
to adjust to the change from unilateral to mutual decision making. The
reinvention of power is thus a contingent ideal and an unpredictable
experiment appropriate for education in a society that calls itself democratic and may yet become so.

Students Authorized as Teachers: The AC Group and the Class

When students assumed some teaching functions in the After-Class
Group, the ACG became an informal "Center for Teaching/Learning in
the Course." In this metaphorical center, the position of "the teacher"
became a multiple function. I was one locus of "the teacher" with my
agendas, executing this function by leading class sessions, by convening
the AC group, and by preparing for class at home. The AC students
with their agendas were another site of "the teacher." They assumed
some of the teaching function through critique of the process, through
participation in the regular class sessions, and through special assignments like evaluating the project committees and designing the end-
term evaluation I will discuss below. Finally, in terms of the multiple
sites of "the teacher," the class members in general, with their protest
rights, frontloaded discourse, project groups, collaborative writing, dialogic inquiries, and student-selected themes, comprised a third locus
sharing the teaching function. However, the most dramatic repositioning of "the teacher" occurred through the ACG, whose roles could be
summarized as follows:

- to offer students and me intense practice in democratic power relations;
- to advise me on how to enact my teaching role by providing me

immediate feedback from students about their experience of the learning process;
   • to socialize students into their teaching role through group reflection
after class;
   • to deliberate on curricular adjustments and then to consult with the
rest of the students about proposals receiving a consensus in the ACG;
   • to preview materials and exercises proposed by me or by students
for class activities;
   • to organize formal evaluations of the learning process;
   • to maintain momentum for democratization against the regressive
pull of traditional power relations (Siberia and teacher-talk).

Nothing this complex had occurred in our experience, so it had to be
invented as we went along.

Inventing as We Learn How to Invent: The Student-Designed Course Evaluation

As the semester reached the end, I asked the AC group to produce an
evaluation form for the class as a whole and an evaluation of the AC
process itself. Through several AC sessions, they proposed questions
to ask about the success of the Utopia class. Each AC student nominated
questions and the group then deliberated on which to include in their
self-designed course evaluation. This process could not be completed
in one day, so I collated their agenda of questions and handed them
back to the AC group for a second round of discussion. We debated
and voted on each question proposed, and those that received a majority
became part of the final evaluation. I then typed the questions and prepared forms for the class, which students replied to anonymously. Here
is the student-authored AC evaluation sheet (the first two questions of
which I already cited in the last chapter):

ENGLISH 359—UTOPIAS—COURSE EVALUATION
1. Has this class opened you up to new ideas and changed your way of
thinking? How?
2. Do you feel motivated to take action in student or civic government
or in other classes to change things?
3. Did we spend too much time on only one book, topic or discussion?
If yes, explain:
4. Were the books used in this class wise choices in teaching us about
Utopian societies? Do you feel motivated to read more Utopian books?

5. Was the use of our "grading contract" a good idea? Explain:

6. Were the CSI and NYC improvement groups a good way to stimulate us into Utopian thinking? Were the presentations a good use of class time?

7. What suggestions would you give the instructor to improve this class in the future?

8. What were the most important things you learned from this class?

9. Would you recommend this class to your friends?

10. What was the best thing you liked about this class?

11. Did the teacher stimulate your interest?

12. Was your presence necessary in this class?

13. Did you do more written work for this class than for other 300-level classes?

14. Did you do more reading in this class than in other 300-level classes?

15. Did you participate more here than in other classes?

16. Is this a good evaluation form? Do you think the questions asked here are good ones?

I suggested question 16, asking students in class to evaluate the AC-designed evaluation sheet itself. In anonymous responses, non-AC students were generally positive about the ACG form:

- "These questions were excellent questions. They precisely demonstrate the way the course was taught and the way the teacher is concerned with student opinion and expression. Once again I was given the opportunity to express my opinion!"
- "Some questions were good, and others can't be answered completely in such a small space. I don't like essay questions on an evaluation form."
- "This evaluation is an excellent idea and essential in learning how your students reacted to your class. These were great questions."
- "Good idea, lets the teacher get feedback and makes it easier to plan curriculum for future classes."

However, as my colleague Diane Tedick pointed out in a note to me, this AC form ignored an important issue—the degree to which students learned from each other. Did they begin experiencing each other as knowledge-makers, or did they remain fixed on the authoritative teacher as the sole source of subject matter? That issue needed a profile on the ACG form.

Still, this student-designed evaluation was situated in the discourse we had been mutually creating, not a computer-scored official form sent in bureaucratically and then sent back out. It differed markedly from the generic evaluation questionnaire required by the College and given out at the end of the term in each class, which asks students for agreement or disagreement with the following:

1. Given the nature of the course, the instructor stimulated my interest.
2. I could NOT tell what the important objectives of the course were.
3. With the instructor I felt comfortable asking questions and/or expressing my opinions.
4. I learned a lot in this course.
5. I found the instructor's classes generally well prepared.
6. The instructor was not available during office hours.
7. I thought the examinations fairly represented the major topics of the course.
8. The instructor did NOT present the topics covered in the course in a logical order.
9. I found the instructor's written comments on my assignments and/or exams helpful.
10. I found the examples effectively clarified the material of the course.
11. The instructor seemed to know when students were having difficulty with the material.
12. The instructor WASTED much of the time in this class.
13. I liked the way the course was taught.

The College form also asked for the following information:

14. So far this semester, how many times has the instructor been absent for the scheduled classes . . .
15. My overall grade point average to date is . . .
16. My expected grade for this course is . . .

Comparing the official and unofficial forms was a good harvest exercise in class. It showed how a negotiated process produces different materials and experiences than a traditional one. Situated in the students' actual experience, the questions on the ACG sheet represent students reflecting on their learning, asking themselves what is important to ask about their education, to know its value in their own terms. In the comparison in class, I was not surprised to find that most students preferred the AC form to the College one. In fact, I later discovered that defiant Angela had written in big letters the following protest on the College sheet: "THIS EVALUATION FORM IS NOT APPLICABLE!"

The ACG form could also be described as an instrument of

domain-specific metacognition, that is, a context-based means through which students can critique their own cognition or learning. It enabled critical reflection by students about a specific domain of their experience. Context-based thinking in the students' own idioms enables critical thought because it structures a close relationship between their language, thought, and reality. Critical reflection in this mode is rhetorical action on the specific materials of an experience. On the ACG form, the questions came from students and were about the students, who possessed the background knowledge needed to make informed judgments. This student-centered model of reflecting on learning (metacognition) facilitates their competence and confidence in thinking critically (Bruer 1993). Thus, before anyone glibly asserts that students "can't think" or "don't think" or "won't think," it is good to question the context and idiom of the rhetorical setting, by asking, "Who is requesting them to think about what, at which moment, in what place, for what purpose, in what way, through what format and what idiom?"

On the whole, in the responses to the ACG evaluation form, I would say that students had largely positive feelings about the class. In their anonymous replies to questions 1 and 2, about how the course affected them, they wrote:

- "I am now more concerned about the environment and how to help save it."
- "I think about things more thoroughly than before."
- "It has made me realize all the serious faults of society and that we can't just sit around and wait for change to happen, we have to get out and become active."
- "The class has definitely changed my ways of thinking because I now know that there is more to problem solving than just coming up with a solution. I am more environmentally aware than I was before I read *50 Simple Things* . . . I will speak up in other classes when I feel the teacher is being unfair or wasting time."
- "I have been questioning the status quo for some time now, but through this course I have gained further awareness and ideas. The course really did not change my way of thinking although it did strengthen my ideas."
- "I learned about alternative life styles and ideas . . . To think beyond how I usually think . . . Being able to disagree and voice opinions . . . The books were good choices as an introduction to Utopian societies."
- "The ability to learn from myself."

- "Before this class, I wasn't so fully aware of the environmental crisis and the things we can do to help. I have changed my way of thinking because I was taught to think and think and think. It was a little frustrating when the thinking and solutions turned out to be dead ends. However, it made me think! . . . Make education happen for you, not to you!"
- "Questioning the status quo, social engineering, and decision-making are different ways of recognizing and solving problems than I have known in the past."
- "I feel that you should read more interesting books but in the future don't make one topic drag on, like the Gulf War and like the groups . . . I like that whenever we had a problem we could discuss it out loud and come to an agreement if we all wanted it or not . . . I felt I could be more open in this Utopia class than I can in any other class. I felt more comfortable in this class."
- "Add a book, use less improvement groups . . . The atmosphere presented by the teacher was a very comfortable speaking forum. I felt comfortable expressing my opinion."
- "I am no longer so easily convinced of anything when I hear things on the news. I have become more critical of the way things are in our society . . . I think we spent too much time on the group reports. We should have read at least one more book . . . Give us more concrete examples we can relate to . . . "
- "Talk a little less . . . Very flexible teacher."
- "I feel more compelled to act upon my futuristic beliefs . . . I've more of an open mind when it comes to problem solving, in regards to the city. In other words, I look at more angles than before . . . I don't think we spent enough time discussing the problems in NYC, because I feel this city needs action now."

Almost half of the students indicated they would consider taking action to make change—"Because things are not going to change on their own," as one wrote. But, others were ambivalent or negative about acting on what they learned:

- "Yes and no. Yes because I am beginning to think that things can change if you make them change—but no because it's not easy and you can run into dead ends."
- "It depends on how I can schedule my time."
- "I am sorry but I am not motivated to take action in student or civic government or other classes because I have 5 courses left."

- "In a way I do but I don't think I ever will. I have become a pessimist over the years and do not think that I can make a big difference."

The choice to become a change-agent in school and society is not an easy one, especially in a political climate dominated by a strident "conservative restoration" (see Shor, *Culture Wars*, 1992a). In everyday life, across three decades of conservative resurgence at the end of the century, the dominant themes were "settling for less," "making do with less," "doing more with less," "working harder for less," and "paying more for less." Budget cuts, tuition rises, regressive tax increases, job losses (corporate "downsizing" and "restructuring"), real wage declines, price increases, and attacks on affirmative action, union rights, civil rights, abortion rights, education rights, and gay rights made the last years of the twentieth century an embattled, "fear of falling" time for average people (see Ehrenreich 1989; Schor 1991; Cassidy 1995; Sheehan 1995).

Besides the austerity of the conservative times in which I experimented with critical pedagogy and power-sharing, there was also a low profile for dissident groups. When social movements and activist organizations are marginal on campus and off, teachers and students have more trouble acting on their social criticisms, their knowledge, and their desires for change. In reactionary times, critical thought and feeling in a single classroom are more isolated from larger contexts which could develop the student's political interests. It takes more energy, courage, idealism, and ingenuity to find dissident space in a conservative climate. Under these conditions, the Utopia class served as a small "safe house" (to use a term from Pratt's theory of "contact zones"), where critical thought about knowledge and society had some protected breathing room (even though the basement space was underground and windowless).

Room to Rethink the Course: What Worked and What Didn't Work

On the evaluation sheet, students expressed split opinions about the project reports on improving New York City and the College. Some said these just dragged on, while others said they deserved more time. Those opposed wrote comments like these:

- "Don't try to cover so much—cut down groups."
- "There were too many groups and not all the students came up with Utopian ideas."

- "I think we spent too much time on the CSI and City improvements. They became long, boring, and tiresome. There should have been a time limit and we should have stuck to it."
- "I believe that too much time was spent on the group presentations. The time spent on the literature and class discussions were of interest."

Those favorable to the project groups wanted more of the same:

- "I feel that all the discussion was useful, and that it's more time we need not less discussion."
- "There was not enough time spent."

On the whole, however, as I indicated before, I agree with the student criticism that we should have had one less round of project reports and should have studied one or two more books.

About the three books we did read, class opinions again varied, with some positive feelings along with the strong dislike of *Walden II*. Many endorsed *50 Simple Things You Can Do To Save the Earth* but didn't want to talk about it in class as much as we did, even though it was an environmental eye-opener and practical "green-consumer" guide they enjoyed. The novel *Ecotopia* was very popular for reading and discussion. This is, I think, partly a tribute to author Ernest Callenbach's engaging style and imagination. He blended a Utopian novel with a political thriller, an imaginary voyage, and a passionate love story, punctuated by some exotic rituals like the notorious War Games I discussed earlier. There were no such narrative pyrotechnics in Skinner's text. Callenbach the imaginative writer did what Skinner the behavioral scientist could not do—tell a love story while inventing a modern Utopia. *Ecotopia* was also popular because it was more contemporary than Skinner's *Walden II*, especially in its attitudes toward sexuality and relationships and in its discussion of themes closer to our times, like racial conflict, high-tech innovation, and environmentalism. Skinner's pedantic narrative was often denounced as boring, as I indicated, but some students did say they liked it and others learned about Utopia from it despite its style. I plan to expand the reading list, to ask students to choose what we should read and in what order. As I said earlier, I did just this in a later course called "The Teaching of Writing," where graduate students brought in reading materials to fill out half the reading list, while I provided the other half. In addition, since the Utopia basement, I routinely ask all of my students to bring in reading material, to choose sections of books for reading, and to set the order of reading as well. More recently, I experimented with a different form of student authority vis-à-vis the reading list: I gave readings each week to one freshman composition class where I asked the students to review the text by rating it from 1 to 10 on a scale of low-interest to high-interest and to write what they think the material is about and why they gave it the score they did. I read their reviews, wrote notes back to them, tabulated the scores, and reported the average score in the next class session, consulting with the students on whether the average score was high enough in their opinion to nominate this specific text for extended discussion and writing. So far, this one class suggested that a minimum score of 8 qualifies a reading for formal inclusion in the syllabus. While these freshman students brought in and reviewed their own reading choices, they gave a score of 8 to *only one* of my selected texts, even though they read and wrote about all of the ones I had suggested. In this power-sharing, my authority to propose and their authority to dispose created a dual reading list—one short and formal, the other long and informal.

I doubt that the troublesome book *Walden II* would score an 8 in student reviews. I've received so much heat about Skinner's text that I often think of eliminating it. Students across several semesters have insisted that *Walden II* is a bloody bore. I find its egalitarian social policies challenging and worthy of discussion. But, I am a professor after all, which means that I have a greater stake in academic texts than they do. It's my job to study important, albeit dull texts, like Skinner's and like Dewey's, where deadly wooden prose abounds. In graduate school, I was trained to tolerate boredom as the price of gaining admission to academe. Knowing the peculiarity of my intellectual development, I have to allow for the students' suggestion that putting up with a book's boredom may not be equal to its rewards. But, it won't be easy for me to let go of some books, especially because I'm a slow reader who talks with a book as I read it.

Negative student evaluation of *Walden II* was accompanied by some other student criticisms of the Utopia class. For example, a group of responses denounced the grading contracts: "Everyone should be required to do the same amount of work and then graded according to what they accomplish," one student wrote. Another also protested that "all students should be expected to do the same amount of required assignments." This sentiment in class preferred traditional grading, with me the teacher exercising unilateral authority. A third student claimed that "Many did not live up to" the contracts. But, in tracking the students' performances, I found that eighteen of the twenty-nine who finished the course lived up to the terms of their contracts. Some claimed that it took too much time to negotiate them, a sentiment I heard again from several students in a later journalism course, even though that class as a whole voted 17 to 7 in favor of the contracting process. Another Utopia student asserted that "I don't want a grade before I have seen what the work is like. I felt I had to choose too early. Grades should be given out at the end." A sixth criticism was that "I don't like sticking to a contract," and a seventh protest was textually yelled at me through abundant use of the exclamation point: "It wouldn't stimulate someone to go for a higher grade if they knew all they had to do was a certain amount of work for a certain grade. Bad idea!!!" Still another student replied that "it will allow people to settle for a grade and know that they can't do better so why try. I feel some of the points may have been too strict, however, I didn't argue that when the contract was being made and that's my fault. In a Utopian society, we would not have grades." For a final protest about contract grading, a student wrote that "this just categorizes students from day one. Someone may have settled for a B so they didn't have to get up in front of the class twice. I don't feel this is fair."

Still, despite the protests and complaints, a majority of students in the Utopia class approved of the contract grading process. Here are some of their positive remarks:

- "It gave students a clear understanding of what was expected of them for whatever grade they wanted to receive."
- "It was an excellent idea. I was definitely motivated to get the grade (A) I contracted for."
- "It was good for me because it gave me a list of things I knew I had to do in order to get the grade I wanted. I knew if I did everything on the list I would get the grade."
- "The criteria wasn't a mystery like in most classes. The grading contract was better than a syllabus."
- "They were a good way to stimulate us but I think we spent too much time on them."
- "It made me feel committed."
- "It gave me an idea of what I am in for as well as what I am responsible for."

In the later journalism class I mentioned, where a majority of students endorsed the contracts, some wrote similar (unedited) comments:

- "The negotiations were great . . . Definitely keep using this system. The classroom shouldn't be a dictatorship, the students should be able to take part in deciding the curriculum."
- "These were great! I wish all classes had contracts. It give us something to live by & strive for."

My habit now with the contract negotiations is to test student resistance with several votes, usually soon after the first day of negotiations, then a week or two later, and then four to six weeks after that. Each time, I ask students to write anonymously their opinions of the contract process. At any time, if 40 percent vote it down I will consult with the ACG about ending the contract and negotiation experiments. Only a strong majority vote authorizes my confidence to keep this practice in place. Another choice students voted for in a more recent class was to treat the contract as general grading guidelines not individually signed by students, so that they have public, visible, negotiated standards to live up to without feeling prematurely constrained to sign up for a specific grade.

While some Utopia students resented contracting and a majority approved it, a response of others was to regularly *renegotiate*. Each session, I would routinely start class by saying out loud the following, "Are there any questions, suggestions, proposals, complaints, or objections?" With this verbal cue followed by my patient look around the room inviting people to speak, some students did ask for various renegotiations. For example, in the Utopia class, one young woman proposed a week's extension on a paper deadline. When I asked for explanation and discussion before we voted on this, she and others said that they have midterms this week in biology, or accounting, or nursing, or mechanical tech, etc., and can't fit in the Utopia paper. I then said, "Why don't you ask the bio professor or the accounting teacher to put off the test until next week because you have a Utopia paper due?" They instantly replied they couldn't do that. "Why not?" I asked. "Because those professors don't negotiate the curriculum," they answered. At this moment, the students were enjoying the negotiating process far more than I was; once again, I was caught in a pickle of my own persuasions and felt morally obliged to extend the deadline. This is another instance of what I mean by "the discomforts of democracy," or more precisely, the contradictions of offering a lone negotiated course in a traditional College where teacher-talk and unilateral authority dominate across the curriculum.

While most students said they couldn't negotiate with other teachers, some wanted to initiate power-sharing in other courses and asked my advice privately. I replied that protest is always risky ("not a weekend on a tropical beach," as Paulo Freire put it [Shor and Freire 1987]). But, protest is harder and more risky when you do it by yourself ("confronting the lion alone," to use another metaphor from Freire). Change-agency tends to be more productive and more secure when attempted collaboratively (safety in numbers) and planned well beforehand. I suggested they could speak with other students outside of their other classes to see if anyone else felt like initiating negotiation. Find out who might join in approaching the professor, I said, and then talk over in advance how to do it and what to ask for, with some sense of priorities, that is, clarify what matters most to negotiate for and what matters least. Allow some "wiggle room" in the negotiations by having fall-back positions from your main objectives that you can live with in case the discussion bogs down. Soften the confrontational aspects by approaching teachers privately, in a quiet group after class, not startling them with unannounced interventions during class, which would likely make teachers angry, defensive, and dig in their heels to show who's boss. In addition, I suggested that it makes sense to approach instructors from the credible position of "good" students who do the work. Being academically serious builds up what I've written about elsewhere as "deviance credits" or the earned right to deviate from and to question the status quo by having participated credibly in some aspects of the existing regime. Further, it's a good idea to "sweeten" the discussion by telling the teacher immediately what you like about the course. A few Utopia students did approach a professor in another course but, unfortunately, were dismissed out of hand by him.

As I've acknowledged often in this book, negotiation and contract grading will not be accepted easily by teachers or students, given the long-term habits we develop for unilateral authority. A grand cultural canyon yawns between education and democracy, which simply represents the distance society itself has to travel to reach the democracy it claims to already offer. To the extent that contract grading can help bridge the gap by extending some authority to students, it is valuable. In some classes, I have reached across the power canyon by using peer-groups to develop individual provisions of the contract rather than deliberating as a "committee of the whole." In the peer-group approach, I asked students to form small groups for each specific item on the proposed contract I handed out. These peer-groups then debated the particular provision I proposed, and recommended its acceptance, amendment, major revision, or rejection. One student in an earlier class wrote about the peer-group form of contracting that

> This exercise made everyone think about a way to make the class meet their standards. Not everyone got their way but they had the chance to state their opinions. This forced the class to negotiate and finally come up with a compromise that pleased the majority of the class. We started off with a set of rules that we had never seen before. We read them over and could have had no choice but to accept them. Instead we began to give our individual thoughts about it. Then we discussed in a group of three. We then compromised in a group of six. We then compromised among the entire class until we came up with a compromise to satisfy the majority, if not the whole class. This was a long process because it becomes complicated when conflicting opinions exist. It is nearly impossible not to have various different positions on issues in a large group. This is what Utopians want to achieve—a better society even if it involves many steps.

In another form of shared authority, in one class the students read and graded each other's written work, in addition to my reading and evaluating their papers. Each student's paper was read by two other students who put comments and grades on it. Every written assignment was brought to class in three xerox copies, one for me and two for peer student readers. This gave students multiple responses to their writing. On the whole, this process took careful organizing and preparatory discussion about giving helpful feedback. It also produced a greatly expanded paper trail (an environmental issue in terms of the paper consumed, which some Utopia students protested) and took up some class time to administrate. In general, though, students have liked peer editing groups, so I will continue this now-familiar activity in English education.

One problem, however, is that students dislike giving grades to each other, a practice that can be dispensed with, I think. They can simply write comments to each other without having to assign a letter grade. In any case, they tend to grade each other high because they want to avoid making enemies. Grading is divisive. It divides teachers from students and students from each other. Some students (and teachers) solve the problem by largesse, sprinkling high grades everywhere. For example, during the Utopia project reports on improving New York and the College, the AC students who evaluated each group's oral presentation often gave A and A−, which I thought was generously high.

Students may give each other high grades, but they do know geese from swans. By that I mean that most can tell a critical, engaging oral report or written paper from a superficial or sloppy one. Some students will bother to exercise careful judgment by writing detailed comments on peer-students' work. But at the point where written evaluation ends and the awarding of a letter grade begins, a political reality comes into play. When it comes to "payday" (giving grades) the decent thing from the students' point of view is to become socialists or to play Santa Claus. They generously distribute the available wealth (high grades) by giving a B+ to an A whenever possible. I don't distribute A grades the way they do when they are asked to grade each other. I would argue that the students' separation of evaluation from grading—that is knowing whether a student performance is A-quality or not while preferring to give at least B+ no matter what the performance—is their way of protecting their relationships, as peers in the same boat reluctant to undermine each other for a teacher or an education system. This is their unacknowledged class solidarity—giving high grades to each other and expecting reciprocal generosity when it comes their turn to be graded. It's an understandable and equitable way to behave.

Giving high grades to peers undermines grading as a discipline device of authority, thus offering students a way to resist control. Through this kind of resistance, students gum up the works, not with frontal assaults but with small opportunistic jabs. Unlike bold Angela, the Utopia timekeeper, most students are more at ease putting up with or quietly undermining the unilateral regime of the teacher and the institution. As Jack in the AC group wrote, "Students will never let a teacher know if they do not like the way the class is being taught. The students will just accept the way a class is taught (no matter how bad) for fear of his or her scholastic standing (the teacher might be biased when grading the student)." Jack is right to beware a teacher's power to flunk him, because grades in education are the equivalent of wages at work. Who can live without money? Who can stay in college with a transcript full of D's or F's?

Grading the Course: Critical Words from Students

What did the students write anonymously as the most important things they learned in the Utopia class?

- "To think beyond how I usually think."
- "To look more toward the future."

- "The ability to learn for myself."
- "Make education happen for you, not to you, and how to speak up and express your opinion honestly and openly."
- "The severe damage going on in our environment! How the budget crisis is severely affecting everyone—it needs to be solved."
- "I learned about Utopian societies and how they differ."
- "How to get to the roots of a problem. To respect nature and our environment. To care about life. To hope for a brighter future."
- "I'm more aware of different angles to look at problems. I feel more compelled to act upon my futuristic beliefs."
- "I learned that life can be much better."

What did they identify as the best thing they liked about the class?

- "Being able to disagree and voice opinions."
- "Ecotopia."
- "Class discussions."
- "Contract grading, Ecotopia, and other students."
- "Open discussion, everyone's opinions welcome."
- "Discussing things in groups, the classroom atmosphere, the fact that it was not a lecture, and there was constant active student participation."
- "There isn't any best thing."
- "Whenever we had a problem we could discuss it out loud and come to an agreement."

What suggestions would they give me to improve this class in the future?

- "Don't try to cover so much."
- "Require more reading material."
- "Cut off discussions when they become too long."
- "Be open about lateness."
- "No opinion."
- "Add a book, use less improvement groups."
- "Spend more time discussing how to change NYC instead of reading books."
- "Read more books."

This motherlode of discourse generated by the AC evaluation form has kept me thinking in the many months since. In a concrete way, the students had become teachers, clarifying for themselves what they had learned and experienced while also teaching me how to become a better teacher.

Evaluating the ACG: The Promise of a Critical-Democratic Process

The ACG itself also needed to be evaluated. From week to week, it had become a small legend to non-AC students. I mentioned earlier that some regular students began visiting after class to sit in on our deliberations, out of curiosity, not for credit. The ACG had a purposefulness and congeniality at the same time that it sometimes made me squirm in my fiberglass seat when the students bluntly criticized my teaching.

The AC students' evaluations of the AC process itself were all favorable except for Stephanie's, which I will present below. First, here is a sampling of the favorable remarks:

LISA: It's a terrible shame that this seems to be the only class I can speak of which drew upon such a valuable resource so efficiently. Most of us have been denied this opportunity for the most part, forced to sit through boring lectures, with only a textbook to rely on.

SAMMY: The after-class group has been one of the best experiences that I have had in my two years of college. Most professors do not care whether students are enjoying their class or if the students have ideas which could improve the class. With the after-class group, we, the students, are involved in a no holds barred discussion where we can express our feelings and ideas about the class . . . I also enjoyed the after-class group because it made me feel important . . . I felt like my voice and opinion did matter. What I said was taken seriously and I was able to see my ideas employed in future class discussions . . . I also found it refreshing to see a teacher open to change and willing to listen to people who challenge his methods. You held no grudges and were always willing to improve or even change your methods. This was something I never got to experience before and greatly appreciated . . . The after-class group, most of all, helped to solidify the ideas I learned in class. The topics which generated the most interest during class were brought out even further in the after-class group . . . In conclusion, the after-class group was a great idea and should be continued. I also feel that more people could benefit from this group. Maybe you could include more people in it. [NOTE: These positive comments were from the business major who complained to me that this was more of a civics course than an English course and who protested that it should be called "How To Become an Activist" instead of "Utopias."]

LAURIE: I must add that we all (including the teacher) looked forward to the after class meetings . . . I think the objective was achieved and then some. Classes seemed to flow smoothly. Students often complained that the class went too fast. I feel that being part of the after class group I gained more out of the class then those who were not part of the group. I say this because when you can talk to the teacher on a level where you are helping him run the class it changes your whole attitude toward the teacher and learning. You feel like your taking hold of your education, like your an inspector making sure you and your class get the most you can out of the experience. . . . I find myself questioning the way other classes are being taught and how effective this after class group would be in all of my classes . . . I think the people in my after class group and I received extra information on the day's lesson. Everyone had good ideas about what happened that day and since the group was small, everyone had the chance to speak . . . I felt that I was sitting in on something new and wonderful. It was a comforting feeling, one that I hope will not end with this class.

JACK: I really liked being part of the after-school evaluation group. I understood the class discussion much better by being part of the group, since we discussed things in more detail after school. We were allowed to state our opinion on how the class was going . . . It was like we made up the schedule for the teacher . . . I wish more teachers would take the time and ask the students how they think the class is going and if they have any advice on how to change it for the better, I feel more students would learn better this way and would be more interested in the class. The after-school evaluating group is a great idea and it should be done in more classes.

MAUREEN: I feel that the after-class group was a great asset to the class. Having this group gave the students a chance to have a say in what goes on in class. Instructors usually have the attitude that they plan the lesson and teach it, with the after-class group we were told what was planned and then asked what we thought about it . . . Many students don't get the privilege of being able to criticize things that the instructor does, this is very important because then the instructor knows what he or she can do to motivate the students. I feel that the group worked extremely well because now as we reach the end I can see that everyone is very honest and open about what they liked and did not like in class, we are not intimidated to tell the instructor how we really feel . . . I think every instructor should have a group like this, then maybe with the help of the students they can make their classes more interesting and keep the students motivated.

JEREMY: The group made the students question the status quo of a situation they were involved in . . . it was a lesson in utopian thinking, which is what we were trying to learn . . . there are many people who almost never question the status quo . . . and when those people do question the status quo they feel as though it can't be changed . . . This group is showing people that it is possible to make changes in the status quo . . . they realize that things don't have to be just the way they are . . . This doesn't mean that every student in the group is going to go out and devote their life to making positive changes in society, but perhaps, when an alternative is brought up they will look upon it with an open mind and take action.

Jeremy, a thoughtful, quiet young activist unique in the class, also had a reservation about the AC group: ". . . it's decisions should never be allowed to go into effect without the class discussing and voting on them (and I don't think they were)." His point was that while the AC group is far more democratic an arrangement than classes run unilaterally by the teacher, the democratic responsibility of the group is to seek the consent of the whole class for its proposals.

The one negative evaluation came from Stephanie, the bright and dissatisfied transfer student I've written much about. She thought that the AC group spent too much time discussing material from the regular class and not enough time critiquing the class process. Stephanie objected to the very thing that most of the others praised, the extra time in a small-group setting to pursue class topics in depth: "Unfortunately, I don't feel that this group really tackled the task it set out to tackle. Too often the group turned into a seminar style continuation of the class it purported to study. When we did actually discuss the class occurrences, we frequently complained about things with which we were unhappy and yet offered few solutions." She also suggested that it would have been better to divide the AC session into three segments: "one in which we individually voiced our opinions about the class, another in which we discussed them as a group and a third in which we offered ways in which to improve the situations." Further, Stephanie proposed that the AC group should do "more frequent evaluations of the class. This would keep us thinking and seeing analytically throughout the semester." I liked some of these suggestions and have been doing more frequent in-class evaluations. In addition, concerning too much time devoted to the seminar aspect of the ACG, I remind myself in current ACGs to bring the discussion back to that issue when it spends too long as a post-class seminar on the subject matter of the course.

Stephanie's final words were disapproving: "What I believed would be an English class turned out to be a civics class . . . the role of the teacher in assisting the student in studying, unraveling and interpreting the text is irreplaceable." Her statement seems to long for the intense, close reading of texts offered in the small classes at the elite private college she left before arriving at our mass institution. The working students who are the typical clients of my College often want intense, small-group education; this is why the AC evaluations stress the value of the smaller group to their learning and why AC groups since then have all spontaneously assumed the mini-seminar format at the students' initiative. I always begin ACG sessions by asking how the class went, what worked well and didn't work well, to focus on reviewing the process, yet students consistently want to examine the subject matter of the previous class in greater detail. The ones who want a post-class mini-seminar are obviously hungry for an intellectual intensity and intimacy which is hard to produce in the large classes of a mass college. They have not had small seminars in their educational lives. These are luxuries available only to an elite at certain high-tuition private schools and colleges. So, they use their authority to make the ACG a small class after the big class, as well as an evaluation process.

Small seminars are a class luxury denied to the students I teach. Through the ACG, a piece of that luxury became available to a handful of students. I was in a position to donate my time to make this small luxury possible, teaching after class without compensation. It was easy for me to do this because I am a college professor who does not have to teach four to five courses on different campuses like some adjuncts do, or teach five classes a day five days a week, like schoolteachers do; I'm employed full-time at the higher salary paid to college faculty as compared with that of adjuncts and schoolteachers; I do not have to moonlight on a second job and am not raising children who require extra income as well as extra attention as soon as parents can get home; I am also a white male teacher whose authority to propose an experimental project benefitted from the privileged position of my race and gender. Thus, I had the time, energy, interest, income, skin color, and gender authority to support my informal teaching of an unpaid experimental seminar after the regular Utopia class. Schoolteachers with greater workloads and lesser pay; adjuncts, part-timers, substitutes, and untenured junior faculty with low-wage jobs and too many courses to teach in too many places; teachers with young children or elderly parents to look after; teachers of color and women; all would generally not have the same freedom or authority I had to stay after class several times a week to benefit my development and that of the students. I'd have to conclude that I occupied a privileged position that helped me schedule in the AC group. Then again, the AC students were also privileged in some ways relative to their peers: They were the students who did not have to run out of the regular class at 3:40 to go to jobs, families, or other classes. They had enough free time just at that moment to take part in something that other students may have had to pass up for lack of hours or income or childcare. These are the constraints we work under at a nonelite commuter college. Despite them, the AC group was still able to break through some limits and open new ground, including the offer of an intense post-class seminar to working students who rarely if ever receive such lavish academic attention.

The ACG was thus legitimized to all but one of the AC students by becoming an intense seminar on the content of the course while critiquing/codeveloping the syllabus. It was not mere talk, I would say. Working students are impatient with talk that is mere intellectualizing. This process was not an abstract exchange of high-status theorizing or a truckload sale of puffed-up professorial words. Instead, the ACG was an experiment within an experiment whose practice involved reflecting on our education so as to take further educated action. It enjoyed an experiential immediacy that made the ACG meaningful to most students, who could use this group to address the concrete and subjective reality of the course itself. As a concrete form of power-sharing, the ACG appeared to increase the cultural capacities of the students, understanding "culture" here in the Deweyan sense of the ability to perceive and to act on meaning in your social experience, and in the Freirean sense of culture being the power to use thought, discourse, and action to understand and change your conditions, which Lev Vygotsky explored as the developmental or "bootstrapping" potential of reflective language. The AC students could see that their deliberations influenced the class as well as influencing their own individual learning via the mini-seminar aspect of the sessions and the cogovernance aspect of the process. This gave tangible purpose to the group and saved it from being a pointless, powerless bull session, rap session, or gripe session. For many students, critical thought is attractive when it connects purposefully to action, subjective feeling, and immediate experience.

If teachers and institutions took the students' advice and made the AC group a credited feature of every course, that would be a major reform in education, a major step toward cultural democracy and against unilateral authority. It would address some, but not all, of the inequity issues in school and society, with questions of gender, race, and sexual orientation still to be dealt with to make the process multi-culturally democratic. And, of course, other global issues would remain: unequal funding of elite and mass institutions, class size, the vast exploitation of adjunct instructors in higher education, the underpayment and overwork of schoolteachers, the ocean of standardized testing, the persistence of tracking, etc. Democratic practices in one classroom do not mean that school and society have been democratized, not even that my Department or my College have been democratized. Students leaving the Utopia class and the AC group faced unilateral authority at every turn, in every course, in every social institution and workplace. The Siberian Syndrome, disrupted but not dispersed in the Utopia basement, remained undisturbed elsewhere, even in classrooms with big windows.

Windows on a Harvest Moon: Angela's Last Word

A final word from Angela the defiant timekeeper can help end this story. Because of her radical intervention against required attendance during the contract negotiation, I was thrown into a quandary in those first hours when I feared losing the class if I agreed to unlimited absences. I also feared undermining the process of negotiation if I simply overruled her. This dilemma led to my intuited offer of protest rights and the AC group. I'm indebted to her for pushing me into things I had not planned to do. I think that she and the others taught me more and changed me more than I was able to teach them or change them.

Angela was the midwife of the AC group but she did not serve in it. She couldn't stay after class because she had to go to work. Her cohort, Doug the tall bio major, couldn't join the ACG either because he was too busy applying to eleven medical schools, one of which belittled his upcoming baccalaureate degree because he attended our no-name budget college, until we both sighed in relief when another school finally accepted him. I still wonder what the ACG might have been like if those two could have stayed. And I would have paid a lot to watch AC debates between Angela from the working class and Stephanie from the elite college. But, *during* class, Angela and Doug were regularly involved, and Angela faithfully performed her role as timekeeper. When 3:40 came, her hand went up, even if I was in mid-sentence, except once, when at 3:40 I was not quite finished with some passionate remarks on Utopia, which I delivered in a style worthy of my doctorate, casting a worried eye in her ticking direction, grateful that she did not swing her unforgiving arm and cut me off, until my last inflated words expired, and then, after a few seconds of silence, her hand flew up, and the basement chamber emptied.

Well, I asked students to write me a letter at the end, after the contracts were fulfilled and the final grades already done, telling me what they had learned in the course. Here is Angela's farewell note:

> Dear Mr. Shor,
>
> During this semester I have learned more in this class than all of my others put together. Most importantly, I learned about the environment and how it is being destroyed. I am leaving this class with a new awareness of the environment, and a new concept of how I think and act. All of the Utopian principles and the 4 R's [repair, recycle, re-use, reduce consumption] will be of use to me in my lifetime. In addition, I have grown mentally from being confronted with large complex problems in our society. Some of the things that you have asked me to think about have pushed my mind to its outermost limits, and that active learning is also a valuable thing to me. To sum it up, this class was very eye opening and I really enjoyed it. I look forward to having you as a teacher next semester.

I thought to myself, Oh, no, another semester of her relentless time-keeping! But, really, I was honored by her letter.

Earlier, during one of our talks about changing the status quo, Angela insisted that she would become a change-agent in society. I asked her if she could keep it up for twenty years or more, because it isn't easy to make important social changes. Would the desire for change run out with her youth, after the routine problems of adult life and the unavoidable setbacks on the road to the future slowed her down? Absolutely not, she declared without hesitation, her sharp eyes fixed on me. So, I made an appointment with her in twenty years. I asked her to meet me in my office on a specific day in the 21st century, so we can compare notes on how we kept trying to change the system. She said she'd be there, and I've kept her sign-in sheet with its address so that I can find her and keep the appointment. That year is approaching. I hope her desires for social change stay warm, bright, and alive, and so do mine.

Afterword

by Lewis Dimmick,
Former Student

Empowering Education (Shor 1992b) was especially interesting for me to read, having formerly been a student in a fiction workshop with Ira Shor. On the first day of class we were given a contract.

> I distribute learning contracts for students to discuss and amend, as another way to negotiate the curriculum. My contracts specify three grade levels, A, B, and C. I say that if any of them start out planning to get a D or an F, I would prefer they drop the class right now, because it is a monumental waste of time to be here . . . For each grade, I usually propose different levels of participation, attendance, length of papers, number of papers, project work, books to read, and so on. I hand out the contracts, ask students to read them, discuss them, and then ask questions for whole-class negotiation. Then I ask them to take them home, think them over, and make one of three choices: sign the contract as proposed and amended in class at a specific grade level, or negotiate further changes with me individually, or throw the contract out and negotiate one of their own design. (p.159)

This was new to me, and I imagine to the rest of the class as well. I remember a student saying: "This explains everything we have to do, but where's your responsibility in all this?"

"My responsibility is to fulfill my end of the bargain," Professor Shor said.

That student did not return to class.

The importance of participation, of sharing writing, reading it aloud in class, was stressed. A student rose and left the room and never came back.

I signed for an A, although I had received very few in my college career. If I remember correctly, an A required: A's on all written work, no more than two absences, and frequent class participation. I wasn't sure if I could do all this, but felt I had to sign for an A. How could I, on the first day of class, not at least plan to do my best?

The contract makes an explicit statement: if you want to do well you have to work hard. It helped me begin with high standards. "To continue codevelopment of the curriculum, I also ask students to bring in materials, such as short stories, news articles, or magazine reports, which they think are relevant to our dialogue" (p. 244). In the fiction course, toward the end of the semester, each student brought a short story to class. Then we met in groups and read each member's story. Each group picked one story for the whole class to read. Our group picked "Lust," by Susan Minot. After the class was over, I read the rest of Minot's collection and recently used the title story in a graduate paper, comparing it with Doris Lessing's "One Off the Short List."

Picking stories to read, however, was not the only way we codeveloped the curriculum. We decided what the class talked about. The class met once a week, devoting each session to discussing one short story. Each student came to class having read the story and written a journal response, which included a question. We met in groups and read our journals aloud. We introduced our questions. We discussed the story. Finally it would be time to discuss the story as a whole class. Each group would pick one question to ask. One person from each group would read their question aloud and Professor Shor would write it down. Then he would read all of them back to us. "Which one would you like to start with?" he'd say.

As a student I was inspired. I looked forward to class. I looked forward to reading and discussing the stories. I had never felt so good about school. Upon reflection, the beautiful simplicity of it all stuns me: we decided what the class talked about. We asked the questions. And we discussed them for hours. We shaped the class. We codeveloped the curriculum. In most of my previous classes, the professor had done all of the talking. Students would doodle or sleep or intentionally disrupt class. Here we did all the talking. And I have never seen another class with students so interested and involved.

About the benefits of dialogue, as opposed to one-way teacher-talk, Shor writes:

Dialogue transforms the teacher's unilateral authority by putting limits on his or her dominating voice and calling on students to codevelop a joint learning process. The teacher opens the process to greater student participation, less student resistance, and more fertile contact with student thought and experience. (p. 90)

As a teacher, I have been inspired as well. I have used these methods in my own classes. I never cease to be amazed by the thoughtful questions students ask and the eagerness with which they involve themselves in class discussion. They know I value their ideas. They know they can say anything. They feel comfortable. They open up completely.

Reading *Empowering Education* has helped me learn to create an environment in which all of this is possible.

Bibliography

Alford, Barry, and Keith Kroll. In press. *Two-year Colleges and the Politics of Writing Instruction*. Portsmouth, NH: Heinemann.

Annas, Pam. 1985. "Style as Politics: A Feminist Approach to the Teaching of Writing." *College English* 47, no. 4: 360–72.

Anyon, Jean. 1979. "Ideology and United States History Textbooks." *Harvard Educational Review* 49 (August): 361–86.

———. 1980. "Social Class and the Hidden Curriculum of Work." *Journal of Education* 162, no. 2: 67–92.

———. 1981. "Social Class and School Knowledge." *Curriculum Inquiry* 11, no. 1: 3–42.

———. 1983. "Workers, Labor and Economic History, and Textbook Content." In *Ideology and Practice in Schooling*, edited by Michael W. Apple and Lois Weis, pp. 37–60. Philadelphia: Temple University Press.

Anzaldua, Gloria. 1987. *Borderlands/la frontera: The New Mestiza*. San Francisco: Spinsters/Aunt Lute.

Apple, Michael. 1990. *Ideology and Curriculum*, 2d ed. New York: Routledge.

Aronowitz, Stanley, and Henry A. Giroux. 1991. *Postmodern Education: Politics, Culture, and Social Criticism*. Minneapolis: University of Minnesota Press.

Atwell, Nancie. 1985. "Everyone Sits at a Big Desk: Discovering Topics for Writing." *English Journal* 74 (September): 35–39.

Auerbach, Elsa Roberts. 1992. *Making Meaning, Making Change*. Washington, DC: Center for Applied Linguistics.

Auerbach, Elsa Roberts, and associates. 1996. *From the Community to the Community: A Guidebook for Participatory Literacy Training*. Mahwah, NJ: Lawrence Erlbaum and Associates.

225

Baker, Houston A., Jr. 1993a. "Local Pedagogy; or, How I Redeemed My Spring Semester." *PMLA* 108 (May): 400–409.

———. 1993b. *Black Studies, Rap, and the Academy.* Chicago: University of Chicago Press.

Bakhtin, M. M. 1981. *The Dialogic Imagination.* Edited by Michael Holquist. Translated by Caryl Emerson and Michael Holquist. Austin: University of Texas Press.

———. 1986. *Speech Genres and Other Late Essays.* Translated by Vern W. McGee. Edited by Caryl Emerson and Michael Holquist. Austin: University of Texas Press.

Banks, James A. 1992. "African American Scholarship and the Evolution of Multicultural Education." *Journal of Negro Education* 63, no. 3: 273–86.

Banks, James A., and Cherry A. McGee Banks. 1995. *Handbook of Research in Multicultural Education.* New York: Macmillan.

Barlett, Donald L., and James B. Steele. 1992. *America: What Went Wrong?* Kansas City: Andrews and McMeel.

Barnes, Douglas. 1991. *From Communication to Curriculum,* 2d ed. Portsmouth, NH: Boynton/Cook. Originally published in 1975.

Bauer, Dale. 1990. "The Other 'F' Word: Feminism in the Classroom." *College English* 52, no. 4: 385–96.

Belanoff, Pat. 1990. "The Generalized Other and Me: Working Women's Language and the Academy." *Pre/text* 11 (1 and 2): 60–74.

Belanoff, Pat, and Marcia Dickson, eds. 1991. *Portfolios: Process and Product.* Portsmouth, NH: Boynton-Cook.

Belenky, Mary Field, and Blythe McVicker Clinchy, Nancy Rule Goldberger, and Jill Mattuck Tarule. 1986. *Women's Ways of Knowing: The Development of Self, Voice, and Mind.* New York: Basic Books.

Berlin, James A. 1984. *Writing Instruction in Nineteenth-Century American Colleges.* Carbondale: Southern Illinois University Press.

———. 1987. *Rhetoric and Reality: Writing Instruction in American Colleges, 1900–1985.* Carbondale: Southern Illinois University Press.

———. 1988. "Rhetoric and Ideology in the Writing Class." *College English* 50, no. 5: 477–94.

———. 1994. "Poststructuralism, Cultural Studies, and the Composition Classroom: Postmodern Theory in Practice." *Rhetoric Review* 11 (Fall): 16–33.

———. 1996. *Rhetoric, Poetics, and Cultures: Refiguring College English Studies.* Urbana, IL: NCTE.

Berlin, James A., and Michael Vivion. 1993. *Cultural Studies in the English Classroom.* Portsmouth, NH: Boynton-Cook, Heinemann.

Berliner, David C., and Bruce J. Biddle. 1995. *The Manufactured Crisis: Myths, Fraud, and the Attack on America's Public Schools.* Reading, MA: Addison-Wesley.

Bibby, Michael. 1993. " 'Where Is Vietnam?' Antiwar Poetry and the Canon." *College English* 55 (February): 158–78.

Bigelow, William. 1989. "Discovering Columbus: Rereading the Past." *Language Arts* 66 (October): 635–43.

———. 1990. "Inside the Classroom: Social Vision and Critical Pedagogy." *Teachers College Record* 91 (Spring): 437–48.

Bigelow, William, and Norman Diamond. 1987. *The Power in Our Hands: A Curriculum on the History of Work and Workers in the United States.* New York: Monthly Review Press.

Bigelow, William, and Barbara Miner. 1991. *Rethinking Columbus: Teaching about the 500th Anniversary of Columbus' Arrival in America.* Milwaukee: Rethinking Schools.

Bizzell, Patricia. 1994. "Contact Zones and English Studies." *College English* 56 (February): 163–69.

Bloome, David, with Rachel Bloomekatz and Petra Sander. 1993. "Literacy, Democracy, and the Pledge of Allegiance." *Language Arts* 70 (December): 655–58.

Boomer, Garth, and Nancy Lester, Cynthia Onore, and Jon Cook. 1992. *Negotiating the Curriculum: Educating for the Twenty-first Century.* London: Falmer Press.

Bowers. C. A. 1984. *The Promise of Theory: Education and the Politics of Cultural Change.* New York: Longman, Green.

Bowles, Samuel, and Herbert Gintis. 1976. *Schooling in Capitalist America: Educational Reform and the Contradictions of Economic Life.* New York: Basic Books.

Bridwell-Bowles, Lillian. 1992. "Discourse and Diversity: Experimental Writing within the Academy." *College Composition and Communication* 43 (October): 349–68.

Brier, Stephen, et al. 1989. *Who Built America: Working People and the Nation's Economy, Politics, Culture, and Society, Volumes 1 and 2.* New York: Pantheon.

Britton, James, and Tony Burgess, Nancy Martin, Alex McLeod, and Harold Rosen. 1975. *The Development of Writing Abilities (11–18).* London: Macmillan.

Brodhagen, Barbara. 1995. "The Situation Made Us Special." In *Democratic Schools,* edited by Michael Apple and James A. Beane, pp. 83–105. Alexandria, VA: Association for Supervision and Curriculum Development.

Brodkey, Linda. 1989. "On the Subjects of Class and Gender in 'the Literacy Letters.'" *College English* 51 (February): 125–41.

———. 1994. "Writing on the Bias." *College English* 56 (September): 527–47.

Brookfield, Stephen. 1987a. *Developing Critical Thinkers: Challenging Adults to Explore Alternative Ways of Thinking and Acting.* San Francisco: Jossey-Bass.

———. 1987b. *Learning Democracy: Eduard Lindeman on Adult Education and Social Change.* London: Croom Helm.

———. 1990. *The Skillful Teacher: On Technique, Trust, and Responsiveness in the Classroom.* San Francisco: Jossey-Bass.

———. 1991. "On Ideology, Pillage, Language, and Risk: Critical Thinking and the Tensions of Critical Practice." *Studies in Continuing Education* 13, no. 1: 1–14.

———. 1993. "Self-directed Learning, Political Clarity, and the Critical Practice of Adult Education." *Adult Education Quarterly* 43 (Summer): 227–42.

———. 1995. *Becoming a Critically Reflective Teacher.* San Francisco: Jossey-Bass.

Brown, Stuart C., and Theresa Enos, eds. 1993. *Defining the New Rhetorics.* Newbury Park, CA: Sage.

Bruer, John T. 1993. *Schools for Thought: A Science of Learning in the Classroom.* Cambridge, MA: MIT Press.

Bruffee, Kenneth. 1984. "Collaborative Learning and the 'Conversation of Mankind.'" *College English* 46 (November): 635–52.

———. 1993. *Collaborative Learning: Higher Education, Interdependence, and the Authority of Knowledge.* Baltimore: Johns Hopkins University Press.

Bruner, Jerome. 1986. *Actual Minds, Possible Worlds.* Cambridge, MA: Harvard University Press.

Bryant, Adam. 1994. Along Digital Path, Dead-End Jobs. *New York Times* 15 February: D1, D5.

Bullock, Richard, and John Trimbur, eds. 1991. *The Politics of Writing Instruction: Postsecondary.* Portsmouth, NH: Boynton-Cook, Heinemann.

Burke, Kenneth. 1969. *A Grammar of Motives.* Berkeley: University of California Press. Originally published in 1945.

Callenbach, Ernest. 1974. *Ecotopia.* New York: Bantam.

Campbell, JoAnn. 1992. "Controlling Voices: The Legacy of English A at Radcliffe College 1883–1917." *College Composition and Communication* 43 (December): 472–85.

Carnoy, M., D. Shearer, and H. M. Levin. 1985. *School and Work in the Democratic State.* Stanford: Stanford University Press.

Carter, Margie, and Deb Curtis. 1994. *Training Teachers: A Harvest of Theory and Practice.* St. Paul, MN: Redleaf Press.

Cassidy, John. 1995. Who Killed the Middle Class? *New Yorker* October 16: 113–16, 119–24.

Cazden, Courtney. 1988. *Classroom Discourse: The Language of Teaching and Learning.* Portsmouth, NH: Heinemann.

Christensen, Linda. 1990. "Teaching Standard English: Whose Standard?" *English Journal* 79 (February): 36–40.

Christopher, Doris Heisig. 1995. "Implementing Critical Pedagogy in Teacher Education: A Study of Student Participation in Program Planning Meetings." Ph.D. diss., University of Minnesota.

Clark, Burton R. 1960. "The Cooling-Out Function in Higher Education." *American Journal of Sociology* 65 (May): 569–76.

———. 1980. "The 'Cooling Out' Function Revisited." In *New Directions for*

Community Colleges, edited by George B. Vaughn, pp. 15–31. San Francisco: Jossey-Bass.

Cochran-Smith, Marilyn. 1991. "Learning to Teach Against the Grain." *Harvard Educational Review* 61 (August): 279–309.

Cohen, Arthur, and Florence Brawer. 1982. *The American Community College.* San Francisco: Jossey-Bass.

Cohen, Jeff, and Normon Solomon. 1993. *Adventures in Medialand: Behind the News, Beyond the Pundits.* Monroe, ME: Common Courage Press.

———. 1995. *Through the Media Looking Glass: Decoding Bias and Blather in the News.* Monroe, ME: Common Courage Press.

Coiner, Constance, ed. 1995a. *Working-Class Studies.* Special issue of *Radical Teacher* 46 (Spring).

———. 1995b. *Better Red: The Writing and Resistance of Tillie Olsen and Meridel Le Suer.* New York: Oxford University Press.

Connelly, Eileen A. J. 1994. "Parking at CSI Still a Hassle." *The Staten Island Advance*, 31 August: A15.

Coontz, Stephanie. 1995. "The American Family and the Nostalgia Trap." *Phi Delta Kappan* March: K1–K20.

Courage, Richard. 1993. "The Interaction of Public and Private Literacies." *College Composition and Communication* 44 (December): 484–96.

Cross, Patricia K. 1971. *Beyond the Open Door.* San Francisco: Jossey-Bass.

Croteau, David, and William Hoynes. 1994. *By Invitation Only: How the Media Limit Political Debate.* Monroe, ME: Common Courage.

Cuban, Larry. 1984. *How Teachers Taught: Constancy and Change in American Classrooms, 1890–1980.* New York: Longmans.

Culley, Margo, and Catherine Portuges. 1985. *Gendered Subjects: The Dynamics of Feminist Teaching.* Boston: Routledge, Kegan and Paul.

Cummins, Jim. 1989. *Empowering Minority Students.* Sacramento: California Association for Bilingual Education.

Dahlin, Amber. 1994. "A Student-written Syllabus for Second-semester English Composition." *Teaching English in the Two-Year College* 21 (February): 27–32.

Darder, Antonia. 1991. *Culture and Power in the Classroom.* Westport, CT: Greenwood, Bergin-Garvey.

DeJoy, Nancy C. 1994a. "Reconfiguring the Grounds of/for Composition: Alternative Routes to Subjectivity in the Work of James A. Berlin." *Mediations* Fall: 37–52.

———. 1994b. "James A. Berlin's Social-Epistemic Rhetoric in a Transformative Frame: A Conversation with Ira Shor." *Mediations* Fall: 5–24.

DeMott, Benjamin. 1990. *The Imperial Middle: Why Americans Can't Think Straight about Class.* New York: William Morrow and Company.

Derman-Sparks, Louise, and the ABC Task Force. 1989. *Anti-bias Curriculum: Tools for Empowering Young Children.* Washington, DC: National Association for the Education of Young Children.

Dewey, John. 1933. *How We Think*. Boston: Heath. Originally published in 1910.

———. 1963. *Experience and Education*. New York: Collier. Originally published in 1938.

———. 1966. *Democracy and Education*. New York: Free Press. Originally published in 1916.

———. 1971. *The Child and the Curriculum*. Chicago: University of Chicago Press. Originally published in 1900.

———. 1975. *Moral Principles in Education*. Carbondale: Southern Illinois University Press. Originally published in 1909.

Dews, C. L. Barney, and Carolyn Leste Law. 1995. *This Fine Place So Far from Home: Voices of Academics from the Working Class*. Philadelphia: Temple University Press.

Dillon, David. 1993. "Review of *Empowering Education*." *English Quarterly* 25, no. 1: 35–36.

Dippo, Don, and Steven A. Gelb. 1991. "Making the Political Personal: Problems of Privilege and Power in Post-secondary Teaching." *Journal of Education* 173, no. 3: 81–95.

Dougherty, Kevin J. 1991. "The Community College at the Crossroads: The Need for Structural Reform." *Harvard Educational Review* 61 (August): 311–36.

———. 1994. *The Contradictory College: The Conflict Origins, Impacts and Futures of the Community College*. Albany: State University of New York Press.

Downing, David B., Patricia Harkin, and James J. Sosnoski. 1994. "Configurations of Lore: The Changing Relations of Theory, Research and Pedagogy." In *Changing Classroom Practices: Resources for Literary and Cultural Studies*, edited by David B. Downing, pp. 3–34. Urbana, IL: National Council of Teachers of English.

Dowst, Kenneth. 1980. "The Epistemic Approach: Writing, Knowing, and Learning." In *Eight Approaches to Teaching Composition*, edited by Timothy R. Donovan and Ben W. McLelland, pp. 65–85. Urbana, IL: National Council of Teachers of English.

Dudley-Marling, Curt, and Dennis Searle. 1995. *Who Owns Learning? Questions of Autonomy, Choice, and Control*. Portsmouth, NH: Heinemann.

Ebert, T. 1991. "The 'Difference' of Postmodern Feminism." *College English* 53, no. 8: 886–904.

Ede, Lisa. 1995. *Work in Progress: A Guide to Writing and Revising*, 3d ed. New York: St. Martin's Press.

Edelsky, Carole. 1994. "Education for Democracy." *Language Arts* 71 (April): 252–57.

Ehrenreich, Barbara. 1989. *Fear of Falling: The Inner Life of the Middle Class*. New York: HarperCollins.

Elbow, Peter. 1981. *Writing with Power*. New York: Oxford University Press.

———. 1986. *Embracing Contraries: Explorations in Learning and Teaching*. New York: Oxford University Press.

———. 1991. "Reflections on Academic Discourse: How It Relates to Freshmen and Colleagues." *College English* 53 (February): 135–55.

Ellsworth, Elizabeth. 1989. "Why Doesn't This Feel Empowering?" *Harvard Educational Review* 59 (August): 297–324.

Elsasser, Nan, and Patricia Irvine. 1992. Literacy as Commodity: Redistributing the Goods. *Journal of Education* 174, no. 3: 26–40.

EXTRA! 1991. *Gulf War Coverage: A One Note Chorus—Special Issue on the Gulf War* 4, no. 3 (May 1991). A publication of Fairness and Accuracy in Reporting, New York.

50 Simple Things You Can Do to Save the Earth. 1990. Earthworks Project. Alhambra, CA: Greenleaf Publishers.

Fine, Michelle. 1987. "Silencing in Public Schools." *Language Arts* 64 (February): 157–74.

Finnan, Christine, and Henry M. Levin. 1994. "Using School Organization and Culture to Raise School Effectiveness." Paper presented at the American Educational Research Association Annual Meeting, April 1994, New Orleans.

Fishman, Stephen M. 1993. "Explicating Our Tacit Tradition: John Dewey and Composition Studies." *College Composition and Communication* 44 (October): 315–29.

Fits, Karen, and Alan W. France, eds. 1995. *Left Margins: Cultural Studies and Composition Pedagogy.* Albany, NY: State University of New York Press.

Foderaro, Lisa W. 1990. "Trying to Hold Down the Garbage Pile." *New York Times* 30 November: B1.

Foucault, Michel. 1977. *Language, Counter-memory, Practice: Selected Essays and Interviews,* translated and edited by D. F. Bouchary. Ithaca: Cornell University Press.

———. 1980. *Power/Knowledge: Selected Interviews and Other Writings,* edited by C. Gordon. New York: Pantheon.

Fox, Thomas. 1990a. *The Social Uses of Writing.* Norwood, NJ: Ablex.

———. 1990b. "Basic Writing as Cultural Conflict." *Journal of Education* 172: 65–83.

———. 1992. "Repositioning the Profession: Teaching Writing to African American Students." *Journal of Advanced Composition* 12 (Fall): 291–303.

Frankenstein, Marilyn. 1989. *Relearning Mathematics: A Different Third R— Radical Maths.* London: Free Association Books.

Freeman, Richard. 1976. *The Overeducated American.* New York: Basic.

Freire, Paulo. 1970. *Pedagogy of the Oppressed.* New York: Seabury.

———. 1981. "The People Speak Their Word: Learning to Read and Write in São Tome and Principe." *Harvard Educational Review* 51 (February): 27–30.

———. 1985. *The Politics of Education: Culture, Power, and Liberation.* Westport, CT: Greenwood, Bergin-Garvey.

———. 1993. *Pedagogy of the City.* New York: Continuum.

———. 1994. *Pedagogy of Hope: Reliving Pedagogy of the Oppressed.* New York: Continuum.

Freire, Paulo, and Donaldo Macedo. 1987. *Literacy: Reading the Word and the World*. Westport, CT: Greenwood, Bergin-Garvey.

Freire, Paulo, and Antonio Faundez. 1989. *Learning to Question: A Pedagogy of Liberation*. New York: Continuum.

Friedman, Susan Stanford. 1988. "Authority in the Feminist Classroom: A Contradiction in Terms?" In *Gendered Subjects*, edited by Margo Culley and Catherine Portuges, pp. 203–8. Boston: Routledge, Kegan and Paul.

Galbraith, John Kenneth. 1967. *The New Industrial State*. Boston: Houghton Mifflin.

Garan, Elaine M. 1994. "Who's in Control? Is There Enough 'Empowerment' to Go Around?" *Language Arts* 71 (March): 192–99.

Geertz, Clifford. 1973. *The Interpretation of Cultures: Selected Essays by Clifford Geertz*. New York: Basic Books.

———. 1983. *Local Knowledge: Further Essays in Interpretative Anthropology*. New York: Basic Books.

Gilyard, Keith. 1991. *Voices of the Self: A Study of Language Competence*. Detroit: Wayne State University Press.

Giroux, Henry A. 1983. *Theory and Resistance in Education: A Pedagogy for the Opposition*. South Hadley, MA: Bergin-Garvey.

———. 1988. *Schooling and the Struggle for Public Life*. Minneapolis: University of Minneapolis Press.

———. 1992. *Border Crossings*. New York: Routledge.

———. 1994. "Slacking Off: Border Youth and Postmodern Education." *Journal of Advanced Composition* 14 (Fall): 347–66.

Goodlad, John. 1984. *A Place Called School: Prospects for the Future*. New York: McGraw-Hill.

Goodman, Jesse. 1995. "Change without Difference: School Restructuring in Historical Perspective." *Harvard Educational Review* 65 (Spring): 1–27.

Gore, Jennifer. 1993. *The Struggle for Pedagogies*. New York: Routledge.

Goswami, Dixie, and Peter R. Stillman. 1987. *Reclaiming the Classroom: Teacher Research as an Agency for Change*. Upper Montclair, NJ: Boynton-Cook.

Graff, Gerald. 1987. *Professing Literature: An Institutional History*. Chicago: University of Chicago Press.

———. 1992. *Beyond the Culture Wars: How Teaching the Conflicts Can Revitalize American Education*. New York: Norton.

Graff, Harvey J. 1987. *The Labyrinths of Literacy: Reflections on Literacy Past and Present*. London: Falmer Press.

Gramsci, Antonio. 1971a. *The Modern Prince and Other Essays*. New York: International.

———. 1971b. *Selections from the Prison Notebooks*. New York: International.

Greene, Maxine. 1988. *The Dialectic of Freedom*. New York: Teachers College Press.

Greenwood, Scott C. 1995. "Learning Contracts and Transaction: A Natural Marriage in the Middle." *Language Arts* 72 (February): 88–96.

Greider, William. 1993. *Who Will Tell the People?* New York: Simon and Schuster.

Gross, Jane. 1993. "Combating Rape on Campus in a Class on Sexual Consent." *New York Times,* 25 September: A1.

Grumet, Madeleine. 1988. *Bitter Milk: Women and Teaching.* Amherst: University of Massachusetts Press.

Gussman, Deborah, and Wendy Hesford. 1992. "A Dialogical Approach to Teaching Introductory Women's Studies." *Feminist Teacher* 6 (Spring): 32–39.

Hacker, Andrew. 1992. *Two Nations: Black and White, Separate, Hostile, Unequal.* New York: Scribner's.

Hall, Stuart. 1980. "Cultural Studies: Two Paradigms." *Media, Culture, and Society* 2, no. 1: 57–72.

Hall, Trish. 1990. "How Youths Rallied to Dolphins' Cause." *New York Times* 18 April: C1.

Haswell, Richard H. 1983. "Minimal Marking." *College English* 45 (October): 600–604.

Harris, Joseph. 1995. "Negotiating the Contact Zone." *Journal of Basic Writing* 14 (Spring): 27–42.

Heath, Shirley Brice. 1978. *Teacher-Talk: Language in the Classroom.* Washington, DC: Center for Applied Linguistics.

———. 1983. *Ways with Words: Language, Life, and Work in Communities and Classrooms.* Cambridge: Cambridge University Press.

Hennessy, Rosemary. 1993. *Materialist Feminism and the Politics of Discourse.* New York: Routledge.

Herman, Edward, and Noam Chomsky. 1988. *Manufacturing Consent: The Political Economy of Mass Media.* New York: Pantheon Press.

Hillocks, George, Jr. 1986. *Research on Written Composition: New Directions for Teaching.* Urbana, IL: ERIC Clearinghouse on Reading and Communication Skills and the National Conference on Research in English.

Hoggart, Richard. 1992 [1957]. *The Uses of Literacy.* New Brunswick, NJ: Transaction Publishers. Originally published in 1957.

Holusha, John. 1993. "A Profitable Xerox Plans to Cut Staff by 10,000." *New York Times* 9 December: D1, D7.

hooks, bell. 1994. *Teaching to Transgress: Education as the Practice of Freedom.* New York: Routledge.

Hopfenberg, Wendy S., Henry M. Levin, and associates. 1993. *The Accelerated Schools Resource Guide.* San Francisco: Jossey-Bass.

Horner, Bruce. 1992. "Rethinking the 'Sociality' of Error: Teaching Editing as Negotiation." *Rhetoric Review* 11 (Fall): 172–99.

Horton, Myles, and Paulo Freire. 1990. *We Make the Road by Walking: Conversations on Education and Social Change.* Philadelphia: Temple University Press.

Horton, Myles, with Judith Kohl and Herbert Kohl. 1990. *The Long Haul: An Autobiography.* New York: Doubleday.

Howell, David. 1994. "The Skills Myth." *The American Prospect* (Summer): 84, 87–90.

Hurlbert, C. Mark, and Michael Blitz, eds. 1991. *Composition and Resistance.* Portsmouth, NH: Boynton-Cook, Heinemann.

Hurlbert, C. Mark, and Samuel Totten, eds. 1992. *Social Issues in the English Classroom.* Urbana, IL: National Council of Teachers of English.

Hymes, D. 1974. *Foundations in Sociolinguistics.* Philadelphia: University of Pennsylvania Press.

Illich, Ivan. 1973. *Tools for Conviviality.* New York: Harper and Row.

Irby, Janet. 1993. "Empowering the Disempowered." *English Journal* 82 (November): 50–54.

Isaac, Katherine. 1992. *Civics for Democracy: A Journey for Teachers and Students.* Washington, DC: Center for Study of Responsive Law.

Jarratt, Susan. 1991. "Feminism and Composition: The Case for Conflict." In *Contending with Words: Composition and Rhetoric in a Postmodern Age,* edited by Patricia Harkin and John Schilb, pp. 105–23. New York: MLA Press.

Jensen, Carl, ed. 1995. *Censored: The News That Didn't Make the News and Why—The Project Censored Yearbook.* New York: Four Walls Eight Windows.

Johnson, Richard. 1987. "What Is Cultural Studies Anyway?" *Social Text* 16: 38–80.

Kagay, Michael R. 1994. "From Coast to Coast, from Affluent to Poor, Poll Shows Anxiety over Jobs." *New York Times* 11 March: A14.

Kanpol, Barry. 1994. *Critical Pedagogy.* Westport, CT: Bergin-Garvey.

Karabel, Jerome. 1972. "Social Stratification and Community Colleges." *Harvard Educational Review.* 42 (November): 521–62.

Karabel, Jerome, and Steven Brint. 1989. *The Diverted Dream: Community Colleges and the Promise of Educational Opportunity in America, 1900–1985.* New York: Oxford.

Katz, Jackson. 1995. "Reconstructing Masculinity in the Locker Room: The Mentors in Violence Prevention Project." *Harvard Educational Review* 65 (Summer): 163–74.

Kirkwood, Gerri, and Colin Kirkwood. 1989. *Living Adult Education: Freire in Scotland.* Milton Keynes, UK: Open University Press.

Knoblauch, C. H., and Lil Brannon. 1984. *Rhetorical Traditions and the Teaching of Writing.* Upper Montclair, NJ: Boynton-Cook.

———. 1993. *Critical Teaching and the Idea of Literacy.* Portsmouth, NH: Boynton-Cook, Heinemann.

Koegel, Robert. 1995. "Responding to the Challenges of Diversity: Domination, Resistance, and Education." *Holistic Education Review* 8 (Summer): 5–17.

Kohl, Herb. 1984. *Basic Skills.* New York: Bantam Books.

———. 1994. *"I Won't Learn from You": And Other Thoughts on Creative Maladjustment.* New York: New Press.

Kozol, Jonathan. 1991. *Savage Inequalities: Children in America's Schools.* New York: Crown.

Kreisberg, Seth. 1992. *Transforming Power: Domination, Empowerment and Education*. Albany: State University of New York Press.

Kretovics, Joseph R. 1985. "Critical Literacy: Challenging the Assumptions of Mainstream Educational Theory." *Journal of Education* 167, no. 2: 50–62.

Kroll, Keith. 1992. "Empowering Faculty as Teacher-Researchers." In *Fostering a Climate for Faculty Scholarship at Community Colleges*, edited by James C. Palmer and George B. Vaughan, chap. 4, pp. 23–37. Washington, DC: American Association of Community and Junior Colleges.

Kuhn, Thomas. 1962. *The Structure of Scientific Revolutions*. Chicago: University of Chicago Press.

Kutz, Eleanor, and Hephzibah Roskelly. 1991. *An Unquiet Pedagogy: Transforming Practice in the English Classroom*. Portsmouth, NH: Boynton-Cook/Heinemann.

Lankshear, C. and M. Lawler. 1987. *Literacy, Schooling, and Revolution*. London: Falmer Press.

Lappé, Frances Moore, and Paul Martin Dubois. 1994. *The Quickening of America*. San Francisco: Jossey-Bass.

Larrabee, Mary Jeanne. 1993. *An Ethic of Care: Feminist and Interdisciplinary Perspectives*. New York: Routledge.

Larson, Richard. 1982. "The Research Paper in the Writing Course: A Nonform of Writing." *College English* 44 (no. 8): 811–16.

Lather, Patti. 1986. "Research as Praxis." *Harvard Educational Review* 56 (August): 257–77.

Lauer, Janice M. 1982. "Writing as Inquiry: Some Questions for Teachers." *College Composition and Communication* 33 (February): 89–93.

———. 1984. "Issues in Rhetorical Invention." In *Essays on Classical Rhetoric and Modern Discourse*, edited by Robert Connors, Lisa Ede, and Andrea Lunsford, pp. 127–39, 227–80. Carbondale, IL: Southern Illinois University Press.

———. 1994. "Persuasive Writing on Public Issues." In *Composition in Context: Essays in Honor of Donald C. Stewart*, edited by W. Ross Winterowd and Vincent Gillespie, pp. 62–72. Carbondale: Southern Illinois University Press.

Lazere, Donald, ed. 1987. *American Media and Mass Culture: Left Perspectives*. Berkeley: University of California Press.

———. 1992a. "Back to Basics: A Force for Oppression or Liberation?" *College English* 54 (January): 7–21.

———. 1992b. "Teaching the Rhetorical Conflicts." *College Composition and Communication* 43 (May): 194–213.

Leistyna, Pepi, Stephen A. Sherblom, and Arlie Woodrum. 1996. *Breaking Free: The Transformative Power of Critical Pedagogy*. Cambridge, MA: Harvard Educational Review.

Lemoyne, James. 1991. "Pentagon's Strategy for the Press: Good News or No News." *New York Times* 17 February: E3.

Levin, Henry M. 1988. *Towards Accelerated Schools*. New Brunswick, NJ: Center for Policy Research in Education.

Levine, Arthur, and Deborah Hirsch. 1990. "Student Activism and Optimism Return to the Campuses." *The Chronicle of Higher Education* 7 November: A48.

Levine, David, and Robert Lowe, Bob Peterson, and Rita Tenorio. 1995. *Rethinking Schools: An Agenda for Change.* New York: New Press.

Lewiecki-Wilson, Cynthia. 1994. "Teaching in the Contact Zone of the Two-year College Classroom: Multiple Literacies, Deep Portfolio." *Teaching English in the Two-Year College* 21 (December): 267–76.

Lindemann, Erika. 1995. *A Rhetoric for Writing Teachers.* New York: Oxford University Press.

Liston, Daniel, and Kenneth Zeichner. 1987. "Critical Pedagogy and Teacher Education." *Journal of Education* 169, no. 3: 117–37.

———. 1991. *Teacher Education and the Social Conditions of Schooling.* New York: Routledge.

Lohr, Steve. 1988. "The Growth of the Global Office." *New York Times,* 18 October: D1, D25.

Loewen, James. 1992. *Lies My Teacher Told Me.* New York: The New Press.

Lu, Min-Zhan. 1990. "Writing as Repositioning." *Journal of Education* 172, no. 1: 18–21.

———. 1992. "Conflict and Struggle: The Enemies or Preconditions of Basic Writing?" *College English* 54 (December): 887–913.

———. 1994. "Professing Multiculturalism: The Politics of Style in the Contact Zone." *College Composition and Communication* 45 (December): 442–59.

Luke, Carmen, and Jennifer Gore, eds. 1992. *Feminisms and Critical Pedagogy.* New York: Routledge.

Maher, Frances A. 1987. "Toward a Richer Theory of Feminist Pedagogy: A Comparison of 'Liberation' and 'Gender' Models for Teaching and Learning." *Journal of Education* 163, no. 3: 91–100.

Matcuk, Matt. 1995. "The Power of Babel: Advertising Rhetoric and Public Discourse." Ph.D. diss. University of Wisconsin—Milwaukee. Ann Arbor: UMI.

Mayher, John. 1990. *Uncommon Sense: Theoretical Practice in Language Education.* Portsmouth, NH: Boynton-Cook, Heinemann.

———. 1993. "Review of *Empowering Education.*" *Journal of the New York Metropolitan Association for Developmental Education* 7 (Spring): 8–10.

Mayo, Peter. 1991. "Pedagogy and Politics in the Work of Paulo Freire." *Education* (Malta) 4, no. 1: 20–28.

———. 1993. "When Does It Work? Freire's Pedagogy in Context." *Studies in the Education of Adults* 25, no. 1: 11–30.

———. 1994. "Synthesizing Gramsci and Freire: Possibilities for a Theory of Radical Adult Education." *The International Journal of Lifelong Education* 13 (March/April): 125–48.

McCarthy, Lucille Parkinson. 1987. "A Stranger in Strange Lands: A College Student Writing across the Curriculum." *Research in the Teaching of English* 21 (October): 233–65.

McCracken, Nancy Mellin, and Bruce C. Appleby. 1992. *Gender Issues in the Teaching of English*. Portsmouth, NH: Heinemann.

McLaren, Peter. 1988. *Schooling as a Ritual Performance: Towards a Political Economy of Educational Symbols and Gestures*. London: Routledge, Kegan, and Paul.

McLaren, Peter, and Henry Giroux. 1994. *Between Borders: Pedagogy and the Politics of Cultural Studies*. New York: Routledge.

McLaren, Peter, and Colin Lankshear. 1993. *Critical Literacy: Radical and Post-modern Perspectives*. Albany: State University of New York Press.

McLaren, Peter, and Peter Leonard. 1993. *Paulo Freire: A Critical Encounter*. New York: Routledge.

McMillan, James H. 1987. "Enhancing College Students' Critical Thinking: A Review of Studies." *Research in Higher Education* 26: 3–29.

McNeil, Linda. 1986. *Contradictions of Control: School Structures and School Knowledge*. New York: Routledge, Kegan, and Paul.

Meier, Terry. 1989. "The Case Against Standardized Achievement Tests." *Re-thinking Schools* 3 (January–February): 9–12.

Menand, Louis. 1995. "The Advocacy Trap." *Lingua Franca* (July/August): 57–61, 72.

Mezirow, Jack, and associates. 1990. *Fostering Critical Reflection in Adulthood: A Guide to Transformative and Emancipatory Learning*. San Francisco: Jossey-Bass.

Miller, Richard E. 1994. "Fault Lines in the Contact Zone." *College English* 56 (April): 389–408.

Miller, Susan. 1991. *Textual Carnivals: The Politics of Composition*. Carbondale: Southern Illinois University Press.

Mortenson, Thomas G. 1991. *Equity of Higher Educational Opportunity for Women, Black, Hispanic, and Low Income Students*. ACT Student Financial Aid Research Report series, no. 91-1, January 1991. Iowa City: American College Testing Program.

———. 1993–94. *Post-secondary Education Opportunity: The Mortenson Report on Public Policy Analysis of Opportunity for Post-secondary Education*. Nos. 10 (February 1993), 13 (May 1993), 16 (September 1993), 24 (June 1994). Iowa City: American College Testing Program.

Mutnick, Deborah. 1996. *Writing in an Alien World: Basic Writing and the Struggle for Equality in Higher Education*. Portsmouth, NH: Boynton/Cook, Heinemann.

Neill, A. S. 1960. *Summerhill: A Radical Approach to Child Rearing*. New York: Hart Publishing Company.

Neverow-Turk, Vara. 1991. "Researching the Minimum Wage: A Moral Economy for the Classroom." *College Composition and Communication* 42 (December): 477–83.

Nieto, Sonia. 1994a. "Lessons from Students on Creating a Chance to Dream." *Harvard Educational Review* 64 (Winter): 392–426.

———. 1994b. *Affirming Diversity: The Sociopolitical Context of Multicultural Education*. White Plains, NY: Longmans. 2d edition: 1996.

North, Stephen. 1987. *The Making of Knowledge in Composition: Portrait of an Emerging Field.* Portsmouth, NH: Boynton-Cook.

Oakes, Jeannie. 1985. *Keeping Track.* New Haven: Yale University Press.

Oakes, Jeannie, and Martin Lipton. 1990. *Making the Best of Schools.* New Haven: Yale University Press.

O'Brien, Sheila Ruzycki. 1992. "Writing to Learn about Gender, Race and Class." *Advanced Composition Forum* 4 (Fall): 1–4.

O'Loughlin, Michael. 1992a. "Engaging Teachers in Emancipatory Knowledge Construction." *Journal of Teacher Education* 43, no. 5: 336–46.

———. 1992b. "Rethinking Science Education: Beyond Piagetian Constructivism toward a Sociocultural Model of Teaching and Learning." *Journal of Research in Science Teaching* 29: 791–820.

Ohmann, Richard. 1976. *English in America: A Radical View of the Profession.* New York: Oxford University Press.

———. 1987. *Politics of Letters.* Middletown: Wesleyan University Press.

———. 1996. *Selling Culture: Magazines, Markets, and Class at the Turn of the Century.* New York: Verso.

Ollman, Bertell. 1993. *Dialectical Investigations.* New York: Routledge.

Oreskes, Michael. 1995. "Profiles of Today's Youth: They Couldn't Care Less." In *Reading Culture,* 2d ed., edited by Diana George and John Trimbur, pp. 67–72. New York: HarperCollins.

Paine, Charles. 1989. "Relativism, Radical Pedagogy, and the Ideology of Paralysis." *College English* 51, no. 6: 557–70.

Paul, Richard. 1993. *Critical Thinking: How to Prepare Students for a Rapidly Changing World.* Rohnert Park, CA: Center for Critical Thinking and Moral Critique.

Perl, Sondra. 1980. "Understanding Composing." *College Composition and Communication* 31 (December): 363–69.

———. 1994a. Composing Texts, Composing Lives. *Harvard Educational Review* 64 (Winter): 427–49.

———, ed. 1994b. *Landmark Essays: On Writing Process.* Davis, CA: Hermagoras Press.

Phelps, Louise Wetherbee. 1988. *Composition as a Human Science: Contributions to the Self-Understanding of a Discipline.* New York: Oxford University Press.

Piaget, Jean. 1979. *Science of Education and the Psychology of the Child.* New York: Penguin. Originally published in 1969.

Pincus, Fred L. 1980. "The False Promises of Community Colleges: Class Conflict and Vocational Education." *Harvard Educational Review* 50 (August): 332–61.

———. 1994. "Statistical Data on Inequality in Higher Education." Department of Sociology and Anthropology. University of Maryland, Baltimore County. Unpublished manuscript.

———. 1995. "Statistics on Race/Ethnic Inequality." Department of Sociology and Anthropology. University of Maryland, Baltimore County. Unpublished manuscript.

Pincus, Fred, and E. Archer. 1989. *The Bridges to Opportunity? Are Community Colleges Meeting the Transfer Needs of Minority Students?* New York: The College Board.

Pincus, Fred, and Howard J. Ehrlich, eds. 1994. *Race and Ethnic Conflict: Contending Views on Prejudice, Discrimination, and Ethnic Violence.* Boulder, CO: Westview Press.

Pratt, Mary Louise. 1991. "Arts of the Contact Zone." In *Profession '91,* pp. 33–40. New York: Modern Language Association.

Rethinking Our Classrooms: Teaching for Equity and Justice. 1994. Milwaukee: Rethinking Schools.

Rich, Adrienne. 1979. "Teaching Language in Open Admissions." In *On Lies, Secrets, and Silence: Selected Prose, 1960–78.* New York: Norton.

Rimer, Sara. 1991. "A Coach Learns Again to Love the Game." *The New York Times* 10 April: B1.

Rivage-Seul, Margaret K. 1987. "Peace Education: Imagination and the Pedagogy of the Oppressed." *Harvard Educational Review* 57 (May): 153–69.

Rohter, Larry. 1989. "Isolated Desert Community Lives by Skinner's Precepts." *New York Times* 7 November: C1.

Rose, Mike. 1990. *Lives on the Boundary.* New York: Penguin Books.

———. 1995. *Possible Lives: The Promise of Public Education in America.* Boston: Houghton Mifflin.

Rosen, Harold. 1972. *Language and Class: A Critical Look at the Theories of Basil Bernstein.* Bristol, UK: Falling Wall Press.

Rothgery, David. 1993. " 'So What Do We Do Now?' Necessary Directionality in Writing Teacher's Response to Racist, Sexist, Homophobic Papers." *College Composition and Communication* 44 (May): 241–47.

Royce, Knut. 1991. "A Trail of Distortion Against Iraq." *Newsday* 21 January: 21.

Russell, David R. 1993. "Vygotsky, Dewey, and Externalism: Beyond the Student/Discipline Dichotomy." *Journal of Advanced Composition* 13 (Winter): 173–97.

Ryan, Jake, and Charles Sackrey. 1984. *Strangers in Paradise: Academics from the Working Class.* Boston: South End Press.

Sapon-Shevin, Mara, and Nancy Schniedewind. 1991. "Cooperative Learning as Empowering Pedagogy." In *Empowerment through Multicultural Education,* edited by Christine Sleeter, pp. 159–78. Albany, NY: State University of New York Press.

Scharle, Catherine M. 1993. "The Lesson that Flew: A Political-Action Primer for Students." *English Journal* 82 (November): 39–43.

Schniedewind, Nancy, and Ellen Davidson. 1987. *Cooperative Learning, Cooperative Lives: A Sourcebook of Learning Activities for Building a Peaceful World.* Dubuque, IA: William C. Brown.

Schon, D. A. 1983. *The Reflective Practitioner: How Professionals Think in Action.* New York: Basic Books.

———. 1987. *Educating the Reflective Practitioner: Toward a New Design for Teaching and Learning in the Professions.* San Francisco: Jossey-Bass.

Schor, Juliet. 1991. *The Overworked American: The Unexpected Decline of Leisure.* New York: Basic Books.

Scribner, Sylvia, and Michael Cole. 1981. *The Psychology of Literacy.* Cambridge, MA: Harvard University Press.

Shannon, Patrick. 1990a. *The* Struggle to Continue: Progressive Reading Instruction in the United States. Portsmouth, NH: Heinemann.

————. 1990b. "Re-searching the Familiar." *Language Arts* 67 (April): 379–87.

————. 1992. *Becoming Political: Readings and Writings in the Politics of Literacy Education.* Portsmouth, NH: Heinemann.

Sheehan, Susan. 1995. "Ain't No Middle Class." *The New Yorker Magazine* (December): 82–93.

Shor, Ira. 1986. "Equality Is Excellence: Transforming Teacher Education and the Learning Process." *Harvard Educational Review* 56 (November): 406–26.

————. 1987a. *Critical Teaching and Everyday Life.* Chicago: University of Chicago Press. Originally published in 1980.

——, ed. 1987b. *Freire for the Classroom: A Sourcebook for Liberatory Teaching.* Portsmouth, NH: Boynton-Cook, Heinemann.

————. 1992a. *Culture Wars: School and Society in the Conservative Restoration, 1969–1991.* Chicago: University of Chicago Press. Originally published in 1986.

————. 1992b. *Empowering Education: Critical Teaching for Social Change.* Chicago: University of Chicago Press.

Shor, Ira, and Paulo Freire. 1987. *A Pedagogy for Liberation: Dialogues on Transforming Education.* Westport, CT: Bergin-Garvey, Greenwood.

Simon, Roger. 1992. *Teaching Against the Grain.* South Hadley, MA: Bergin-Garvey.

Simon, Roger, and Don Dippo. 1987. "What Schools Can Do: Designing Programs for Work Education that Challenge the Wisdom of Experience." *Journal of Education* 169, no. 3: 101–16.

Sizer, Theodore. 1984. *Horace's Compromise: The Dilemmas of the American High School.* Boston: Houghton-Mifflin.

Sledd, Andrew. 1988. "Readin' Not Riotin': The Politics of Literacy." *College English* 50, no. 5: 495–508.

————. 1994. "Pigs, Squeals, and Cow Manure: Or Power, Language, and Multicultural Democracy." *Journal of Advanced Composition* 14 (Fall): 547–58.

Sledd, James. 1969. "Bi-dialecticism: The Linguistics of White Supremacy." *English Journal* 58: 1307–15.

Sleeter, Christine E., ed. 1991. *Empowerment through Multicultural Education.* Albany, NY: State University of New York Press.

Smith, Frank. 1993. *Whose Language? What Power?: A Universal Conflict in a South African Setting.* New York: Teachers College Press.

Smitherman, Geneva. 1993 [1977]. *Talkin' and Testifyin': The Language of Black America.* Detroit: Wayne State University Press. Originally published in 1977.

Smitherman-Donaldson, Geneva. 1987. "Toward a National Public Policy on Language." *College English* 49 (January): 29–36.

Soliday, Mary. 1994. "Translating Self and Difference through Literacy Narratives." *College English* 56, no. 5: 511–26.

Solorzano, Daniel G. 1989. "Teaching and Social Change: Reflections on a Freirean Approach in a College Classroom." *Teaching Sociology* 17 (April): 218–25.

Spring, Joel. 1989. *The Sorting Machine Revisited: National Educational Policy since 1945.* White Plains, NY: Longman.

Stein, Nan, Nancy L. Marshall, and Linda R. Tropp. 1993. *Secrets in Public: Sexual Harassment in Our Schools.* Wellesley, MA: Center for Research on Women, Wellesley College.

Sternglass, Marilyn S. 1993. "Writing Development as Seen Through Longitudinal Research." *Written Communication* 10 (April): 235–61.

Stuckey, J. Elspeth. 1991. *The Violence of Literacy.* Portsmouth, NH: Boynton-Cook.

Sutphin, Christine. 1992. "The Inclusion/Exclusion Issue: Including Students in Choosing Texts." *Feminist Teacher* 7 (Fall): 31–34.

Tayko, Gail, and Jonathan Tassoni. 1996. *Sharing Pedagogies: Students and Teachers Respond to English Curricula.* Portsmouth, NH: Boynton-Cook.

Thomas, William. 1995. "When 'Student Empowerment' Works Too Well: Adventures in Publishing by a Former High School Newspaper Sponsor." *English Journal* 84 (November): 58–64.

Tinberg, Howard B. 1989. "Ethnography in the Writing Classroom." *College Composition and Communication* 40 (February): 79–82.

Tokarcyzk, Michelle M., and Elizabeth A. Fay. 1993. *Working-class Women in the Academy: Laborers in the Knowledge Factory.* Amherst: University of Massachusetts Press.

Tremmel, Robert. 1993. "Zen and the Art of Reflective Practice in Teacher Education." *Harvard Educational Review* 63 (Winter): 434–49.

Trimbur, John. 1988. "Cultural Studies and Teaching Writing." *Focuses* 1, no. 2: 5–18.

Uchitelle, Louis. 1990. "Not Getting Ahead? Better Get Used to It." *New York Times* 16 December: E1, E6.

———. 1991. "Trapped in the Impoverished Middle Class." *New York Times* 17 November: Section 3, 1, 10.

———. 1994a. "Job Losses Don't Let Up Even as Hard Times Ease." *New York Times* 22 March: A1, D5.

———. 1994b. "Moonlighting Plus: 3-job Families on the Rise." *New York Times* 16 August: A1.

Villanueva, Victor. 1993. *Bootstraps: From an American Academic of Color.* Urbana, IL: National Council of Teachers of English.

Vygotsky, Lev. 1962. *Thought and Language.* Cambridge: MIT Press.

———. 1978. *Mind in Society: The Development of Higher Psychological Processes.* Cambridge: Harvard University Press.

Walker, Constance I., and Diane J. Tedick. 1994. "Creating a Culture of Reform and Reflection." *Teaching Education* 6, no. 2: 81–95.

Wallerstein, Nina, and Edward Bernstein. 1988. "Empowerment Education: Freire's Ideas Adapted to Health Education." *Health Education Quarterly* 15 (Winter): 379–94.

Weiler, K. 1987. *Women Teaching for Change: Gender, Class, Power.* South Hadley, MA: Bergin-Garvey.

———. 1991. "Freire and a Feminist Pedagogy of Difference." *Harvard Educational Review* 61 (November): 449–74.

Wertsch, James V. 1985. *Vygotsky and the Social Formation of Mind.* Cambridge: Harvard University Press.

Williams, Carole. 1993. "Social Action Begins at School: The Research Paper Revisited." *English Journal* 82 (November): 44–49.

Williams, Meredith. 1989. "Vygotsky's Social Theory of Mind." *Harvard Educational Review* 59 (February): 108–26.

Williams, Raymond. 1977. *Marxism and Literature.* Oxford: Oxford University Press.

———. 1983. *Culture and Society.* New York: Columbia University Press. Originally published in 1958.

Willis, Paul. 1981. *Learning to Labor: How Working Class Kids Get Working Class Jobs.* New York: Columbia University Press.

Wilson, John K. 1996. *The Myth of Political Correctness: The Conservative Attack on Higher Education.* Durham, NC: Duke University Press.

Wirth, Arthur G. 1992. *Education and Work for the Year 2000: Choices We Face.* San Francisco: Jossey-Bass.

Woodward, Helen. 1994. *Negotiating Evaluation: Involving Children and Parents in the Process.* Portsmouth, NH: Heinemann.

Zandy, Janet. 1990. *Calling Home: Working Class Women's Writings.* New Brunswick: Rutgers University Press.

———. 1994. "Human Labor and Literature: A Pedagogy from a Working-Class Perspective." In *Changing Classroom Practices: Resources for Literary and Cultural Studies,* edited by David B. Downing, pp. 37–52. Urbana, IL: National Council of Teachers of English.

———. 1995. *Liberating Memory: Our Work and Working-Class Consciousness.* New Brunswick: Rutgers University Press.

Zebroski, James, and Nancy Mack. 1992. "Ethnographic Writing for Critical Consciousness." In *Social Issues in the English Classroom,* edited by C. Mark Hurlbert and Samuel Totten, chap. 10, pp. 196–205. Urbana, IL: National Council of Teachers of English.

Zeichner, Kenneth M., and Daniel P. Liston. 1987. "Teaching Student Teachers to Reflect." *Harvard Educational Review* 57 (February): 1–22.

Zinn, Howard. 1980. *A People's History of the United States.* New York: Harper and Row.

Index